Late Life

Tiffany Field

Rev. date: 07/26/2023

To order additional copies of this book, contact:
Xlibris
844-714-8691
www.Xlibris.com
Orders@Xlibris.com
853375

The Negatives

The Positives

Review Article   **IJPRR (2023) x:xx**

International Journal of Psychological Research and Reviews
(ISSN:2639-6041)

Loneliness in Aging Adults: A Narrative Review

Tiffany Field, PhD

University of Miami/Miller School of Medicine and Fielding Graduate University

ABSTRACT

The recent literature on loneliness in aging adults (last five years) is predominantly focused on negative effects of being lonely along with some studies on risk factors, buffers, and interventions. Aging is typically defined as ages starting at 60 or 65. The prevalence rates for loneliness in aging adults were highly variable in this literature, ranging from a low of 11% in Norway to a high of 76% in San Diego. Negative effects have included ageism attitudes, anxiety, depression, memory loss, low heart rate variability, short telomere length, frailty, frequent falls and trips to the emergency room. Risk factors have included aging anxiety, sensory loss, neuroticism, losing a partner, and COVID-19. Buffers/protective factors have included being in a relationship, continued working, internet use and being with pets and robots. And personality traits have been protective including agreeableness, wisdom, and narcissism. Interventions have included social networking, personal voice assistants, writing and laughter therapy. Although the recent research suggests that loneliness and aging are related on some variables like frailty, it has not suggested that loneliness is more prevalent among the aging than younger adults. In addition, most of the data are based on self-report surveys that have yielded mixed results across countries.

*Correspondence to Author:
Tiffany Field, PhD
University of Miami/Miller School of Medicine and Fielding Graduate University

How to cite this article:
Tiffany Field. Loneliness in Aging Adults: A Narrative Review. International Journal of Psychological Research and Reviews, 2023, x:xx

eSciPub LLC, Houston, TX USA.
Website: https://escipub.com/

This narrative review involved entering the terms loneliness and aging into PubMed and PsycINFO. The search yielded 197 papers for the last five years. However, following exclusion criteria including case studies and non-English papers, this review is a summary of the research reported in 47 papers. The recent literature on loneliness in aging adults is predominantly focused on negative effects of being lonely along with some studies on risk factors, buffers and interventions. This narrative review is accordingly divided into sections on prevalence, effects, risk factors, buffers and interventions.

Prevalence of Loneliness in Aging Adults

Loneliness has been defined as a subjective, negative experience of being isolated and having an inadequate meaningful connection. It has been differentiated from social isolation which has been defined as the objective state of having fewer or infrequent social relationships. Aging is typically defined as ages starting at 60 or 65. The prevalence of the aging population is expected to double from 420 million in 2002 to 973 million in 2030 (Nguyen et al, 2021). The prevalence rates for loneliness in aging adults have been highly variable, ranging from a low of 11% in Norway (Ormstad et al, 2020) to a high of 76% in San Diego (Lee et al, 2019) (see table 1). The high prevalence in San Diego was explained by lumping different age groups that had the greatest prevalence of loneliness including those in their late 20s, mid 50s and late 80s.

Other prevalence rates include 23% from Canada (Chamberlain et al, 2022) to a range of 30 to 40% in western countries (Spreng et al, 2021) and to 60% in Sweden (Svensson et al, 2022). This significant variability in prevalence doesn't seem to be explained by long winters given that Norway had a low prevalence of 11% while Sweden had a high of 60% and it didn't seem to relate to COVID given that a couple rates during the COVID years were low while the highest rates were reported for non-COVID years. This range may simply be cultural variation on factors like average retirement age,

government support, extended family size or any of the risk factors noted below.

Negative Effects of Loneliness on Aging Adults

The negative effects of loneliness on aging adults have also been highly variable across studies, typically depending on the "pet variables" of the researchers. These have focused on psychological distress including ageism attitudes, anxiety and depression (see table 2). Physiological effects have included low heart rate variability and short telomere length. Surprisingly very few studies have focused on cognitive function except for memory loss in the case of two studies. Physically, the aging have been affected by inflammation and frailty which probably, in turn, explains the limited activities of daily living for the aging adults, their frailty, their frequent falls and their trips to the emergency room. Data on these problems have resulted in references to morbidity and mortality related to loneliness in aging adults.

Psychological Effects

In the survey on western countries, several negative effects were noted including susceptibility to psychiatric disorders as serious as suicidality, cognitive decline and dementia, hypertension and immune system dysfunction (Spreng et al, 2021). The authors referred to these conditions as being greater than obesity and smoking more than 15 cigarettes per day. In their discussion, they suggested that the default network was affected involving the connection of regions located in the brain's midline with a spatial overlap with the social brain that is vulnerable to age-related decline. They further referred to it as a "neural substrate linking loneliness, aging and brain health". Unfortunately and surprisingly, the fMRI data they referred to do not appear in the recent literature.

Ageism. In a study that was focused on ageism or aging anxiety and negative attitudes towards aging, ageism was a moderator of loneliness effects on anxiety and depression in a sample of

1038 aging adults (Bergman et al, 2021). That negative attitudes towards aging might moderate effects of loneliness on negative mood states is not surprising. Negative attitudes about aging would be expected to exacerbate the negative effects of loneliness on depression and anxiety. Ageism might have also been a risk factor for loneliness via rejection by aging peers if the variables of interest had been entered into data analysis differently, especially when they are collected cross-sectionally rather than longitudinally, as in this study.

Psychological Distress. Psychological distress in general has been noted to occur in aging adults. For example, in a Canadian longitudinal study (N= 30,079 aging adults), a logistic regression analysis was performed on the variables of loneliness and social isolation combined (Menec et al, 2020). The results suggested that although being socially isolated and lonely led to a greater likelihood of psychological distress, loneliness was the more significant predictor of psychological distress in this sample.

Similar findings were noted among older people in Ghana (Gyasi et al, 2019). Again, loneliness and living alone contributed to greater psychological distress. These studies highlight the importance of examining profiles that combine both social isolation and loneliness in terms of identifying the profile that is most indicative of the need for intervention.

Depression. Loneliness has also been more prevalent than social isolation in some samples including from a Swedish population study (N = 5804) (Svensson et al, 2022). In this study, 60% reported being lonely occasionally while only 6% were socially isolated. Greater loneliness led to increased symptoms ranging from 67% for gastrointestinal-urinary problems to 96% for depression in those who were experiencing constant loneliness. These surprisingly different rates between loneliness and social isolation highlight the probability that social isolation may not be a necessary or sufficient condition for

loneliness and that aging adults can be lonely without being socially isolated.

Loneliness has also been entered as a mediator variable in a couple studies. For example, in a study entitled "Self-perceptions of aging and depressive symptoms: the mediating role of loneliness", the Health and Retirement Survey spanning eight years suggested that the self-perception of aging leads to depression with loneliness as the mediator (Segel-Karpas et al, 2022). The a priori selection of each type of variable for the analysis in several studies like this one is seemingly arbitrary.

In a similar longitudinal study on 75-year-old adults who were followed for 11 years in Amsterdam, decreased physical function and social network size led to increased depression via loneliness and further decreases in social network size (Domenech-Abrlla et al, 2021). These results are based on a very complex cross-legged panel analysis which has technical problems in that the chosen time lag may not be appropriate for each effect. In addition, the authors suggested that the differential loss to follow-up and collider bias in the study may have led to an underestimation of effects (a distortion that modifies an association between an independent and dependent variable by trying to control for a common effect of those variables).

Anxiety and depression. In contrast, a recent study has reported that older adults have less anxiety and sadness and loneliness than middle-age and younger groups (Liruela-Baltar et al, 2020). In this study on 18-to-88-year-olds (N= 1501), those participants who had high levels of comorbid anxiety and sadness had more negative self–perceptions of aging. This study, like many others, was limited by being a correlation study which cannot interpret findings as suggestive of causality or direction of effects.

Physiological Effects

Only one study could be found on physiological effects that is entitled "Loneliness and telomere length: immune and parasympathetic function are associated with accelerated aging" (Wilson et al, 2019). In this sample of 40-to-85-year-olds (N=113), lonelier people with lower heart rate variability had viral reactivation and shorter telomere length (a biological marker of aging). In those with higher heart rate variability, there was no association with loneliness, viral reactivation or telomere length, However, this is not a longitudinal study, so directionality again cannot be determined.

Cognitive Effects

The shorter telomere length may contribute to the cognitive deficits that have been noted in aging inasmuch as it is a biomarker for Alzheimer's and dementia. Surprisingly, only two studies addressed the relationship between loneliness and cognitive deficits. In a study on a Canadian sample, loneliness was correlated with memory loss three years later (Kyrolainen et al, 2020). But only one item was used for loneliness in the study and predictive validity as well as test-retest reliability were very low. In a longer longitudinal study, a similar relationship was reported. In this 10-year longitudinal study, loneliness was related to poor memory and verbal fluency at baseline and a stronger rate of memory and verbal fluency loss occurred over 10 years (Yin et al, 2019). This linear increase in memory loss was related to an increase in loneliness in a relationship that was likely bidirectional, suggesting that loneliness could lead to memory loss and memory loss, in turn, could contribute to loneliness.

Physical Effects

Frailty. Frailty is one of the most frequently studied physical effects of loneliness in aging adults. In a longitudinal study from England (N=2,817 adults older than 60), high levels of loneliness led to greater frailty over a six-year period (Gale et al, 2018). High social isolation also led to frailty, but only in men for some unknown reason. Similar findings were noted in the Survey of Health, Aging and Retirement in Europe (Jrach et al, 2021). In this sample of 13,069 aging adults, average and high levels of loneliness and social isolation were associated with robust people becoming frail and people who were frail at baseline becoming more frail. Because this is a cross-sectional study, not a longitudinal survey, it is conceivable that these effects were bidirectional. The degree to which loneliness and social isolation contributed to the effects of the frailty was also unclear.

Frailty has also been studied in a community dwelling sample of adults greater than age 65 (N= 1427) (Hoogendijk et al, 2020). In this sample, the prevalence of frailty was 13%, frailty plus loneliness was 5.9%, and frailty plus social isolation was 6.2%. It's not clear whether the sample of frailty plus loneliness was the same sample or overlapped with the frailty plus social isolation sample.

In a scoping review of the literature on 26 studies, frailty contributed to greater health problems but was unrelated to loneliness and social isolation (Mehrabi et al, 2020). This finding was surprising given the positive relationship between loneliness and frailty in the studies previously described. Loneliness may have been a mediator of the effects of frailty on poor health but was not analyzed as a mediator.

Limited Activities of Daily Living. The significant increase in frailty may have contributed to limited activities of daily living, the falls and trips to the emergency room that have been related to loneliness in this literature, although frailty has not been mentioned in these studies. In the report on activities of daily living, for example, loneliness was associated with increasing difficulties with activities of daily living but frailty was not measured (Shankar et al, 2017). In this sample from the English Longitudinal Study of Aging (N=3070 adults whose mean age was 69), loneliness was also related to reduced gait speed, although the relationship between gait speed and activities of daily living was not given.

Falls. Frailty might also contribute to the frequency of falls reported in this literature. In a study from the National Social Life, Health and Aging project that was a longitudinal study over five years, 51% had at least one fall and 23% had greater than two falls (Zeytinoglo et al,

2021). an Increased odds of loneliness related to falls in the 65-to-85-year-old group. Although this is a longitudinal sample and loneliness was said to predict falls, the greater incidence of falling may have also predicted loneliness, again as in a bidirectional relationship.

Emergency Room Visits. Frequent falling would be expected to lead to emergency room (ER) visits. The only study on emergency room visits, however, related those to loneliness, not falling (Chamberlain at all, 2022). In this sample (N= 44,413) from the Canadian Longitudinal Study of Aging, the prevalence of loneliness was 23% and the prevalence of emergency room visits was 27%. Greater odds were noted for the lonely visiting the ER and loneliness was associated with ER visits more frequently in women which might have related to their greater frailty, although that variable wasn't included in the data analysis. One of the limitations of the study is that the multivariate logistic regression that was used to analyze the data controlled for variables that were not the primary variables of interest but that might have been significant predictors such as frailty. In addition, both the loneliness and emergency room visits were dichotomous variables which have limited reliability.

Morbidity and Mortality. Reaching 90 years of age was negatively correlated with social loneliness in a longitudinal study from Amsterdam on 64-90-year-old men and women (N=2,080) (Brandts et al, 2021). Greater morbidity and mortality have been associated with loneliness. In a review of the literature, increased morbidity predicted greater loneliness and loneliness predicted morbidity (Nguyen et al, 2021). These authors spoke of "deaths of despair" due to suicide and opioid abuse in lonely aging adults which they claimed contributed to more deaths than those secondary to lung cancer or stroke. The increased odds of mortality for lonely aging adults was 30%. In a study they described, loneliness mediated the relationship between pain and suicidal ideation in 200 elderly unmarried men (single, divorced, widowed) but not partnered or married men (Lutzman et al, 2020). In addition, they suggested that it was data like these that led the UK to appoint a minister for loneliness in 2018 and WHO (the World Health Organization) to create the Global Network of Age Friendly Cities and Communities.

Risk Factors/Predictors for Loneliness in Aging Adults

It should be noted that many of the effects just discussed could also be considered risk factors in the same way that the following risk factors could be treated as effects of loneliness (see table 3). Examples of these reciprocal or bidirectional relationships are reduced physical function as related to frailty which has been noted as an effect of loneliness while it is also a risk factor (Shankar et al, 2017). The same could be said about memory loss (Kyrolainen et al, 2020) and about aging anxiety (Hu et al, 2022) that have both led to loneliness. These factors have been arbitrarily assigned in this review according to the direction in which they have been analyzed, namely as independent or dependent variables. In this section the risk factors of aging anxiety, sensory loss, neuroticism, losing a partner COVID-19 risk factors are reviewed.

Table 1. Prevalence of loneliness in aging adults.

Prevalence	First Author
11% Norway	Ormstad
76% San Diego	Lee
23% Canada	Chamberlain
30-40% western countries	Spreng

Table 2. Negative effects of loneliness on aging adults.

Effects	First Author
Psychological	
Suicidality, cognitive decline	Spreng
Anxiety and depression	Bergman
Psychological distress	Menee, Gyasi
Depression	Domenech-Abrilla, Losada-Baltar, Segel-Karpas, Svennson
Suicidal ideation	Lutzman
Physiological	
Lower heart rate variability, viral reactivation, shorter telomere length	Wilson
Cognitive	
Memory loss	Kyrolainen, Yin
Verbal fluency loss	Yin
Physical	
Frailty	Gale, Jrach, Mehrabi, Hoogendijk
Limited activities of daily living	Shankar
Falls	Zeytinoglo
Emergency room visits	Chamberlain
Morbidity	Nguyen
Mortality	Brandts

Table 3. Risk factors for loneliness in aging adults.

Risk Factors	First Author
Aging anxiety	Ayalon, Hu
Sensory loss	Mick
Neuroticism	Wang, Ormstad
Agreeableness in women	Ormstad
Functional limitations, low family support and strained friendships	Hawkley
Losing a partner	Boger
COVID-19	Peng, Field, Losada-Baltar, Chamberlain

Table 4. Buffers for loneliness in aging adults.

Buffers	First Author
Social factors	
Being in a relationship	Itzick
Intergeneration relationship quality	Liu
Neighborhood cohesiveness	Gam
"Aging in place"	Umer
Continued working	Cheng, Itzick
Internet use	Yu, Casanova
Pets, robots and interactive manikins	Ramesh, Chiu
Personality traits	
Agreeableness in men	Itzick
Wisdom	Lee, Nguyen
Narcissism	Carter

Table 5. Interventions for loneliness in aging adults.

Interventions	First Author
Social networking	Heins
Personal voice assistants (Alexa)	Jones
Writing therapy	Moieno
Laughter therapy	Kuru

6

Aging Anxiety

Aging anxiety or negative attitudes towards aging have received most of the attention as risk factors. In some studies they've been treated as effects, as discussed in that section. But, in other studies they have been treated as risk factors. Aging anxiety has been defined as worries from imagining negative consequences and losses associated with old age (Ayalon et al, 2018). In this study on adult day care funded by the government as compared to continuing care retirement communities in Israel, the adult daycare aging adults reported more loneliness and negative attitudes regarding aging. Inasmuch as the government supported daycare centers likely served lower socioeconomic (SES) folks, these results would suggest that lower SES may be related to negative attitudes about aging and greater loneliness.

In an eight-year longitudinal study (N = 3597 adults), latent growth curve modeling and path analysis were performed (Hu et al, 2022). In this sample, negative self-perceptions of aging had a direct effect on loneliness and an indirect effect on social disconnectedness via loneliness. The origins of the self-perceptions of aging were not addressed, but were clearly influential on loneliness.

Sensory Loss

Sensory loss including loss of vision and audition has been associated with loneliness in the Canadian Longitudinal Study on Aging (Mick et al, 2018). Having a sensory loss would not only be stigmatic in terms of socializing but would also make it more difficult to communicate in interactions with others. Less socializing, in turn, would be expected to lead to greater loneliness.

Neuroticism

Neuroticism has been a risk factor for loneliness in a study on Chinese adults (N= 3157) living in Chicago (Wang et al, 2018). In a logistic regression that adjusted for confounding factors, high levels of neuroticism led to 3.59 times greater likelihood of feeling lonely. In contrast, high consciousness led to a 24% lower risk of

loneliness. Again, directionality cannot be determined from cross-sectional data and the designation of dependent versus independent variables is arbitrary. Further, the logistic regression may have removed confounding variables that are risk factors.

Neuroticism has also been a risk factor for loneliness in a five-year follow-up study, but only for men (Ormstad et al, 2020). High neuroticism, low agreeableness and low conscientiousness led to loneliness in men while, surprisingly, high agreeableness in women contributed to their loneliness which is difficult to interpret. In this sample, loneliness occurred in 14% of the women and in 11% of the men. These data are tenuous, however, as they may not be as relevant today as they were two decades ago when they were collected (between 2002 and 2007).

Multiple Variables

Multiple variable studies may yield more valid predictors as the data analyses have less often controlled for confounding variables. Multiple risk factors contributed to the frequency of loneliness in the five-year follow-up of the National Social Life, Health and Aging project (Hawkley et al, 2018). The predictive factors included functional limitations and low family support as well as strained friendships. Another interesting aspect of this study was the reporting of the factors explaining the changes from lonely to non-lonely and non-lonely to lonely. The factors that were associated with transitioning from being lonely to non-lonely status included better self-related health and greater socializing as well as less family strain.

Losing a Partner

Losing a partner would be expected to be a significant variable in the relationship between aging and loneliness, but it was only reported in one study in this recent literature. In this study, the authors addressed the predictive validity of losing a partner resulting in loneliness (Boger et al, 2020). Surprisingly, with advancing age, partnership status was less predictive of

7

loneliness. This finding was noted in the German Aging Survey on 40-to-85-year-old adults (N=6188). The authors concluded that the relevance of partnership for social well-being was neither universal nor stable but appeared to decrease in the course of aging as well as across historical time. Although these are old data from 2014, continuity of these results might be expected. A possible reason for the decreasing relationship between partnerships and loneliness with increasing age is that older adults are more likely living in communities where they have formed friendships that attenuate the effects of loss on loneliness. Friends and caregivers may be buffers for the loss of partnerships.

COVID-19 as a Risk Factor

COVID-19 was explored as a risk factor for loneliness and aging in a few studies. In the two waves of the longitudinal Health and Retirement Study on adults older than 50 years, changes from 2016 to 2020 occurred including increased physical isolation and social isolation (Peng et al, all, 2022). However, there was no change in digital isolation or loneliness probably related to more time on social media. In a Survey during the COVID-19 lockdown, the young living alone experienced more loneliness than the old living alone, probably because the old were more accustomed to living alone (Field et al, 2021). In similar results from another study during the COVID-19 lockdown, psychological distress was noted to be less in the aging adults (Losada-Baltar et al, 2022). In this sample from Spain (N= 1549), the authors interpreted their results as the aging adults being more resilient. The results could also be interpreted as the older adults being accustomed to being lonely or at least living alone.

In contrast, in a study from Canada (N= 12,469), loneliness was measured by the three-item UCLA Loneliness Scale which was associated with depression (Chamberlain et al, 2022). However, covariates were also associated with depression including caregivers, working and having greater than two chronic diseases.

Nonetheless, the covariates were controlled by the data analysis so that only loneliness and depression remained as the primary variables. The UCLA Loneliness Scale only has three items including how often do you feel left out, isolated from others and not having companions.

Buffers for Loneliness in Aging Adults

Buffers /protective factors have been more frequently researched than risk factors in this recent literature on loneliness in the aging. These have included social factors and personality traits (see table 4).

Social Factors

Being in a Relationship. In a study on predictors of loneliness among older men in Israel (N=392), being in a relationship was associated with lower levels of loneliness (Itzick et al, 2020). Given that there were no women in this study, the data are not generalizable.

Intergenerational Relationship Quality. High quality relationships with younger generation family members have also been a buffer for loneliness as well as for greater attitudes toward later life in a study on adults greater than 50-years-old (N=801) (Lru et al, 2022). That relationships with adult children would decrease loneliness and enhance more positive attitudes toward later life is not surprising but is not often mentioned in this literature as a buffer for loneliness.

Neighborhood Cohesiveness. Friends in the neighborhood have also been a protective factor in the Canadian Longitudinal Study (N=14,301) (Gan et al, 2022). In this study, loneliness mediated 27 to 29% of environmental influences on mental well-being versus walking only mediated .4 −.9% of those influences. Social support and socialization related to neighborhood cohesion would be expected to reduce loneliness.

"Aging in place". This phenomenon relates to social support. In a study entitled "The relationship among aging in place, loneliness, and life satisfaction in the elderly in Turkey, the Aging in Place Scale was used (Umer et al,

2022). The Aging in Place Scale includes items on perceived social support, physical competence, and achievable social support. These qualities led to increased life satisfaction and lower scores on the Loneliness Scale for the Elderly. Although this is a correlation study, it suggests that "Aging in Place" can decrease loneliness.

Continued Working. Working and the workplace has also been a source of social contact for aging adults. In a study on adults over 60 years of age (N= 2037), continued working and volunteering led to not only less loneliness but also less depression (Cheng et al, 2021). These data were not surprising inasmuch as the workplace would offer more opportunities for socialization. In the study already discussed on older men in Israel, being employed was also a protective factor for loneliness (Itzick et al, 2020).

Internet Use. Social contact has also been facilitated by Internet use which, in turn, has reduced loneliness. In a sample from the Health and Retirement Study, internet use led to decreased loneliness as well as increased social contact over the eight years of the study (Yu et al, 2021). Unfortunately, as in several of these studies, loneliness was measured by only three items on the UCLA Loneliness Scale and internet use was a dichotomous measure, limiting the reliability of these data.

In a review of 11 papers on social network use and old people's well-being in relation to loneliness, social network use led to less loneliness, although the causal relationship was weak (Casanova et al, 2021). This is a surprising finding in that it is the opposite of the negative effects of Internet use on adolescents (Field, 2021).

Pets, Robots and Interactive Manikins. Increasingly, the aging population has turned to pets and novel technologies in the form of robots and interactive mannikins for companionship (Ramesh et al,2021). In a study entitled "Associations between loneliness and acceptance of using robots and pets as companions among older Chinese", 68% of the participants who felt lonely, accepted companionship of robots and 58% accepted pets (Chiu et al, 2022).

Personality Traits

Personality traits have been researched as buffers/protective factors for loneliness in aging adults. These include agreeableness, wisdom, and narcissism.

Agreeableness. Agreeableness was a buffer for the loneliness of older men in the study from Israel (Itzick et al, 2020). However, In another study, agreeableness was not a protective factor but a risk factor for women (Ormstad et al, 2020).

Wisdom. Wisdom has been considered a buffer for loneliness in aging adults in at least two studies. In a study entitled "High prevalence and adverse health effects of loneliness in community dwelling adults across the lifespan: the role of wisdom as a protective factor ", the San Diego Wisdom Scale was used (Lee et al, 2019). In this sample (N= 340), 76% experienced moderate to high levels of loneliness. No sex differences were noted on the prevalence or severity of loneliness. However, age differences were noted including that loneliness was most prevalent in the late 20s, mid 50s and late 80s. Wisdom based on the San Diego Wisdom Scale accounted for as much as 45% of the variance in the UCLA-3 Loneliness Scale.

In a review paper entitled "Wisdom as a potential antidote to loneliness in the aging" , wisdom was defined as a prosocial behavior involving emotion regulation, self-reflection, acceptance of divergent values, decisiveness and social advising (Nguyen et al, 2021). The authors suggested that the neurocircuitry of wisdom involves the prefrontal cortex and limbic striatum. Across the 36 studies reviewed, loneliness was strongly negatively correlated with wisdom (r= .50–.60). Most particularly, the prosocial behavior factor of the wisdom scale (empathy, compassion, and social cooperation) moderated the relationship between social network and loneliness. Wisdom is likely a buffer for many social–emotional problems, although it is rarely considered that way.

Narcissism. Narcissism was also surprisingly a buffer for loneliness. In a study entitled "The aging narcissist: just a myth?" 100 middle-age (Mean= 48 years) and 100 older age adults (Mean= 70 years) were given the 3-item UCLA Loneliness Scale and the 40-item Narcissism Scale (Carter et al, 2018). In this study, narcissism decreased over age and moderated (lessened) the relationship between age and loneliness. These results were surprising inasmuch as narcissism has typically been considered a negative trait, although narcissistic folks notably have good social, mental and physical health and reputedly live longer and certainly would not be lonely. The methodological problem for this study is that loneliness was measured by a 3-item scale and narcissism by a 40-item scale raising the question of the differential reliability of these measures.

Interventions for Loneliness in Aging Adults

Only a handful of intervention studies have been found in this recent literature on loneliness in aging adults. The interventions have varied widely from social networking to personal voice assistants to writing exercises and to laughter therapy (see table 5).

Social Networking

In a review of 36 studies on technological interventions, most of the studies evaluated social networking technology and Internet training (Heins et al, 2021). Limited effects were noted for these interventions on loneliness, social isolation and social support. Further, the studies were of very limited methodological quality.

Personal Voice Assistants

In a study on 75-year-old adults (N= 16), the participants used personal voice assistants such as Amazon Echo (Alexa) for eight weeks (Jones et al, 2021). After four weeks of using Alexa,

loneliness was significantly decreased. Themes were coded and the semantic analysis suggested that they were 1) greetings to a close friend; 2) second person comments/questions; 3) polite interactions; and 4) interactions with Alexa. The relational greetings especially led to decreased loneliness in the first four weeks, and baseline loneliness led to increased greetings over the eight-week intervention. Surprisingly, the greetings had greater effects than the interactions with Alexa.

Writing Therapy

In a study that involved writing about life experiences and sharing advice with others, 73 women were randomly assigned to six weeks of that condition or a control group that involved writing about neutral topics (Moieno et al, 2021). Those participants who expressed more positive expectations regarding aging also perceived more social support and had less loneliness. Given that this sample was exclusively women, it's not clear that it would generalize to a sample that included both women and men. This study was unusual in that it randomly assigned participants to intervention and control groups and the results highlighted the positive effects of writing especially about positive expectations regarding aging. However, it is a small sample study that needs to be replicated.

Laughter Therapy

In a laughter therapy study, 20 participants from a nursing home were given laughter therapy two times per week for five weeks and compared to a control group. (Kuru et al, 2018). The total scores for the long scale for loneliness called the DeJong Giervald Loneliness Scale and its subscale scores for emotional and social loneliness were decreased in the intervention group. No differences were noted on the death uncertainty and pain scales. Although the scale includes 11 items making it a more comprehensive measure than the three-item UCLA Loneliness Scale, the responses are simply yes, more or less or no, as in a dichotomous rating scale. The scale has been popularly used likely because it has been translated in several languages.

Methodological Limitations

Several methodological limitations can be noted about these recent studies on loneliness in aging adults. Significant variability has been reported on the sampling methods, on the sample sizes, and the prevalence and results of the studies. Most of the methods have been self-report surveys.

The key variables, as often happens, have been pet variables or those favored by the authors And often the data have been analyzed via logistic regression analysis which controls for confounding variables that might instead be risk factors or mediating/moderating variables if they had been analyzed by mediation/moderation or structural equations analysis.

More studies have appeared on buffers or protective factors versus risk factors. Several of the effects that have been noted could also be risk factors as in bidirectional, reciprocal variables.

Several of the scales are short as in the UCLA three item measure or simply dichotomous as in lonely or not lonely which limits the reliability of these measures. Directionality cannot be determined as most of the studies are correlational and others that are longitudinal have simply analyzed cross-sectional data.

Many of the results are relationships between loneliness and other effects, risk variables or protective factors selected by the researchers. Rarely has loneliness been compared in the aging versus the young adults. And when that comparison was made in at least one study, loneliness was most prevalent in the late 20s, mid 50s and late 80s (Lee et al, 2019). Surprisingly, sex differences have been rare, although several studies were exclusively male or female, limiting generalizability. The prevalence of loneliness, its measures and its effects are so variable that reviews have been inconclusive and meta-analyses have not been conducted.

Virtually no mechanism studies appear in this literature and potential mechanisms have not been discussed. And, only a few intervention studies could be found in this recent literature. Despite these methodological limitations, the recent literature highlights the relationships between loneliness and aging, although it doesn't conclude that aging is associated with more loneliness necessarily than other stages of life.

Conclusion

The recent literature on loneliness in aging adults is predominantly focused on negative effects of being lonely along with some studies on risk factors, buffers, and interventions. Aging is typically defined as ages starting at 60 or 65. The prevalence rates for loneliness in aging adults have been highly variable, ranging from a low of 11% in Norway to a high of 76% in San Diego. Negative effects have included ageism attitudes, anxiety, depression, memory loss, low heart rate variability, short telomere length, frailty, frequent falls and trips to the emergency room. Risk factors have included aging anxiety, sensory loss, neuroticism, losing a partner, and COVID-19. Buffers/protective factors have included being in a relationship, continued working, internet use and being with pets and robots. And personality traits have been protective including agreeableness, wisdom, and narcissism. Interventions have included social networking, personal voice assistants, writing and laughter therapy. Although the recent research suggests that loneliness and aging are related on some variables like frailty, it has not suggested that loneliness is more prevalent among the aging than younger adults. In addition, most of the data are based on self-report surveys that have yielded mixed results across countries.

References

[1]. Ayalon L. Loneliness and Anxiety About Aging in Adult Day Care Centers and Continuing Care Retirement Communities. Innov Aging. 2018 Jul 27;2(2):igy021. doi: 10.1093/geroni/igy021. PMID: 30480141; PMCID: PMC6177038.

[2]. Bergman YS, Segel-Karpas D. Aging anxiety, loneliness, and depressive symptoms among middle-aged adults: The moderating role of ageism. J Affect Disord. 2021 Jul 1;290:89-92. doi: 10.1016/j.jad.2021.04.077. Epub 2021 May 4. PMID: 33993085.

[3]. Böger A, Huxhold O. The Changing Relationship Between Partnership Status and Loneliness: Effects Related to Aging and Historical Time. J Gerontol B Psychol Sci Soc Sci. 2020 Aug 13;75(7):1423-1432. doi: 10.1093/geronb/gby153. PMID: 30590817.

[4]. Brandts L, van Tilburg TG, Bosma H, Huisman M, van den Brandt PA. Loneliness in Later Life and Reaching Longevity: Findings From the Longitudinal Aging Study Amsterdam. J Gerontol B Psychol Sci Soc Sci. 2021 Jan 18;76(2):415-424. doi: 10.1093/geronb/gbaa145. PMID: 32880641; PMCID: PMC7813181.

[5]. Carter GL, Douglass MD. The Aging Narcissus: Just a Myth? Narcissism Moderates the Age-Loneliness Relationship in Older Age. Front Psychol. 2018 Jul 24;9:1254. doi: 10.3389/fpsyg.2018.01254. PMID: 30087636; PMCID: PMC6066667.

[6]. Casanova G, Zaccaria D, Rolandi E, Guaita A. The Effect of Information and Communication Technology and Social Networking Site Use on Older People's Well-Being in Relation to Loneliness: Review of Experimental Studies. J Med Internet Res. 2021 Mar 1;23(3):e23588. doi: 10.2196/23588. PMID: 33439127; PMCID: PMC7961406

[7]. Chamberlain SA, Savage R, Bronskill SE, Griffith LE, Rochon P, Batara J, Gruneir A. Examining the association between loneliness and emergency department visits using Canadian Longitudinal Study of Aging (CLSA) data: a retrospective cross-sectional study. BMC Geriatr. 2022 Jan 22;22(1):69. doi: 10.1186/s12877-022-02763-8. PMID: 35065598; PMCID: PMC8783523.

[8]. Cheng GH, Chan A, Østbye T, Malhotra R. Productive engagement patterns and their association with depressive symptomatology, loneliness, and cognitive function among older adults. Aging Ment Health. 2021 Feb;25(2):332-340. doi: 10.1080/13607863.2019.1686458. Epub 2019 Nov 13. PMID: 31718250.

[9]. Chiu CJ, Lo YH, Ho MH, Montayre J, Zhao IY. Association between loneliness and acceptance of using robots and pets as companions among older Chinese immigrants during the COVID-19 pandemic. Australas J Ageing. 2022 Sep;41(3):414-423. doi: 10.1111/ajag.13075.

Epub 2022 Apr 19. PMID: 35438833; PMCID: PMC9111400.

[10]. Domènech-Abella J, Mundó J, Switsers L, van Tilburg T, Fernández D, Aznar-Lou I. Social network size, loneliness, physical functioning and depressive symptoms among older adults: Examining reciprocal associations in four waves of the Longitudinal Aging Study Amsterdam (LASA). Int J Geriatr Psychiatry. 2021 Oct;36(10):1541-1549. doi: 10.1002/gps.5560. Epub 2021 May 9. PMID: 33908639.

[11]. Field internet use in adolescents

[12]. Field et al loneliness in the young alone

[13]. Gale CR, Westbury L, Cooper C. Social isolation and loneliness as risk factors for the progression of frailty: the English Longitudinal Study of Ageing. Age Ageing. 2018 May 1;47(3):392-397. doi: 10.1093/ageing/afx188. PMID: 29309502; PMCID: PMC5920346.

[14]. Gan DRY, Wister AV, Best JR. Environmental Influences on Life Satisfaction and Depressive Symptoms Among Older Adults With Multimorbidity: Path Analysis Through Loneliness in the Canadian Longitudinal Study on Aging. Gerontologist. 2022 Jul 15;62(6):855-864. doi: 10.1093/geront/gnac004. PMID: 35034124; PMCID: PMC9290896.

[15]. Gyasi RM, Yeboah AA, Mensah CM, Ouedraogo R, Addae EA. Neighborhood, social isolation and mental health outcome among older people in Ghana. J Affect Disord. 2019 Dec 1;259:154-163. doi: 10.1016/j.jad.2019.08.024. Epub 2019 Aug 15. PMID: 31445342.

[16]. Hawkley LC, Kocherginsky M. Transitions in Loneliness Among Older Adults: A 5-Year Follow-Up in the National Social Life, Health, and Aging Project. Res Aging. 2018 Apr;40(4):365-387. doi: 10.1177/0164027517698965. Epub 2017 Mar 17. PMID: 29519211; PMCID: PMC6355458.

[17]. Heins P, Boots LMM, Koh WQ, Neven A, Verhey FRJ, de Vugt ME. The Effects of Technological Interventions on Social Participation of Community-Dwelling Older Adults with and without Dementia: A Systematic Review. J Clin Med. 2021 May 25;10(11):2308. doi: 10.3390/jcm10112308. PMID: 34070660; PMCID: PMC8198527.

[18]. Hoogendijk EO, Smit AP, van Dam C, Schuster NA, de Breij S, Holwerda TJ, Huisman M, Dent E, Andrew MK. Frailty Combined with Loneliness or Social Isolation: An Elevated Risk for Mortality in Later Life. J Am Geriatr Soc. 2020 Nov;68(11):2587-2593. doi: 10.1111/jgs.16716. Epub 2020 Jul 23. PMID: 32700319; PMCID: PMC7689758.

[19]. Hu RX, Li LW. Social Disconnectedness and Loneliness: Do Self-Perceptions of Aging Play a Role? J Gerontol B Psychol Sci Soc Sci. 2022 May 5;77(5):936-945. doi: 10.1093/geronb/gbac008. PMID: 35085397; PMCID: PMC9071429.

[20]. Itzick M, Kagan M, Zychlinski E. The Big Five Personality Traits as Predictors of Loneliness among Older Men in Israel. J Psychol. 2020;154(1):60-74. doi: 10.1080/00223980.2019.1653250. Epub 2019 Sep 16. PMID: 31524563.

[21]. Jarach CM, Tettamanti M, Nobili A, D'avanzo B. Social isolation and loneliness as related to progression and reversion of frailty in the Survey of Health Aging Retirement in Europe (SHARE). Age Ageing. 2021 Jan 8;50(1):258-262. doi: 10.1093/ageing/afaa168. PMID: 32915990; PMCID: PMC7793602.

[22]. Jones VK, Hanus M, Yan C, Shade MY, Blaskewicz Boron J, Maschieri Bicudo R. Reducing Loneliness Among Aging Adults: The Roles of Personal Voice Assistants and Anthropomorphic Interactions. Front Public Health. 2021 Dec 10;9:750736. doi: 10.3389/fpubh.2021.750736. PMID: 34957013; PMCID: PMC8702424.

[23]. Kuru Alıcı N, Zorba Bahceli P, Emiroğlu ON. The preliminary effects of laughter therapy on loneliness and death anxiety among older adults living in nursing homes: A nonrandomised pilot study. Int J Older People Nurs. 2018 Dec;13(4):e12206. doi: 10.1111/opn.12206. Epub 2018 Jul 13. PMID: 30004172.

[24]. Kyröläinen AJ, Kuperman V. The Effect of Loneliness on Cognitive Functioning Among Healthy Individuals in Mid- and Late-Adulthood: Evidence From the Canadian Longitudinal Study on Aging (CLSA). Front Psychol. 2021 Sep 3;12:701305. doi: 10.3389/fpsyg.2021.701305. PMID: 34539500; PMCID: PMC8448416.

[25]. Lee EE, Depp C, Palmer BW, Glorioso D, Daly R, Liu J, Tu XM, Kim HC, Tarr P, Yamada Y, Jeste DV. High prevalence and adverse health effects of loneliness in community-dwelling adults across the lifespan: role of wisdom as a protective factor. Int Psychogeriatr. 2019 Oct;31(10):1447-1462. doi: 10.1017/S1041610218002120. PMID: 30560747; PMCID: PMC6581650.

[26]. Liqing L, Ding H, Li Z. Does Internet Use Impact the Health Status of Middle-Aged and Older Populations? Evidence from China Health and Retirement Longitudinal Study (CHARLS). Int J Environ Res Public Health. 2022 Mar 18;19(6):3619. doi: 10.3390/ijerph19063619. PMID: 35329305; PMCID: PMC8954843.

[27]. Liu C, Zhou S, Bai X. Intergenerational relationship quality, sense of loneliness, and attitude toward later life among aging Chinese adults in Hong Kong. Front Psychol. 2022 Aug 9;13:930857. doi: 10.3389/fpsyg.2022.930857. PMID: 36017420; PMCID: PMC9397484.

[28]. Losada-Baltar A, Martínez-Huertas JÁ, Jiménez-Gonzalo L, Pedroso-Chaparro MDS, Gallego-Alberto L, Fernandes-Pires J, Márquez-González M. Longitudinal Correlates of Loneliness and Psychological Distress During the Lockdown Situation due to COVID-19. Effects of Age and Self-Perceptions of Aging. J Gerontol B Psychol Sci Soc Sci. 2022 Apr 1;77(4):652-660. doi: 10.1093/geronb/gbab012. PMID: 33438002; PMCID: PMC7928595.

[29]. Mehrabi F, Béland F. Effects of social isolation, loneliness and frailty on health outcomes and their possible mediators and moderators in community-dwelling older adults: A scoping review. Arch Gerontol Geriatr. 2020 Sep-Oct;90:104119. doi: 10.1016/j.archger.2020.1041

[30]. Menec VH, Newall NE, Mackenzie CS, Shooshtari S, Nowicki S. Examining social isolation and loneliness in combination in relation to social support and psychological distress using Canadian Longitudinal Study of Aging (CLSA) data. PLoS One. 2020 Mar 23;15(3):e0230673. doi: 10.1371/journal.pone.0230673. PMID: 32203553; PMCID: PMC7089537.

[31]. Mick P, Parfyonov M, Wittich W, Phillips N, Guthrie D, Kathleen Pichora-Fuller M. Associations between sensory loss and social networks, participation, support, and loneliness: Analysis of the Canadian Longitudinal Study on Aging. Can Fam Physician. 2018 Jan;64(1):e33-e41. Erratum in: Can Fam Physician. 2018 Feb;64(2):92. PMID: 29358266; PMCID: PMC5962968.

[32]. Moieni M, Seeman TE, Robles TF, Lieberman MD, Okimoto S, Lengacher C, Irwin MR, Eisenberger NI. Generativity and Social Well-Being in Older Women: Expectations Regarding Aging Matter. J Gerontol B Psychol Sci Soc Sci. 2021 Jan 18;76(2):289-294. doi: 10.1093/geronb/gbaa022. PMID: 32064530; PMCID: PMC7813180.

[33]. Nguyen TT. Wisdom as a potential antidote to loneliness in aging. Int Psychogeriatr. 2021 May;33(5):429-431. doi: 10.1017/S1041610220001660. PMID: 34057066; PMCID: PMC8247117.

[34]. Ormstad H, Eilertsen G, Heir T, Sandvik L. Personality traits and the risk of becoming lonely in old age: A 5-year follow-up study. Health Qual Life Outcomes. 2020 Feb 28;18(1):47. doi: 10.1186/s12955-020-01303-5. PMID: 32111214; PMCID: PMC7049219.

[35]. Peng S, Roth AR. Social Isolation and Loneliness Before and During the COVID-19 Pandemic: A Longitudinal Study of U.S. Adults Older Than 50. J Gerontol B Psychol Sci Soc Sci. 2022 Jul 5;77(7):e185-e190. doi: 10.1093/geronb/gbab068. PMID: 33870414; PMCID: PMC8083229.

[36]. Ramesh A, Issac TG, Mukku SSR, Sivakumar PT. Companionship and Sexual Issues in the Aging Population. Indian J Psychol Med. 2021 Sep;43(5 Suppl):S71-S77. doi: 10.1177/02537176211045622. Epub 2021 Oct 5. PMID: 34732958; PMCID: PMC8543609.

[37]. Segel-Karpas D, Cohn-Schwartz E, Ayalon L. Self-perceptions of aging and depressive symptoms: the mediating role of loneliness. Aging Ment Health. 2022 Jul;26(7):1495-1501. doi: 10.1080/13607863.2021.1991275. Epub 2021 Oct 20. PMID: 34669540.

[38]. Shankar A, McMunn A, Demakakos P, Hamer M, Steptoe A. Social isolation and loneliness: Prospective associations with functional status in older adults. Health Psychol. 2017 Feb;36(2):179-187. doi: 10.1037/hea0000437. Epub 2016 Oct 27. PMID: 27786518.

[39]. Spreng RN, Bzdok D. Loneliness and Neurocognitive Aging. Adv Geriatr Med Res. 2021;3(2):e210009. doi: 10.20900/agmr20210009. Epub 2021 Mar 29. PMID: 33880462; PMCID: PMC8055264.

[40]. Svensson M, Rosso A, Elmståhl S, Ekström H. Loneliness, social isolation, and health complaints among older people: A population-based study from the "Good Aging in Skåne (GÅS)" project. SSM Popul Health. 2022 Nov 7;20:101287. doi: 10.1016/j.ssmph.2022.101287. PMID: 36387019; PMCID: PMC9649938.

[41]. Tümer A, Dönmez S, Gümüşsoy S, Balkaya NA. The relationship among aging in place, loneliness, and life satisfaction in the elderly in Turkey. Perspect Psychiatr Care. 2022 Apr;58(2):822-829. doi: 10.1111/ppc.12855. Epub 2021 May 20. PMID: 34018200.

[42]. Wang B, Dong X. The Association Between Personality and Loneliness: Findings From a Community-Dwelling Chinese Aging Population. Gerontol Geriatr Med. 2018 Jul 17;4:2333721418778181. doi: 10.1177/2333721418778181. PMID: 30035191; PMCID: PMC6050618.

[43]. Wilson SJ, Woody A, Padin AC, Lin J, Malarkey WB, Kiecolt-Glaser JK. Loneliness and Telomere Length: Immune and Parasympathetic Function in Associations With Accelerated Aging. Ann Behav Med. 2019 May 3;53(6):541-550. doi: 10.1093/abm/kay064. PMID: 30107521; PMCID: PMC6499407.

[44]. Wister A, Li L, Levasseur M, Kadowaki L, Pickering J. The Effects of Loneliness on Depressive Symptoms Among Older Adults During COVID-19: Longitudinal Analyses of the Canadian Longitudinal Study on Aging. J Aging Health. 2022 Nov 16:8982643221129686. doi: 10.1177/08982643221129686. Epub ahead of print. PMID: 36383045; PMCID: PMC9672981.

[45]. Yin J, Lassale C, Steptoe A, Cadar D. Exploring the bidirectional associations between loneliness and cognitive functioning over 10 years: the English longitudinal study of ageing. Int J Epidemiol. 2019 Dec 1;48(6):1937-1948. doi: 10.1093/ije/dyz085. PMID: 31056641; PMCID: PMC6929532.

[46]. Yu K, Wu S, Chi I. Internet Use and Loneliness of Older Adults Over Time: The Mediating Effect of Social Contact. J Gerontol B Psychol Sci Soc Sci. 2021 Feb 17;76(3):541-550. doi: 10.1093/geronb/gbaa004. PMID: 31942629.

[47]. Zeytinoglu M, Wroblewski KE, Vokes TJ, Huisingh-Scheetz M, Hawkley LC, Huang ES. Association of Loneliness With Falls: A Study of Older US Adults Using the National Social Life, Health, and Aging Project. Gerontol Geriatr Med. 2021 Jan 29;7:2333721421989217. doi: 10.1177/2333721421989217. PMID: 33614830; PMCID: PMC786845

Review Article

AJPRR (2023) x:xx

American Journal of Psychiatric Research and Reviews
(ISSN:2637-479X)

Inactivity and Sedentary Behavior in Aging Adults: A Narrative Review

Tiffany Field, PhD

University of Miami/Miller School of Medicine and Fielding Graduate University

ABSTRACT

The recent literature (last five years) on inactivity and sedentary behavior in aging (ageing) adults is predominantly focused on negative effects of inactivity/sedentary behavior along with some studies on predictors/risk variables and interventions. Aging has been typically defined as starting as early as 60 or 65. And, inactivity has been defined as reduced time being active and/or increased time being sedentary. The prevalence rates for inactivity in aging adults have been highly variable in this literature, ranging from a low of 21% to a high of 79%. Negative effects have included cognitive impairment, reduced muscle strength, frailty, depression and mortality. The Negative biological effects have included increased cytokines and triglycerides as well as increased hippocampal volume and white matter hyperintensities. Predictors/risk factors have been social isolation, loneliness, inadequate nutrition and multiple demographic variables. Interventions have been effective including stepping, Pilates and mobile health exercises. More well-designed longitudinal studies are needed as well as more robust randomized controlled trials.

*Correspondence to Author:
Tiffany Field, PhD
University of Miami/Miller School of Medicine and Fielding Graduate University

How to cite this article:
Tiffany Field. Inactivity and Sedentary Behavior in Aging Adults: A Narrative Review. American Journal of Psychiatric Research and Reviews, 2023; x:xx

eSciPub LLC
Website: https://escipub.com/

This narrative review involved entering the terms inactivity, sedentary behavior and aging (ageing) into PubMed and PsycINFO. The search yielded 209 papers for the last five years. However, following exclusion criteria including case studies and non-English language papers, this review is a summary of the research reported in 47 papers. This recent literature is predominantly focused on negative effects of inactivity/sedentary behavior on aging adults along with studies on predictors/risk factors and interventions. This narrative review is accordingly divided into sections on prevalence of inactivity/sedentary behavior in aging adults, negative effects, predictors/risk factors and interventions. These are followed by a section on methodological limitations of the research.

Definitions of Inactivity and Sedentary Behavior

In this literature, inactivity and sedentary behavior have sometimes been used interchangeably and sometimes operationally defined differently and measured in tandem. Both physical inactivity and sedentary behavior have frequently been assessed by the Physical Activity Scale for the Elderly (Klicnik et al, 2022) and occasionally by accelerometer (Rodriguez-Gomez et al, 2018). According to the Copenhagen Consensus Statement, "Physical activity entails body movement that increases energy expenditure relative to rest and is often characterized in terms of intensity from light to moderate to rigorous "(Bangsbro et al,2019).

Prevalence of Inactivity and Sedentary Behavior in Aging Adults

The prevalence of inactivity and sedentary behavior in older adults has varied widely across cultures from a low of 21% inactivity in Malaysia (Ibrahim et al, 2022) to a high of 79% sedentary behavior in European older adults (Gine-Garriga et al, 2020) (see table 1). In the latter study, an accelerometer was used to measure physical activity in 1360 adults (mean age=75 years). Based on the accelerometer data, 19% engaged

in light intensity physical activity, and only 3% engaged in moderate to vigorous activity.

The prevalence of inactivity and sedentary behavior in aging adults in other countries include 30% for France (Pierre et al, 2022), 34% for Singapore (Aithal et al, 2022) and 58% for Brazil (Christofoletti et al, 2022). The prevalence has also varied by year of the study. For example, studies from Malaysia indicated a prevalence of 49% in 2019 (Chan et al, 2019), but 30% in 2020 (Chan et al, 2020) and 21% in 2022 (Ibrahim et al, 2022), suggesting that the prevalence of inactivity in aging adults had been decreasing in that country.

Inactivity has also been measured by hours per day. So, for example, in a study that used two devices for assessing activity (ActivPAL and ActiGraph), sedentary behavior was noted to occur approximately 10 hours per day, light intensity activity 5 hours per day, and moderate to vigorous activity 1 hour per day (Rosenberg et al, 2020). In this sample (mean age=77 years), different types of activity were also noted including sitting 10 hours per day, standing 4 hours per day, and stepping 1 hour per day.

Effects of Inactivity and/or Sedentary Behavior on Aging Adults

The effects of inactivity and/or sedentary behavior on aging adults are also highly variable, and typically depend on the interests of the researchers (see table 2). The negative effects include cognitive impairment, limited activities of daily living, blood pressure dysregulation, limited muscle strength, frailty, Sarcopenia, bone loss, depression, and mortality. Of these negative effects, the most frequently studied were cognitive impairment followed by depression.

Cognitive Impairment

Reports on the associations between inactivity, sedentary behavior and cognitive impairment have been highly variable. In one study (N =3780, 55 to 87-year-olds), sitting time greater than 75% of daily activity related to a 60% greater odds of cognitive impairment (Gafni et al, 2022). These authors also reported that not meeting physical activity guidelines related to 27% greater odds of cognitive impairment.

In another study entitled "Profiles of sedentary behaviors in the oldest old" (N =852 adults greater than 80-years-old), the most passive group had lower cognitive function (Zhou et al, 2022). That group also had more difficulties with activities of daily living.

More specific cognitive functions were explored in a study on 75 old adults (mean age=75 years) (Coelho et al, 2020). In this sample, total sedentary time was associated with several measures of executive function (e.g. planning and time management) and memory problems. Less cognitive demanding sedentary behavior (TV viewing and napping) was associated with worse performance on executive function and memory tasks (e.g. building times on Lego towers). Executive function was the most compromised in older adults who were physically inactive.

Memory, language and executive function problems have been reported in still another study on aging adults (Moreira et al, 2022). In this study, the type of sedentary behavior was again a factor. Engaging in mentally active sedentary behavior as, for example, occupational screen time, did not lead to inferior cognitive function. Similarly, in a systematic review, sedentary behavior for reading and computer use was positively associated with cognitive function (Mellow et al, 2022). In this review of 23 studies (N= 23,000 old adults, mean age=71 years), greater physical activity and less sedentary behavior were related to greater cognitive function. In addition, cognitive function was related to sleep as an inverted U-shaped function with too few and too many hours of sleep being associated with inferior cognitive function.

As in all of these cross-sectional studies, direction of effects cannot be determined. Inactivity could be disturbing sleep which, in turn, impairs cognitive function or vice versa or the problems could be bi-directional or reciprocal.

Physical Health

Sedentary behavior has been explored for its association with health in later life (Russell et al, 2019). In this sample from the National Health and Aging Trends Study (N= 1587), multivariate models were used to explore the association of time and six sedentary behaviors including TV, sitting and talking, hobbies, computers, driving, and resting. TV watching was the most frequent and resting the least frequent of the sedentary behaviors, but both TV and resting were associated with worse health.

In a paper entitled "Physical activity and sedentarism among seniors in France and their impact on health", "sedentarity" was noted in 30% of the sample (Pierre et al, 2022). The criterion for sedentarism was adults who failed to meet the WHO recommended physical activity levels (N = 1155 greater than 55–year-old adults). Older adults in this sample averaged six hours per day in sedentary activities which contributed to their ill health.

Muscle Strength

Muscle strength has been notably associated with physical activity of older adults. Low grip strength is one example of inactivity effects (Wang et sl, 2019). Low grip strength has also been associated with greater sedentary behavior (Ramsey et al, 2021). In this sample, greater sedentary behavior was also associated with lower body muscle strength and inferior performance on the chair-to-stand test. Grip strength (hand grip) has also been studied in older Brazilian adults (Christofoletti et al, 2022). In this sample, low grip strength occurred in 58% of all-day sitters, 23% of sitters and 19% of active sitters.

Frailty

Frailty has also resulted from inactivity. In a sample from the Toledo Study for Healthy Aging (N=771), greater frailty, along with less physical function, was reported for the physically inactive and high sedentary group (Manas et al,2019). As others have noted, "heterogeneity in aging can be explained by frailty" (Kehler et al, 2019).

These authors also suggested that long sedentary bouts and sedentary time are risk factors for mortality in frail individuals, but not in fit individuals.

Sarcopenia

Given that sarcopenia (loss of muscle mass) is highly associated with frailty (multi-system impairment), it is not surprising that sedentary behavior has also affected sarcopenia (deSouza et al, 2022). In that sample (N=1165), sedentary behavior, as measured by the International Physical Activity Questionnaire and a report of greater than two hours watching TV or video, was related to sarcopenia. Sarcopenia was measured by the amount of time over 5 trials that exceeded 15 seconds in the sit-to-stand test.

Bone Loss

Bone loss typically accompanies frailty and sarcopenia. In a study on bone and skeletal muscle change in "oldest–old women" (greater than 75-years-old), systematic declines in bone and muscle were associated with physical inactivity (Cavedon et al, 2030). Dual energy x-ray absorptiometry revealed that whole body bone mineral density was decreased by 15%. In another study on associations between sedentary time, physical activity and bone health (N =871), physical activity was measured by an accelerometer and bone mass by bone densitometry (Rodriguez-Gomez et al, 2018). The combined effect of all movement (physical inactivity and sedentary behavior) was associated with whole body, leg and femoral region bone mass in the entire sample. Leg and pelvic bone were more affected in males and whole body, arm, and leg bone in females. More vigorous activity led to greater bone mass, most especially in males. A physical activity increase and sedentary behavior decrease were associated with reduced bone fracture risk in women.

Negative Affect and Depression

Negative affect and depression have also been associated with sedentary behavior and inactivity in older adults. For example, in a sample from the Swedish National Study on Aging and Care (N=595 greater than 65--year-old adults), a greater amount of sitting and less physical activity led to negative affect (Chen et al, 2021). Social participation and support lessened this association.

Although COVID has been noted to exacerbate sedentary behavior and inactivity, engaging in vigorous and moderately vigorous activity has led to greater resilience, positive affect and less depression in one sample during COVID (N=483 in greater than 60-year-old adults) (Camedo et al,2020).

In a systematic review and meta-analysis of 24 studies on physically active adults greater than 60-years-old, there was a lesser risk of depression (Cunningham et al, 2020). In this meta-analysis, physical activity also decreased the risk of breast and prostate cancer, fractures, falls, activities of daily living disability, cognitive decline, dementia, Alzheimer's, other morbidities and mortality.

Physiological and Biochemical Effects

Physiological and biochemical effects of inactivity in aging adults have included blood pressure dysregulation, increased cytokines and triglycerides and decreased hippocampal volume. In a paper entitled "Sedentary behavior is associated with reduced cardiovagal baroreflex sensitivity in healthy adults", greater sedentary behavior was associated with dysregulation of arterial blood pressure (Mori et al, 2022). This was particularly noted in males.

Sedentary behavior has also been associated with alterations in cytokines and chemokines (MacNeil et al, 2021). The metabolic profiles of old adults being physically inactive and sedentary have also included higher cholesterol LDL and triglyceride levels and lower cholesterol HDL (Tian et al. 2021).

In a review of the literature on sedentary behavior and the biological hallmarks of aging, several effects have been noted (Raffin et al, 2023). These include genomic instability, telomere attrition, epigenetic, alterations, loss of proteostasis (protein homeostasis), dysregulated nutrient sensing, mitochondrial dysfunction, cellular senescence, stem cell exhaustion, and altered intercellular communication. These measures have not been made on the same individuals, so their relative effects are not known.

In a paper entitled "Hemodynamic and structural brain measures in high and low sedentary older adults", data were reviewed from the Irish Longitudinal Study on Aging (N=718) (Massakkers et al, 2021). High sedentary individuals had less hippocampal volumes and greater white matter hyperintensities. These findings could relate to the cognitive deficits that have been noted in sedentary old adults, e. g. poor memory.

Mortality

In a paper called "Associations between sedentary time and six–year all–cause mortality", a large sample (N=17,048) was followed for six years (Li et al, 2022). When a group who spent less than four hours in sedentary time per day was compared to a group who were sedentary 8 to 11 hours per day, the higher sedentary folks were more likely to experience all–cause mortality. For each one hour per day of sedentary time, the risk increased 3% for all-cause mortality.

Risk Factors/Predictors

Several risk factors/predictors have been reported in this recent literature on inactivity/ sedentary behavior in aging adults (see table 3). They include age itself, social isolation, loneliness, and studies in which multiple factors were explored.

Age

Despite a significant literature on centenarians suggesting that they have reached that age because they continue to be active and have a healthy diet (Field, 2023), at least one study in this literature suggests that centenarians versus nongenarians (90 years plus) had less steps per day on the accelerometer, but also fewer breaks (Hernandez–Vicente et al, 2019). The greatest

activity in both groups occurred between 10 am and noon. These data are limited for their small and unequal sample sizes (only 18 centenarians and 11 nongenarians).

Social Isolation

Social isolation has been noted to lead to inactivity in the SHARE project (Survey of Health, Aging and Retirement in Europe) (N =67,173 adults from 17 European countries) (Matos et al, 2021). in this sample, greater social isolation led to greater inactivity and a less healthy diet (too few fruits and vegetables).

In a study, entitled "Social contact impacts physical activity and sedentary behavior among older adults in Japan due to COVID–19"(N=1925, mean age = 74), sedentary time increased six hours per week during COVID (Otaki et al, 2022). Also during COVID, social contact decreased in 76% of the sample and virtual contact decreased in 39% of the sample. The physical activity decrease was associated with the decrease in social participation and interactions with friends.

Loneliness

Social isolation would be expected to lead to loneliness. Loneliness has been a predictor, variable for fatigue, inactivity and cognitive impairment. In a study entitled "Is loneliness, a predictor of the modern geriatric giants?", four syndromes were researched including frailty (linked to fatigue and physical inactivity), Sarcopenia , anorexia of aging and cognitive impairment (the four giants) (Gine-Garriga et al, 2021). The prevalence of each of these was noted for the sample from the Survey of Health, Aging and Retirement of Europe project (N= 17,742). The prevalence of loneliness was given at 9 to 12%, fatigue at 16%, physical inactivity at 10%, Sarcopenia at 6%, anorexia at 5% and cognitive impairment at 10%.

In another study, however, loneliness and/or social isolation was reported in both physically, active and physically inactive older adults (deJoning et al, 2021). This study may have been under- powered and gender-biased with only 24 women (mean age=73) being interviewed and transcripts being thematically analyzed.

Multiple Risk Factor Studies

A number of researchers have reported multiple risk factors. For example, in a study, entitled "Prevalence and factors associated with physical inactivity among older adults in Malaysia" (N=3969, greater than 60-year-old adults), the Global Physical Activity Questionnaire was given during a face-to-face interview (Chan et al, 2020). Physical inactivity was noted in 30% of this sample and the risk factors were being greater than 80 years, being unemployed, having functional limitations, and having diabetes and dementia.

Surprisingly, one year earlier, the same research group reported a significantly greater prevalence in this sample from the National Health and Morbidity Survey (N=equals 3790 greater than 60-year-old-adults) (Chan et al, 2019). These authors reported 48% prevalence of physical inactivity in this 2019 study and 30% in their 2020 study, suggesting that the prevalence was decreasing in Malaysia. Multiple risks were identified in this sample as well including being female, older age, single, having no formal education, spending greater than seven hours in sedentary time, diabetes, anemia, and mobility impairment. The two different time samples shared the risk factors of being female and older age and having diabetes.

In a study by a different group in Malaysia, a sample (N=555) was followed for three years and the Physical Activity Scale for the Elderly was used to assess physical activity (Ibrahim et al, 2022). Inactivity was noted in 21% of the sample and the predictors of inactivity were older age, smoking, lower gait speed and lower cognitive status. In this literature, inactivity and sedentary behavior have sometimes been used interchangeably and sometimes operationally defined differently and measured in tandem.

In a study already described, in which 79% of time was spent in sedentary behavior and 90% time in light intensity physical activity, females were noted to engage in light physical activity and males in moderate physical activity (Gine-Garriga et al, 2020). Although the sample was said to watch TV and read 47% of the time, the risk factors for sedentary behavior were older age, being female, single, taking more meds, being obese or overweight, and having a slower gait.

Finally, in a sample from Singapore (N= 2240 greater than 60-year-old adults), insufficient activity was noted in 34% and sedentary behavior (defined as greater than seven hours per day) was seen in 17% of the aging adults (Aithal et al, 2022). The risk factors in this sample were being an older female, residing in smaller housing, living with a child without a spouse, functional limitations and sensory impairment.

Protective Factors

The few buffers or protective factors for physical inactivity that have been noted in this literature on aging adults include retirement, a walkable location, and a greener environment (see table 4). Retirement has, surprisingly, favored activity. In a paper entitled "Objectively measured sedentary time before and after transition to retirement, a sample from the Finnish Retirement and Aging Study was assessed (N= 478, mean age=63) (Suorsa et al, 2020). Based on monitoring by a wrist ActiGraph accelerometer, pre-retirement activity averaged eight hours and 10 minutes in females and nine hours and 49 minutes in males. Post retirement activity increased 29 minutes for females, although there was no change for males.

In another study, greater sedentary time but also greater physical activity were noted at a non-home environment on weekdays, and at home on weekends in a sample of 53 retirees and 137 workers (Pasadena et al. 2021). Greater moderately vigorous physical activity was noted on days off (34 minutes more). No difference was noted for the retirees at 33 minutes more activity on days off.

Table 1. Prevalence of inactivity and sedentary behavior in aging adults.

Prevalence	First author
21% Malaysia	Ibrahim
30% France	Pierre
30% Malaysia	Chan, 2020
34% Singapore	Aithal
49% Malaysia	Chan, 2019
58% Brazil	Christofoletti
79% European countries	Gine-Garriga

Table 2. Effects of inactivity and sedentary behavior in aging adults.

Effects	First author
Cognitive impairment	Gafni, Zhou, Coelho, Moreira, Melluw
Physical health	Russell, Pierre
Muscle strength	Wang, Ramsey, Christofoletti
Frailty	Manas
Sarcopenia	deSouza
Bone loss	Cavedon, Rodriguez-Gomez
Negative affect and depression	Chen, Camedo, Cunningham
Physiological and biochemical effects	
Dysregulated arterial blood pressure	Mori
Cytokines and chemokines	MacNei
>LDL and triglycerides and <HDL	Tian
Telomere attrition	Raffin
<hippocampal volume	Massakers
>mortality	Li

Table 3. Risk factors/predictors of inactivity and sedentary behavior in aging adults.

Risk factor	First author
Age	Hernandez-Vicente
Social isolation	Matos, Otaki
Loneliness	Gine-Garriga, DeJonning
Multiple factors	Chan, Ibrahim, Gine-Garriga, Aithal

Table 4. Protective factors of inactivity and sedentary behavior in aging adults.

Protective factor	First author
Retirement	Suorsa, Pasadena
Neighborhood walkability	Greenwood-Hickman
Denser greenness	Kienik

Table 5. Interventions for inactivity and sedentary behavior in aging adults.

Interventions	First author
"stand up and move"	Crombie
Home-square stepping	Lees
Mobile health	Niemicz
Pilates	Soori

In a paper, entitled "Associations between perceived neighborhood walkability and device/based physical activity and sedentary behavior patterns in older adults" (N=1077), the participants were given the Physical Activity Neighborhood Environment Scale. (Greenwood-Hickman et al, 2022). Greater scores on neighborhood walkability were associated with more steps and sit-to-stand transitions.

In a paper entitled "Leisure sedentary time and physical activity are higher in neighborhoods with denser greenness" (N=36,580 Canadians), both sedentary time and physical activity as assessed by the Physical Activity for Elderly Scale were greater in those aging adults living in neighborhoods with greater greenness (Klienik et al, 2022).

Interventions

Interventions have enhanced activity level in inactive aging adults (see table 5). Those interventions that were found in the current literature on aging adults include "stand-up-and-move", stepping, mobile health and Pilates. In a paper entitled "The feasibility and effectiveness of a community-based intervention to reduce sedentary behavior", sedentary behavior was defined as sitting more than 6 hours per day (Crombie et al, 2021). The "stand-up-and-move" intervention done at home significantly reduced sedentary behavior.

In another intervention study entitled "Potential value of home square–stepping exercise for inactive, older adults", a sample of 10 adults older than 65 engaged in a three-week square-stepping intervention (Lees et al, 2022). Based on pedometer measures, stepping increased 12% and 8 of the 10 adults reached moderate intensity activity levels.

In a review paper entitled, "mHealth supported intervention with potential to address sedentary behavior in older adults: a scoping review", physical activity was noted to increase following mobile health exercises. But the results are tenuous given that mobile health was combined with non-mobile health exercises in 13 studies, and only three of those addressed sedentary behavior (Schepens Niemicet al, 2022).

In the only other intervention study that could be found in this literature, aerobic exercises were compared with Pilates in a sample of 75 inactive older women (Soori et al, 2022). Following 12 weeks of Pilates and aerobics, activity levels increased for both groups, but the Pilates versus the aerobics group experienced a greater decrease in depression. This could relate to a larger portion of the body being exercised in the Pilates group. If more pressure receptors are being stimulated, greater vagal activity and serotonin release would be expected leading to less depression (Field, 2022).

Methodological Limitations

Some methodological limitations can be noted for these recent studies on inactivity and sedentary behavior in aging adults. All aspects of the studies have been highly variable including the sampling methods, the sample sizes, the measures, the prevalence, the effects and the risk factors. Aging has been variously defined as starting at 60 or 65 or at 80 or 85. And the different age adult groups have rarely been compared except for the comparison of nongenarians and centenarians (Hernandez-Vicente et al, 2019). Although the age range of the samples typically spanned 10 years, age was not considered as a potential risk factor for inactivity or sedentary behavior but was treated as a covariate in most of the data analyses.

The researchers have primarily used self-report scales like the Physical Activity Scale for the Elderly, although some have used accelerometers and actigraphs to record activity. But even those more objective measures yielded variable results. In a systematic review of 95 studies (93% from high-income countries), for example, the researchers reported on the impact of different ways of distributing and using accelerometers (Pulsford et al, 2023). This review revealed that consent and adherence were greater for devices delivered in person and accelerometers worn on the wrist versus the waist. These results were not surprising in that older adults frequently appreciate social interaction and dislike waist measurements.

Inactivity and sedentary behavior have sometimes been used interchangeably and sometimes differently defined and measured in tandem, and in at least one study, both physical activity and sedentary time had positive effects. The variability in the age groups sampled, the various definitions of inactivity and the different measures used have made it difficult to conduct systematic reviews and meta-analyses, resulting in very few of those in this literature. Based on the variability of the measures, the prevalence rates for inactivity in aging adults have also been highly variable, ranging from a low of 21% to a high of 79%, although some of the variance may relate to cultural and location (e. g. urban/rural) differences in the samples.

The research has been primarily focused on the negative effects of inactivity/sedentary behavior. Although several negative effects have been reported, ranging from cognitive impairment to frailty to mortality, the studies have focused on these as single variables rather than exploring multiple negative effects for their relative contributions to the variance in the outcomes. And, virtually no positive effects have been reported for either inactivity or sedentary behavior. The predictor variables have also been typically treated as individual risk factors such as social isolation. And, surprisingly, diabetes was the only chronic illness that repeatedly emerged as a risk factor, although several medical conditions would be expected to limit activity.

Most of the studies are cross-sectional, making directionality impossible to determine. Some of the variables could be treated as effects or as risks. For example, depression was treated as a negative effect of inactivity, although depression could also be a risk factor for inactivity. And, social isolation was treated as a risk factor, although it could also be seen as a negative effect of inactivity.

Some conditions that have favorably affected activity in aging adults include retirement, walkable neighborhoods and greener neighborhoods. Interventions have included physical activities like "stand-up-and-move", stepping and Pilates. But these interventions have not been compared, so their relative effectiveness for inactivity/sedentary behavior in aging adults is not known.

For future directions, beyond correcting methodological limitations of the existing literature, several topics seem to be missing from this literature. Surprisingly, bad nutrition, which has contributed significantly to frailty in aging adults, did not appear in this literature. And, the Silver Sneakers activity programs that have served many seniors was only mentioned as continuing during COVID on video programs.

Conclusions

Recent literature on inactivity and sedentary behavior in aging adults has been predominantly focused on their negative effects. Those have included cognitive impairment, reduced muscle strength, frailty, depression and mortality and biological effects have included increased cytokines, triglycerides, hippocampal volume and white matter hyperintensities. Social isolation, loneliness, inadequate nutrition and multiple demographics have been identified as significant predictor variables. Stepping, Pilates and mobile health exercises have been effective interventions. Although more longitudinal studies and robust randomized controlled trials are needed, this literature highlights the negative effects of inactivity and sedentary behavior on aging adults.

References

[1]. Aithal S, Visaria A, Malhotra R. Prevalence, Sociodemographic, and Health Correlates of Insufficient Physical Activity and High Sedentary Behavior Among Older Adults in Singapore. J Aging Phys Act. 2022 Feb 24;30(6):922-935. doi: 10.1123/japa.2021-0324. PMID: 35203055.

[2]. Bangsbo J, Blackwell J, Boraxbekk CJ, Caserotti P, Dela F, Evans AB, Jespersen AP, Gliemann L, Kramer AF, Lundbye-Jensen J, Mortensen EL, Lassen AJ, Gow AJ, Harridge SDR, Hellsten Y,

Kjaer M, Kujala UM, Rhodes RE, Pike ECJ, Skinner T, Skovgaard T, Troelsen J, Tulle E, Tully MA, van Uffelen JGZ, Viña J. Copenhagen Consensus statement 2019: physical activity and ageing. Br J Sports Med. 2019 Jul;53(14):856-858. doi: 10.1136/bjsports-2018-100451. Epub 2019 Feb 21. PMID: 30792257; PMCID: PMC6613739.

[3]. Carriedo A, Cecchini JA, Fernandez-Rio J, Méndez-Giménez A. COVID-19, Psychological Well-being and Physical Activity Levels in Older Adults During the Nationwide Lockdown in Spain. Am J Geriatr Psychiatry. 2020 Nov;28(11):1146-1155. doi: 10.1016/j.jagp.2020.08.007. Epub 2020 Aug 22. PMID: 32919872; PMCID: PMC7443087.

[4]. Cavedon V, Milanese C, Laginestra FG, Giuriato G, Pedrinolla A, Ruzzante F, Schena F, Venturelli M. Bone and skeletal muscle changes in oldest-old women: the role of physical inactivity. Aging Clin Exp Res. 2020 Feb;32(2):207-214. doi: 10.1007/s40520-019-01352-x. Epub 2019 Sep 18. PMID: 31535334.

[5]. Chan YY, Lim KK, Omar MA, Mohd Yusoff MF, Sooryanarayana R, Ahmad NA, Abd Razak MA, Baharudin Shaharuddin A, Mahmud NA, Mahmud MAF, Abdul Mutalip MH, Mohd Hairi NN. Prevalence and factors associated with physical inactivity among older adults in Malaysia: A cross-sectional study. Geriatr Gerontol Int. 2020 Dec;20 Suppl 2:49-56. doi: 10.1111/ggi.13977. PMID: 33370865.

[6]. Chan YY, Sooryanarayana R, Mohamad Kasim N, Lim KK, Cheong SM, Kee CC, Lim KH, Omar MA, Ahmad NA, Mohd Hairi NN. Prevalence and correlates of physical inactivity among older adults in Malaysia: Findings from the National Health and Morbidity Survey (NHMS) 2015. Arch Gerontol Geriatr. 2019 Mar-Apr;81:74-83. doi: 10.1016/j.archger.2018.11.012. Epub 2018 Nov 26. PMID: 30521992.

[7]. Chen S, Calderón-Larrañaga A, Saadeh M, Dohrn IM, Welmer AK. Correlations of Subjective and Social Well-Being With Sedentary Behavior and Physical Activity in Older Adults-A Population-Based Study. J Gerontol A Biol Sci Med Sci. 2021 Sep 13;76(10):1789-1795. doi: 10.1093/gerona/glab065. PMID: 33674835; PMCID: PMC8436992.

[8]. Christofoletti M, Sandreschi PF, Manta SW, Confortin SC, Delevatti RS, D'Orsi E, Benedetti TRB, Rech CR, Matias TS. Clustering of Physical Activity and Sedentary Behavior Associated With Body Composition in Brazilian Older Adults. J Aging Phys Act. 2022 Feb 1;30(1):107-113. doi: 10.1123/japa.2020-0157. Epub 2021 Aug 27. PMID: 34453012.

[9]. Coelho L, Hauck K, McKenzie K, Copeland JL, Kan IP, Gibb RL, Gonzalez CLR. The association between sedentary behavior and cognitive ability in older adults. Aging Clin Exp Res. 2020 Nov;32(11):2339-2347. doi: 10.1007/s40520-019-01460-8. Epub 2020 Jan 2. PMID: 31898168.

[10]. Crombie KM, Leitzelar BN, Almassi NE, Mahoney JE, Koltyn KF. The Feasibility and Effectiveness of a Community-Based Intervention to Reduce Sedentary Behavior in Older Adults. J Appl Gerontol. 2022 Jan;41(1):92-102. doi: 10.1177/0733464820987919. Epub 2021 Jan 27. PMID: 33504249; PMCID: PMC8313650.

[11]. Cunningham C, O' Sullivan R, Caserotti P, Tully MA. Consequences of physical inactivity in older adults: A systematic review of reviews and meta-analyses. Scand J Med Sci Sports. 2020 May;30(5):816-827. doi: 10.1111/sms.13616. Epub 2020 Feb 4. PMID: 32020713.

[12]. de Koning J, Richards SH, Wood GER, Stathi A. Profiles of Loneliness and Social Isolation in Physically Active and Inactive Older Adults in Rural England. Int J Environ Res Public Health. 2021 Apr 9;18(8):3971. doi: 10.3390/ijerph18083971. PMID: 33918808; PMCID: PMC8070246.

[13]. de Souza LF, Danielewicz AL, Rech CR, d'Orsi E, Mendonça VA, Lacerda ACR, de Avelar NCP. How much time in sedentary behavior is associated with probable sarcopenia in older adults? Geriatr Nurs. 2022 Nov-Dec;48:127-131. doi: 10.1016/j.gerinurse.2022.09.007. Epub 2022 Oct 5. PMID: 36208539.

[14]. Delerue Matos A, Barbosa F, Cunha C, Voss G, Correia F. Social isolation, physical inactivity and inadequate diet among European middle-aged and older adults. BMC Public Health. 2021 May 15;21(1):924. doi: 10.1186/s12889-021-10956-w. PMID: 33992074; PMCID: PMC8122541.

[15]. Field, T. (2022). Touch for social engagement and therapy: A narrative review. International Journal of Psychology Research and Reviews. 2022.

[16]. Gafni T, Shuval K, Weinstein G, Barlow CE, Gabriel KP, Willis BL, Leonard D, Haskell WL, DeFina LF. Sitting Time, Physical Activity, and Cognitive Impairment in Midlife and Older Adults. J Aging Phys Act. 2022 Jun 1;30(3):355-363. doi: 10.1123/japa.2020-0473. Epub 2021 Aug 27. PMID: 34453026.

[17]. Giné-Garriga M, Jerez-Roig J, Coll-Planas L, Skelton DA, Inzitari M, Booth J, Souza DLB. Is loneliness a predictor of the modern geriatric giants? Analysis from the survey of health, ageing, and retirement in Europe. Maturitas. 2021 Feb;144:93-101. doi:

10.1016/j.maturitas.2020.11.010. Epub 2020 Dec 2. PMID: 33358215.

[18]. Giné-Garriga M, Sansano-Nadal O, Tully MA, Caserotti P, Coll-Planas L, Rothenbacher D, Dallmeier D, Denkinger M, Wilson JJ, Martin-Borràs C, Skjødt M, Ferri K, Farche AC, McIntosh E, Blackburn NE, Salvà A, Roqué-I-Figuls M. Accelerometer-Measured Sedentary and Physical Activity Time and Their Correlates in European Older Adults: The SITLESS Study. J Gerontol A Biol Sci Med Sci. 2020 Sep 16;75(9):1754-1762. doi: 10.1093/gerona/glaa016. PMID: 31943000; PMCID: PMC7494025.

[19]. Greenwood-Hickman MA, Walker R, Bellettiere J, LaCroix AZ, Kim B, Wing D, Richmire K, Crane PK, Larson EB, Rosenberg DE. Associations Between Perceived Neighborhood Walkability and Device-Based Physical Activity and Sedentary Behavior Patterns in Older Adults. J Aging Phys Act. 2022 Feb 1;30(1):98-106. doi: 10.1123/japa.2020-0387. Epub 2021 Aug 13. PMID: 34388701; PMCID: PMC8843243.

[20]. Hernández-Vicente A, Santos-Lozano A, Mayolas-Pi C, Rodríguez-Romo G, Pareja-Galeano H, Bustamante N, Gómez-Trullén EM, Lucia A, Garatachea N. Physical Activity and Sedentary Behavior at the End of the Human Lifespan. J Aging Phys Act. 2019 Dec 1;27(4):899-905. doi: 10.1123/japa.2018-0122. PMID: 31034321.

[21]. Ibrahim AM, Singh DKA, Mat S, Mat Ludin AF, Shahar S. Incidence and Predictors of Physical Inactivity Among Malaysian Community-Dwelling Older Persons. J Aging Phys Act. 2022 Jul 13;31(1):105-116. doi: 10.1123/japa.2021-0390. PMID: 35894915.

[22]. Kehler DS, Theou O. The impact of physical activity and sedentary behaviors on frailty levels. Mech Ageing Dev. 2019 Jun;180:29-41. doi: 10.1016/j.mad.2019.03.004. Epub 2019 Mar 26. PMID: 30926562.

[23]. Klicnik I, Cullen JD, Doiron D, Barakat C, Ardern CI, Rudoler D, Dogra S. Leisure sedentary time and physical activity are higher in neighbourhoods with denser greenness and better built environments: an analysis of the Canadian Longitudinal Study on Aging. Appl Physiol Nutr Metab. 2022 Mar;47(3):278-286. doi: 10.1139/apnm-2021-0438. Epub 2021 Nov 8. Erratum in: Appl Physiol Nutr Metab. 2022 Sep 1;47(9):979. PMID: 34748418.

[24]. Lees MA, Edwards J, McCain JE, Bouchard DR. Potential value of home square-stepping exercises for inactive older adults: an exploratory case study. BMC Geriatr. 2022 Jan 3;22(1):14.

doi: 10.1186/s12877-021-02712-x. PMID: 34979952; PMCID: PMC8722225.

[25]. Lees MA, Edwards J, McCain JE, Bouchard DR. Potential value of home square-stepping exercises for inactive older adults: an exploratory case study. BMC Geriatr. 2022 Jan 3;22(1):14. doi: 10.1186/s12877-021-02712-x. PMID: 34979952; PMCID: PMC8722225.

[26]. Li Y, Zhou Q, Luo X, Li H, Feng Y, Zhao Y, Yang X, Wu Y, Han M, Qie R, Wu X, Zhang Y, Huang S, Li T, Yuan L, Zhang J, Hu H, Liu D, Hu F, Zhang M, Hu D. Association between Sedentary Time and 6-Year All-Cause Mortality in Adults: The Rural Chinese Cohort Study. J Nutr Health Aging. 2022;26(3):236-242. doi: 10.1007/s12603-022-1727-6. PMID: 35297465.

[27]. Maasakkers CM, Thijssen DH, Knight SP, Newman L, O'Connor JD, Scarlett S, Carey D, Buckley A, McMorrow JP, Leidhin CN, Feeney J, Melis RJ, Kenny RA, Claassen JA, Looze C. Hemodynamic and structural brain measures in high and low sedentary older adults. J Cereb Blood Flow Metab. 2021 Oct;41(10):2607-2616. doi: 10.1177/0271678X211009382. Epub 2021 Apr 17. PMID: 33866848; PMCID: PMC8504407.

[28]. MacNeil LG, Tarnopolsky MA, Crane JD. Acute, Exercise-Induced Alterations in Cytokines and Chemokines in the Blood Distinguish Physically Active and Sedentary Aging. J Gerontol A Biol Sci Med Sci. 2021 Apr 30;76(5):811-818. doi: 10.1093/gerona/glaa310. PMID: 33289019; PMCID: PMC8087278.

[29]. Mañas A, Del Pozo-Cruz B, Rodríguez-Gómez I, Leal-Martín J, Losa-Reyna J, Rodríguez-Mañas L, García-García FJ, Ara I. Dose-response association between physical activity and sedentary time categories on ageing biomarkers. BMC Geriatr. 2019 Oct 15;19(1):270. doi: 10.1186/s12877-019-1284-y. PMID: 31615446; PMCID: PMC6794876.

[30]. Mellow ML, Crozier AJ, Dumuid D, Wade AT, Goldsworthy MR, Dorrian J, Smith AE. How are combinations of physical activity, sedentary behaviour and sleep related to cognitive function in older adults? A systematic review. Exp Gerontol. 2022 Mar;159:111698. doi: 10.1016/j.exger.2022.111698. Epub 2022 Jan 11. PMID: 35026335.

[31]. Moreira PA, Matos SMA, Pitanga FJG, Giatti L, Barreto SM, Harter Griep R, Almeida MDCC, Santos CAST. Association between Sedentary Behavior and Cognitive Performance in Middle-Aged and Elderly Adults: Cross-Sectional Results from ELSA-Brasil. Int J Environ Res Public Health. 2022 Oct 31;19(21):14234. doi:

10.3390/ijerph192114234. PMID: 36361115; PMCID: PMC9654160.

[32]. Mori S, Kosaki K, Matsui M, Takahashi K, Yoshioka M, Tarumi T, Sugawara J, Shibata A, Kuro-O M, Saito C, Yamagata K, Oka K, Maeda S. Sedentary behavior is associated with reduced cardiovagal baroreflex sensitivity in healthy adults. Hypertens Res. 2022 Jul;45(7):1193-1202. doi: 10.1038/s41440-022-00904-5. Epub 2022 Apr 4. PMID: 35379916.

[33]. Otaki N, Yokoro M, Yano M, Imamura T, Akita M, Tanino N, Fukuo K. Social contact impacts physical activity and sedentary behavior among older adults in Japan due to COVID-19. BMC Geriatr. 2022 Jun 8;22(1):491. doi: 10.1186/s12877-022-03188-z. PMID: 35676622; PMCID: PMC9174618.

[34]. Pasanen S, Halonen JI, Pulakka A, Kestens Y, Thierry B, Brondeel R, Pentti J, Vahtera J, Leskinen T, Stenholm S. Contexts of sedentary time and physical activity among ageing workers and recent retirees: cross-sectional GPS and accelerometer study. BMJ Open. 2021 May 18;11(5):e042600. doi: 10.1136/bmjopen-2020-042600. PMID: 34006539; PMCID: PMC8149443.

[35]. Pierre J, Collinet C, Schut PO, Verdot C. Physical activity and sedentarism among seniors in France, and their impact on health. PLoS One. 2022 Aug 18;17(8):e0272785. doi: 10.1371/journal.pone.0272785. PMID: 35981054; PMCID: PMC9387786.

[36]. Pulsford RM, Brocklebank L, Fenton SAM, Bakker E, Mielke GI, Tsai LT, Atkin AJ, Harvey DL, Blodgett JM, Ahmadi M, Wei L, Rowlands A, Doherty A, Rangul V, Koster A, Sherar LB, Holtermann A, Hamer M, Stamatakis E. The impact of selected methodological factors on data collection outcomes in observational studies of device-measured physical behaviour in adults: A systematic review. Int J Behav Nutr Phys Act. 2023 Mar 8;20(1):26. doi: 10.1186/s12966-022-01388-9. PMID: 36890553; PMCID: PMC9993720.

[37]. Raffin J, de Souto Barreto P, Le Traon AP, Vellas B, Aubertin-Leheudre M, Rolland Y. Sedentary behavior and the biological hallmarks of aging. Ageing Res Rev. 2023 Jan;83:101807. doi: 10.1016/j.arr.2022.101807. Epub 2022 Nov 22. PMID: 36423885.

[38]. Ramsey KA, Meskers CGM, Maier AB. Every step counts: synthesising reviews associating objectively measured physical activity and sedentary behaviour with clinical outcomes in community-dwelling older adults. Lancet Healthy Longev. 2021 Nov;2(11):e764-e772. doi:

10.1016/S2666-7568(21)00203-8. Epub 2021 Nov 3. PMID: 36098033.

[39]. Ramsey KA, Rojer AGM, D'Andrea L, Otten RHJ, Heymans MW, Trappenburg MC, Verlaan S, Whittaker AC, Meskers CGM, Maier AB. The association of objectively measured physical activity and sedentary behavior with skeletal muscle strength and muscle power in older adults: A systematic review and meta-analysis. Ageing Res Rev. 2021 May;67:101266. doi: 10.1016/j.arr.2021.101266. Epub 2021 Feb 16. PMID: 33607291.

[40]. Rodríguez-Gómez I, Mañas A, Losa-Reyna J, Rodríguez-Mañas L, Chastin SFM, Alegre LM, García-García FJ, Ara I. Associations between sedentary time, physical activity and bone health among older people using compositional data analysis. PLoS One. 2018 Oct 22;13(10):e0206013. doi: 10.1371/journal.pone.0206013. PMID: 30346973; PMCID: PMC6197664.

[41]. Rosenberg D, Walker R, Greenwood-Hickman MA, Bellettiere J, Xiang Y, Richmire K, Higgins M, Wing D, Larson EB, Crane PK, LaCroix AZ. Device-assessed physical activity and sedentary behavior in a community-based cohort of older adults. BMC Public Health. 2020 Aug 18;20(1):1256. doi: 10.1186/s12889-020-09330-z. PMID: 32811454; PMCID: PMC7436994.

[42]. Russell D, Chase JD. The Social Context of Sedentary Behaviors and Their Relationships With Health in Later Life. J Aging Phys Act. 2019 Dec 1;27(4):797-806. doi: 10.1123/japa.2018-0109. PMID: 30859891.

[43]. Schepens Niemiec SL, Cariño B, Chatfield AJ, Quan K. mHealth-Supported Interventions With Potential to Address Sedentary Behavior in Older Adults: A Scoping Review. J Aging Phys Act. 2022 Mar 30;30(6):1085-1100. doi: 10.1123/japa.2021-0338. PMID: 35354668.

[44]. Soori S, Heirani A, Rafie F. Effects of the aerobic and Pilates exercises on mental health in inactive older women. J Women Aging. 2022 Jul-Aug;34(4):429-437. doi: 10.1080/08952841.2021.1924576. Epub 2021 May 16. PMID: 33998393.

[45]. Suorsa K, Pulakka A, Leskinen T, Heinonen I, Heinonen OJ, Pentti J, Vahtera J, Stenholm S. Objectively Measured Sedentary Time Before and After Transition to Retirement: The Finnish Retirement and Aging Study. J Gerontol A Biol Sci Med Sci. 2020 Sep 16;75(9):1737-1743. doi: 10.1093/gerona/glz127. PMID: 31095675.

[46]. Tian Q, Corkum AE, Moaddel R, Ferrucci L. Metabolomic profiles of being physically active and less sedentary: a critical review.

Metabolomics. 2021 Jul 10;17(7):68. doi: 10.1007/s11306-021-01818-y. PMID: 34245373.

[47]. Wang T, Feng W, Li S, Tan Q, Zhang D, Wu Y. Impact of obesity and physical inactivity on the long-term change in grip strength among middle-aged and older European adults. J Epidemiol Community Health. 2019 Jul;73(7):619-624. doi: 10.1136/jech-2018-211601. Epub 2019 Mar 8. PMID: 30850389.

[48]. Zhou W, Webster KE, Veliz PT, Larson JL. Profiles of sedentary behaviors in the oldest old: findings from the National Health and Aging Trends Study. Aging Clin Exp Res. 2022 Sep;34(9):2071-2079. doi: 10.1007/s40520-022-02157-1. Epub 2022 Jun 8. PMID: 35676552.

Review Article   IJPRR (2023) x:xx

International Journal of Psychological Research and Reviews

(ISSN:2639-6041)

Frailty in Aging Adults : A Narrative Review

Tiffany Field, PhD

University of Miami/Miller School of Medicine and Fielding Graduate University

ABSTRACT

The recent literature (last five years) on frailty in aging (ageing) adults is predominantly focused on predictors/ risk factors for frailty along with some studies on negative effects and interventions. Aging has been typically defined as starting as early as 60 or 65. And, frailty has been defined as reduced physiological and functional reserve or measured by grip strength, weakness, exhaustion and social isolation or by longer assessments like The Frailty Index for Elders. The prevalence rates for frailty in aging adults have been highly variable in this literature, ranging from a low of 5% to a high of 51% depending on the severity of the frailty. Negative effects have included falls and mortality. Predictors/risk factors have included social isolation, lack of exercise, bad nutrition, anemia, anorexia, depression and multiple demographic variables. Interventions have included physical activity, Mediterranean-style diet, combinations of exercise and diet and the anti-aging drug metformin. Potential underlying mechanisms for frailty have been the negative effects of inflammation and the positive effects of Klotho, an aging suppressor gene. More well-designed longitudinal studies are needed as well as more robust randomized controlled trials.

*Correspondence to Author:
Tiffany Field, PhD
University of Miami/Miller School of Medicine and Fielding Graduate University

How to cite this article:
Tiffany Field. Frailty in Aging Adults : A Narrative Review. International Journal of Psychological Research and Reviews, 2023, x:xx

eSciPub LLC
Website: https://escipub.com/

This narrative review involved entering the terms frailty and aging (ageing) into PubMed and PsycINFO. The search yielded 238 papers for the last five years. However, following exclusion criteria including case studies and non-English language papers, this review is a summary of the research reported in 34 papers. This recent literature is predominantly focused on predictors/risk factors for frailty in aging adults along with studies on negative effects and interventions. This narrative review is accordingly divided into sections on prevalence of frailty in aging adults, negative effects, predictors/risk factors and interventions. These are followed by sections on potential underlying mechanisms for frailty and methodological limitations of the research.

Operational Definitions of Frailty and Aging

Aging has been typically operationally defined as starting as early as age 60 or 65 in the literature on frailty in aging adults. And frailty has been variously defined as reduced physiological and functional reserve (Thillainadeson et al, 2020) or a decline in physiological functions that leads to dependency as well as vulnerability to stressors leading to high risk for adverse health outcomes (Vatic et al, 2020). And, it has been measured by various frailty instruments including grip strength, weakness, exhaustion and social isolation (Jang et al, 2022) and the presence of 3 out of 5 symptoms including unintentional weight loss, exhaustion, sedentariness, muscle weakness and slow walking (Shardell et al, 2019). And some have used even longer instruments like The Frailty Index for Elders (FIFE) (Schoufour et al, 2019). This index includes 10 items as follows: 1) help in or out of bed, 2), help washing or bathing, 3) lost or gained 10 pounds in the last six months, 4) tooth or mouth problems, hard to eat, 5) poor appetite and quickly feel full, 6) physical health or emotional problems interfering with social activities, 7) health fair or poor, 8) tired easily, 9) hospitalized during the last three months, and 10) emergency room during the last three

months. The scores are 1 to 3 for risk and four or greater for frailty.

Prevalence Rates for Frailty in Aging Adults

The prevalence rates for frailty in aging adults have been highly variable in this literature, ranging from a low of 5% to a high of 51% depending on the severity of the frailty (Zhou et al, 2018) (see table 1). This range was based on a meta-analysis of 5 studies (N=3268) from China. Other studies from China have cited other prevalence based on classification or severity of frailty. At least two other studies from China have classified aging adults as frailty, pre-frailty and robust. In one of these based on several assessments of Chinese community adults (N=1072 greater than 60-year-old adults), 14% were called frail, 55% pre-frail and 31% robust (Lin et al, 2022). In another study on a much larger sample of Chinese adults across a greater age range from 30-79 years (N=512,723) based on the Frailty Index, only 3% were classified as frail, 40% as pre-frail and 57% as robust (Fan et al, 2020). The low prevalence of frailty in this study can likely be attributed to the younger age group included in this sample (the less than 60-year-old adults). In a sammpe of Taiwanese adults greater than 60 (N=1833), the corresponding figures were 7% for frail and 40% for pre-frail.

Using a different classification of mild to severe, trajectories of frailty in aging were given in a longitudinal study of adults who were followed for 12 years (N=681 adults, mean age =75 years) (Verghese et al, 2021). In this sample, 36% were considered mild, 24% moderate and 5% severe. And 34% were considered relatively stable. These results were based on a latent class modeling of 4 distinct frailty trajectories derived from the Frailty Index.

Negative Effects of Frailty

The research on negative effects of frailty on aging adults have primarily included falling and mortality, although those effects have often been confounded by comorbidities (see table 2). For example, in a meta-analysis of 34 studies on 22 factors, several comorbid conditions were noted along with frailty-related falls including a previous history of falls, cardiac disease, hypertension, diabetes, stroke, depression, Parkinson's and pain (Xo et al, 2022). In a study from Spain on adults greater than 70-years-old (N=527), frailty was noted in 20% of the sample (Machon et al,2018). However, this prevalence was based on as many as 44 health deficits on a Frailty Index including activities of daily living (basic and instrumental), chronic diseases and psychological factors, whereas other studies have only addressed physical frailty or cognitive frailty. For example, in a sample from Taiwan (N=1115 greater than 65-year-old adults), cognitive frailty was assessed on the Mini Mental State Examination and was noted to be present in 4% of the sample.

In another review on frailty, the negative effects included the risk of falling, increased morbidity and mortality (Natic et al, 2020). In the study from Spain, frailty led to poor diet, depression, polypharmacy and falling, although the direction of effects is not clear here given the cross-sectional nature of the data (Machon et al, 2018). In a study on trajectories of frailty and aging across a period of 12 years, frailty of all degrees led to greater mortality (Verghese et al, 2021). And, in one of the studies on Chinese adults, an association was noted between scores on the Frailty Index and all-cause mortality (Fan et al, 2020).

Predictors/Risk Factors

Multiple Predictor Variable Studies

Predictors/risk factors have included depression, anemia, anorexia, bad nutrition, inactivity and multiple demographic variables (see table 3). Although most of the studies in the current literature on predictors/risk factors for frailty have focused on a single predictor variable, a few researchers have explored multiple variables. For example, in a study from Korea (N= 9775), latent growth modeling was used to determine the predictors of frailty as assessed by grip strength, weakness, exhaustion and social isolation (Jang et al,

2022). The authors classified older adults as maintaining robustness, pre-frailty or changing from frailty to pre-frailty. The predictors for frailty were lack of regular exercise, cognitive dysfunction and limited social participation.

In a sample from China, the risk factors for frailty were age, appendicular skeletal muscle mass index, sarcopenia, less education, bad nutrition, weakness and falls (Lin et al, 2022). Of these predictor variables, sarcopenia, nutrition and falls were the most predictive. Surprisingly, mental and psychological status were not associated with frailty.

Single Predictor Variable Studies

The single variable predictor studies have focused on depression, walking, diet, biomarkers and telomeres. In a review paper entitled "The frail depressed patient", depression and frailty were bidirectionally associated (Aprahamian et al, 2022). The authors noted that more falls were due to antidepressants and recommended that dopaminergic antidepressants be used for frail, depressed patients.

In the sample from Spain (N=577 greater than 70-years-old), poor diet and obesity were significant predictors of frailty (Machon et al, 2018). The authors suggested a diet of fruits and vegetables as antioxidants, fish for protein for increasing muscle strength, nuts and legumes for preserving muscle mass and milk products for decreasing the risk of osteoporosis. Similarly, in the Taiwan study, cognitive frailty was inversely associated with dairy products, whole grains, vegetables, fruit, fish and seafood, nuts, tea, and coffee.

In a review entitled "Dietary protein, exercise, and frailty domains", the authors suggested that low protein as well as a lack of physical activity leads to physical frailty (Schoufour et al, 2019). They emphasized that frailty not only includes physical frailty, but also mood, cognition, and comorbidity. In the study on trajectories of frailty in aging, a clinical risk profile was formulated, which suggested that the greatest risk factors

Table 1. Prevalence of frailty in aging adults (and first authors).

Prevalence	First authors
5-51%	Zhou
14%	Lin
3%	Fan
5%	Verghese

Table 2. Negative effects of frailty on aging adults (and first authors).

Negative effects	First authors
Comorbidities	Xo, Machon
Falls	Xo, Natic
Mortality	Natic, Verghese, Fan

Table 3. Predictors/risk factors for frailty in aging adults (and first authors).

Predictors/risk factors	First authors
Inactivity	Jang, Schoufour, Verghese
Cognitive dysfunction	Jang
Limited social participation	Jang
Sarcopenia	Lin
Less education	Lin, Verghese
Bad nuitrition	Lin, Machon, Schoufour
Weakness	Lin
Falling	Lin
Depression	Aprahamian
Obesity	Machon, Verghese
Living alone	Verghese
Difficulty walking	Garcia-Pena
Anemia	Palmer, Sanford
Anorexia	Palmer
Telomere shortening	Assar, Lorenzi, Carvalho, Zhou

Table 4. Interventions for frailty in aging adults (and first authors).

Interventions	First authors
Mediterranean diet	Lachlainn, Feart
Exercise training	Lachlainn, Puts
Physical activity plus nutrition	Ngent
Metformin	Piskovatska, Mohammed, Triggle

Table 5. Potential underlying mechanisms for frailty in aging adults (and first authors).

Mechanism	First author
Hypthalamic pituitary adrenal (HPA) dysregulation	Kamwa
Insulin resistance	Kamwa
Low vitamin D	Kamwa
Insulin-like growth factor-1 (IGF-1)	Chen, Goncalves
Inflammation ("inflammaging")	Natic, Sendoma
Klotho	Shardell, Veronsi

were obesity, physical inactivity, and slower walking while talking (Verghese et al, 2021). These risk factors were confounded by low levels of education and living alone.

In a study entitled "Network analysis of frailty and aging" (N=10,983 greater than 50-year-old adults), the Deficit Frailty Index was formulated (Garcia – Pena et al, 2019). In this index of 34 factors, self-report of health and difficulty walking a block were the best predictors of frailty.

The physical conditions of anemia and anorexia have also been risk factors for frailty. In a meta-analysis of 19 studies on the relationship between anemia and frailty, 49% of those with anemia had pre-frailty and 24% of those with anemia were classified as frail (Palmer et al, 2018). Those with anemia had a two-fold odds of frailty. The authors suggested the need for longitudinal research on changes in anemia and treatment effects. In a study on anorexia in aging adults and its role in frailty, decreasing appetite was related to impaired smell and taste, alterations in stress hormones and inflammatory mediators (Sanford et al, 2017).

Telomere shortening has also been associated with aging. However, the research on its relationship with frailty has been very mixed. For example, in a review of five studies (N= 3268), frailty was noted in 5 to 51% of the aging, but no associations were noted between frailty and telomere length (Zhou et al, 2018. The authors suggested that well designed, prospective studies were needed. In another study, telomere length and frailty were related at baseline, but telomere length failed to predict frailty or mortality 35 years later (Assar et al, 2021). Further, in a review on telomere length and frailty, telomere length could not be considered as a single predictive measure or a biological marker for age-related conditions such as frailty (Lorenzi et al, 2018). However, in still another systematic review and meta-analysis, telomere length was shorter for frail adults based on the Frailty Index, but only in the Hispanic sample (Carvalho et al, 2019).

Interventions

Exercise, diet, and metformin (a medication for diabetes) have been the most frequently reported interventions in the literature on frailty in aging (see table 4). The Mediterranean diet has been cited in several studies. For example, in a systematic review, a Mediterranean diet was notably protective (Lochlainn et al, 2021). Specifically, a diet of fruit and veggies and less consumption of processed foods were noted by these authors. In addition, many of the studies included exercise training. In a study entitled "Nutrition and frailty: current knowledge", the Mediterranean diet contributed to 60% reduced risk of frailty based on three meta-analyses (Feart et al, 2019).

In a review of 14 intervention studies designed to reduce the level of frailty including 12 randomized controlled trials, activity interventions (all types and combinations) were noted to reduce frailty markers (Puts et al, 2017). A methodological problem noted by these authors was the variability in definitions of frailty in the 14 studies.

In another meta-analysis (N=5262, participants in eight different intervention studies), physical activity and physical activity plus nutrition contributed to a 71 to 100 percent reduced likelihood of frailty (Ngem et al, 2019). The authors suggested that more robust randomized controlled trials were needed.

Metformin, a medication used for glucose management in patients with diabetes, reputedly has an anti-aging effect (Piskovatska et al, 2020). It has been known to decrease the risk of age- related diseases, including cardiometabolic disorders, neurodegeneration, chronic inflammation and frailty. It is controversial as to whether it's protective of those who are free of diabetes (Mohammed et al, 2032). According to these authors, the reduced risk of age – related disease may be an indirect effect of cellular metabolism, anti-hypoglycemic – action that enhances insulin sensitivity and the reduction of oxidative stress. Others have also attributed the clinical benefits of metformin to its antihyperglycemic effects leading to reduced risk for a number of diseases and thereby enhancing "healthspan" (Triggle et al, 2022).

Potential Underlying Mechanisms

Several potential underlying mechanisms have been suggested for frailty, including hypothalamic pituitary adrenal axis (HPA) dysregulation, the production of insulin-like growth factor-one (IGF-1), inflammation and Klotho (see table 5). HPA has been reputedly involved in the pathogenesis of both frailty and sarcopenia (low muscle mass and strength associated with aging and reduced physical performance), indicating the severity of the condition (Kamwa et al, 2021). Sarcopenia is a key feature of the frailty phenotype. These authors suggested that insulin resistance and low vitamin D status may have confounded the negative effects of the HPA dysregulation. More robust randomized trials are needed.

IGF-1 was associated with reduced frailty, lean muscle mass and bone mineral density in the Taiwan study (Chen et al, 2018). In that sample (N=1833 greater than 60-year-old adults), IGF-1 was positively correlated with lean body mass, bone mineral density and hand grip strength, and negatively correlated with weakness.

Inflammation has been the focus of many studies on frailty in the aging and has been termed "inflamm-ageing", "oxi-inflamm-ageing" and "inflamm-inactivity" by some (Natic et al, 2020). Given that the biomarkers including inflammation, oxidative, stress, and muscle protein turnover are related to physical inactivity, these authors and many others have recommended exercise training and nutritional counseling to reduce the inflammation related to frailty.

In another paper on the resolution of inflammation, a low level of chronic inflammation called "inflammaging" in this case was again said to contribute to diseases of aging, such as sarcopenia and frailty (Sendama et al, 2019). These authors suggested that the presence of "inflammaging" indicates a failure of the cell

clearance mechanisms that ordinarily resolve the inflammation after the infiltration of pathogens or tissue injury.

Other authors have elaborated on the frailty biomarkers as being the growth factors (IGF-1, SIRJ-1, GDF15) and inflammation markers (IL –6, CRP and TF- alpha) (Goncalves et al, 2022). As they suggested, these biomarkers provide the best evidence for the significance of inflammation and nutrient sensing for frailty.

Still another potential underlying mechanism is the aging suppressor gene called klotho. In a sample of 774 Italians greater than 65-years-old, those who had higher levels of plasma klotho had lesser odds of exhaustion, weight loss, weakness and frailty (Shardell et al, 2019). In a systematic review on 16 studies, the authors reported a positive association between klotho, muscle strength and physical activity and a negative association between klotho and frailty, disability and mortality (Veronesi et al, 2021).

Methodological Limitations

Several methodological limitations can be noted about these recent studies on frailty in aging adults. The sampling methods, the sample sizes, the prevalence and the results of the studies have been highly variable. Aging has been typically defined as starting at 60 or 65 which seems early given that life expectancy is now somewhere in the 70s-80s in most countries and increasing numbers of centenarians are being identified.

The researchers have primarily used self-report symptoms and scales rather than medical data that might have been more reliable, although standard medical physicals do not typically include frailty measures. Frailty has been variously defined as reduced physiological and functional reserve or it has been measured by grip strength, weakness, exhaustion and social isolation or by longer instruments like The Frailty Index for Elders. This wide variety of measures has made it difficult to conduct systematic reviews and meta-analyses resulting in very few of those in the literature. Based on the variability of these measures, the prevalence rates for frailty in aging adults have also been highly variable in this literature, ranging from a low of 5% to a high of 51% depending on the severity of the frailty.

The research has been primarily focused on predictors/risk factors for frailty, although they have only included a few variables, e. g. depression, anemia, anorexia and multiple demographic variables. The outcome measures have also been limited to falls and mortality. Both the predictors and the outcome variables appear to be obvious. However, although multiple variables would be predictive, they have often been treated as covariates in the data analyses rather than assessing the degree to which multiple variables contribute to the variance in the outcome. And, although variables often seem like mediators or moderators, mediation/moderation or structural equations analyses have rarely been used.

Although most of the studies are correlational or cross-sectional, making directionality difficult to determine, the variables that could be bi-directional or reciprocal seem to be arbitrarily treated as predictors or outcome variables. The longitudinal studies with mortality as an outcome have likely been limited by high attrition, although that methodological problem has rarely been reported.

Interventions have included physical activity, Mediterranean-style diet, combinations of exercise and diet and the anti-aging drug metformin that has reduced the risk of age-related diseases. These interventions haven't been compared as in a random assignment to different interventions, making it difficult to know the relative effectiveness of the interventions for frailty in aging adults.

Potential underlying mechanisms for frailty have been the negative effects of "inflammaging" and the positive effects of Klotho, the "aging suppressor gene". These have not been considered in the same study, so their relative validity as underlying mechanisms is unknown. As some have suggested, more well-designed prospective studies are needed as well as more robust randomized controlled trials.

Conclusions

The recent literature (last five years) on frailty in aging (ageing) adults is predominantly focused on predictors/ risk factors for frailty along with some studies on negative effects and interventions. Aging has been typically defined as starting at 60 or 65. And, frailty has been defined as reduced physiological and functional reserve or measured by grip strength, weakness, exhaustion and social isolation or by longer instruments like The Frailty Index for Elders. The prevalence rates for frailty in aging adults have been highly variable in this literature, ranging from a low of 5% to a high of 51% depending on the severity of the frailty. Negative effects have included falls and mortality. Predictors/risk factors have included depression, anemia, anorexia and multiple demographic variables. Interventions have included physical activity, Mediterranean-style diet, combinations of exercise and diet and the anti-aging drug metformin that has reduced the risk of age-related diseases. The potential underlying mechanisms for frailty have been the negative effects of "inflammaging" and the positive effects of Klotho, the "aging suppressor gene". More well-designed longitudinal studies are needed as well as more robust randomized controlled trials. Nonetheless, this recent literature has identified frailty as both an effect of inactivity and limited diet in aging adults and a contributor to mortality, highlighting the importance of continuing research on this problem.

References

[1]. Álvarez-Bustos A, Carnicero-Carreño JA, Sanchez-Sanchez JL, Garcia-Garcia FJ, Alonso-Bouzón C, Rodríguez-Mañas L. Associations between frailty trajectories and frailty status and adverse outcomes in community-dwelling older adults. J Cachexia Sarcopenia Muscle. 2022 Feb;13(1):230-239. doi: 10.1002/jcsm.12888. Epub 2021 Dec 23. PMID: 34951157; PMCID: PMC8818602.

[2]. Aprahamian I, Borges MK, Hanssen DJC, Jeuring HW, Oude Voshaar RC. The Frail Depressed Patient: A Narrative Review on Treatment Challenges. Clin Interv Aging. 2022 Jun 22;17:979-990. doi: 10.2147/CIA.S328432. PMID: 35770239; PMCID: PMC9234191.

[3]. Araújo Carvalho AC, Tavares Mendes ML, da Silva Reis MC, Santos VS, Tanajura DM, Martins-Filho PRS. Telomere length and frailty in older adults-A systematic review and meta-analysis. Ageing Res Rev. 2019 Sep;54:100914. doi: 10.1016/j.arr.2019.100914. Epub 2019 Jun 3. PMID: 31170457.

[4]. Chen LY, Wu YH, Liu LK, Lee WJ, Hwang AC, Peng LN, Lin MH, Chen LK. Association Among Serum Insulin-Like Growth Factor-1, Frailty, Muscle Mass, Bone Mineral Density, and Physical Performance Among Community-Dwelling Middle-Aged and Older Adults in Taiwan. Rejuvenation Res. 2018 Jun;21(3):270-277. doi: 10.1089/rej.2016.1882. Epub 2017 May 9. PMID: 28351218.

[5]. El Assar M, Angulo J, Carnicero JA, Walter S, García-García FJ, Rodríguez-Artalejo F, Rodríguez-Mañas L. Association between telomere length, frailty and death in older adults. Geroscience. 2021 Apr;43(2):1015-1027. doi: 10.1007/s11357-020-00291-0. Epub 2020 Nov 15. PMID: 33190211; PMCID: PMC8110679.

[6]. Fan J, Yu C, Guo Y, Bian Z, Sun Z, Yang L, Chen Y, Du H, Li Z, Lei Y, Sun D, Clarke R, Chen J, Chen Z, Lv J, Li L; China Kadoorie Biobank Collaborative Group. Frailty index and all-cause and cause-specific mortality in Chinese adults: a prospective cohort study. Lancet Public Health. 2020 Dec;5(12):e650-e660. doi: 10.1016/S2468-2667(20)30113-4. PMID: 33271078; PMCID: PMC7708389.

[7]. Feart C. Nutrition and frailty: Current knowledge. Prog Neuropsychopharmacol Biol Psychiatry. 2019 Dec 20;95:109703. doi: 10.1016/j.pnpbp.2019.109703. Epub 2019 Jul 17. PMID: 31325470.

[8]. García-Peña C, Ramírez-Aldana R, Parra-Rodriguez L, Gomez-Verjan JC, Pérez-Zepeda MU, Gutiérrez-Robledo LM. Network analysis of frailty and aging: Empirical data from the Mexican Health and Aging Study. Exp Gerontol. 2019 Dec;128:110747. doi: 10.1016/j.exger.2019.110747. Epub 2019 Oct 25. PMID: 31665658; PMCID: PMC7493650.

[9]. Gonçalves RSDSA, Maciel ÁCC, Rolland Y, Vellas B, de Souto Barreto P. Frailty biomarkers under the perspective of geroscience: A narrative review. Ageing Res Rev. 2022 Nov;81:101737. doi: 10.1016/j.arr.2022.101737. Epub 2022 Sep 23. PMID: 36162706.

[10]. Huang WC, Huang YC, Lee MS, Chang HY, Doong JY. Frailty Severity and Cognitive Impairment Associated with Dietary Diversity in Older Adults in Taiwan. Nutrients. 2021 Jan 28;13(2):418. doi: 10.3390/nu13020418. PMID: 33525496; PMCID: PMC7911853.

[11]. Jang AR, Sagong H, Yoon JY. Frailty trajectory among community-dwelling middle-aged and older adults in Korea: evidence from the Korean Longitudinal Study of Aging. BMC Geriatr. 2022 Jun 25;22(1):524. doi: 10.1186/s12877-022-03229-7. PMID: 35752752; PMCID: PMC9233334.

[12]. Kamwa V, Welch C, Hassan-Smith ZK. The endocrinology of sarcopenia and frailty. Minerva Endocrinol (Torino). 2021 Dec;46(4):453-468. doi: 10.23736/S2724-6507.20.03198-3. Epub 2020 Dec 17. PMID: 33331737.

[13]. Lin H, Wang D, Ma S, Suo Y, Zhou P, Zhao Q, Liu J, Ding G. Frailty's Prevalence and the Association with Aging-Related Health Conditions in Chinese Community Dwelling Elderly. Comput Intell Neurosci. 2022 Aug 16;2022:1748162. doi: 10.1155/2022/1748162. PMID: 36017459; PMCID: PMC9398729.

[14]. Lorenzi M, Bonassi S, Lorenzi T, Giovannini S, Bernabei R, Onder G. A review of telomere length in sarcopenia and frailty. Biogerontology. 2018 Jul;19(3-4):209-221. doi: 10.1007/s10522-018-9749-5. Epub 2018 Mar 16. PMID: 29549539.

[15]. Machón M, Mateo-Abad M, Vrotsou K, Zupiria X, Güell C, Rico L, Vergara I. Dietary Patterns and Their Relationship with Frailty in Functionally Independent Older Adults. Nutrients. 2018 Mar 24;10(4):406. doi: 10.3390/nu10040406. PMID: 29587356; PMCID: PMC5946191.

[16]. Mohammed I, Hollenberg MD, Ding H, Triggle CR. A Critical Review of the Evidence That Metformin Is a Putative Anti-Aging Drug That Enhances Healthspan and Extends Lifespan. Front Endocrinol (Lausanne). 2021 Aug 5;12:718942. doi: 10.3389/fendo.2021.718942. PMID: 34421827; PMCID: PMC8374068.

[17]. Negm AM, Kennedy CC, Thabane L, Veroniki AA, Adachi JD, Richardson J, Cameron ID, Giangregorio A, Petropoulou M, Alsaad SM, Alzahrani J, Maaz M, Ahmed MM, Kim E, Tehfe H, Dima R, Sabanayagam K, Hewston P, Abu Alrob H, Papaioannou A. Management of Frailty: A Systematic Review and Network Meta-analysis of Randomized Controlled Trials. J Am Med Dir

Assoc. 2019 Oct;20(10):1190-1198. doi: 10.1016/j.jamda.2019.08.009. PMID: 31564464.

[18]. Ni Lochlainn M, Cox NJ, Wilson T, Hayhoe RPG, Ramsay SE, Granic A, Isanejad M, Roberts HC, Wilson D, Welch C, Hurst C, Atkins JL, Mendonça N, Horner K, Tuttiett ER, Morgan Y, Heslop P, Williams EA, Steves CJ, Greig C, Draper J, Corish CA, Welch A, Witham MD, Sayer AA, Robinson S. Nutrition and Frailty: Opportunities for Prevention and Treatment. Nutrients. 2021 Jul 9;13(7):2349. doi: 10.3390/nu13072349. PMID: 34371858; PMCID: PMC8308545.

[19]. Palmer K, Vetrano DL, Marengoni A, Tummolo AM, Villani ER, Acampora N, Bernabei R, Onder G. The Relationship between Anaemia and Frailty: A Systematic Review and Meta-Analysis of Observational Studies. J Nutr Health Aging. 2018;22(8):965-974. doi: 10.1007/s12603-018-1049-x. PMID: 30272101.

[20]. Piskovatska V, Storey KB, Vaiserman AM, Lushchak O. The Use of Metformin to Increase the Human Healthspan. Adv Exp Med Biol. 2020;1260:319-332. doi: 10.1007/978-3-030-42667-5_13. PMID: 32304040.

[21]. Puts MTE, Toubasi S, Andrew MK, Ashe MC, Ploeg J, Atkinson E, Ayala AP, Roy A, Rodríguez Monforte M, Bergman H, McGilton K. Interventions to prevent or reduce the level of frailty in community-dwelling older adults: a scoping review of the literature and international policies. Age Ageing. 2017 May 1;46(3):383-392. doi: 10.1093/ageing/afw247. PMID: 28064173; PMCID: PMC5405756.

[22]. Sanford AM. Anorexia of aging and its role for frailty. Curr Opin Clin Nutr Metab Care. 2017 Jan;20(1):54-60. doi: 10.1097/MCO.0000000000000336. PMID: 27749690.

[23]. Schoufour JD, Overdevest E, Weijs PJM, Tieland M. Dietary Protein, Exercise, and Frailty Domains. Nutrients. 2019 Oct 8;11(10):2399. doi: 10.3390/nu11102399. PMID: 31597289; PMCID: PMC6835617.

[24]. Sendama W. The effect of ageing on the resolution of inflammation. Ageing Res Rev. 2020 Jan;57:101000. doi: 10.1016/j.arr.2019.101000. Epub 2019 Dec 17. PMID: 31862417; PMCID: PMC6961112.

[25]. Shardell M, Semba RD, Kalyani RR, Bandinelli S, Prather AA, Chia CW, Ferrucci L. Plasma Klotho and Frailty in Older Adults: Findings From the InCHIANTI Study. J Gerontol A Biol Sci Med Sci. 2019 Jun 18;74(7):1052-1057. doi: 10.1093/gerona/glx202. PMID: 29053774; PMCID: PMC6580690.

[26]. Thillainadesan J, Scott IA, Le Couteur DG. Frailty, a multisystem ageing syndrome. Age Ageing. 2020 Aug 24;49(5):758-763. doi: 10.1093/ageing/afaa112. PMID: 32542377.

[27]. Triggle CR, Mohammed I, Bshesh K, Marei I, Ye K, Ding H, MacDonald R, Hollenberg MD, Hill MA. Metformin: Is it a drug for all reasons and diseases? Metabolism. 2022 Aug;133:155223. doi: 10.1016/j.metabol.2022.155223. Epub 2022 May 29. PMID: 35640743.

[28]. Vatic M, von Haehling S, Ebner N. Inflammatory biomarkers of frailty. Exp Gerontol. 2020 May;133:110858. doi: 10.1016/j.exger.2020.110858. Epub 2020 Jan 31. PMID: 32007546.

[29]. Verghese J, Ayers E, Sathyan S, Lipton RB, Milman S, Barzilai N, Wang C. Trajectories of frailty in aging: Prospective cohort study. PLoS One. 2021 Jul 12;16(7):e0253976. doi: 10.1371/journal.pone.0253976. PMID: 34252094; PMCID: PMC8274857.

[30]. Veronesi F, Borsari V, Cherubini A, Fini M. Association of Klotho with physical performance and frailty in middle-aged and older adults: A systematic review. Exp Gerontol. 2021 Oct 15;154:111518. doi: 10.1016/j.exger.2021.111518. Epub 2021 Aug 15. PMID: 34407459.

[31]. Xu Q, Ou X, Li J. The risk of falls among the aging population: A systematic review and meta-analysis. Front Public Health. 2022 Oct 17;10:902599. doi: 10.3389/fpubh.2022.902599. PMID: 36324472; PMCID: PMC9618649.

[32]. Zhou J, Wang J, Shen Y, Yang Y, Huang P, Chen S, Zou C, Dong B. The association between telomere length and frailty: A systematic review and meta-analysis. Exp Gerontol. 2018 Jun;106:16-20. doi: 10.1016/j.exger.2018.02.030. Epub

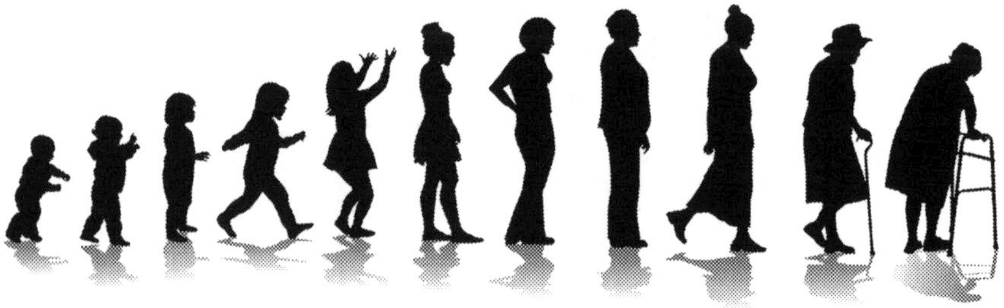

International Journal of Geriatrics and Gerontology

Field T. Bordelon C. Int J Geriatr Gerontol 6: 149.

www.doi.org/10.29011/2577-0748.100049

www.gavinpublishers.com

OPEN ACCESS

GAVIN PUBLISHERS

Review Article

Sleep Problems in Aging (Ageing) Adults: A Narrative Review

Tiffany Field*

University of Miami/Miller School of Medicine and Fielding Graduate University, USA

*Corresponding author: Tiffany Field, University of Miami/Miller School of Medicine and Fielding Graduate University, USA

Citation: Field T (2023) Sleep Problems in Aging (Ageing) Adults: A Narrative Review. Int J Geriatr Gerontol 6: 149. DOI: 10.29011/2577-0748.100049

Received Date: 23 February, 2023; Accepted Date: 03 March, 2023; Published Date: 08 March, 2023

Abstract

The recent literature on sleep problems in aging (ageing) adults has primarily focused on negative effects as well as risk factors, buffers, and interventions. The sleep problems have typically been self-reported or measured by actigraphy. The prevalence rates for sleep problems starting at age 60 have been variable, ranging from a low of 18% in the UK to a high of 50% in China, a variability that may relate to the type of sleep data and/or cross-cultural variation. Psychological effects have included dissatisfaction with life, unhealthy aging and affective/depressive mood states. Physical effects have included elevated blood pressure, impaired functionality, frailty, comorbidity and immune dysfunction. Cognitive impairment has also resulted from sleep problems, and aging brain biomarkers have included shorter telomere length, reduced gray matter volume and earlier mortality. Psychological risk factors have included meta-cognitive beliefs, worrying, loneliness, poor relationships and depression. Physical risk factors have included inactivity, napping and comorbidity. Buffers/protective factors have included retirement, light exercise, consumption of vegetables and melatonin as a sleep medication. Only a couple interventions could be found in this recent literature on sleep in aging adults including Cognitive Behavior Therapy and exercise. A few potential underlying mechanisms for disturbed sleep in aging adults include decreased vagal activity, increased connectivity in the brain making disconnecting for sleep difficult, inflammation and orexins. Although the data highlight the severity of sleep problems in the aging, they have been primarily based on self-report surveys that have yielded mixed results across samples.

Sleep Problems in Aging (Ageing) Adults: A Narrative Review

This narrative review involved entering the terms sleep and aging (ageing) into PubMed and PsycINFO. The search yielded 735 papers for the last five years. However, following exclusion criteria including case studies and non-English language papers, this review is a summary of the research reported in 67 papers. The recent literature is predominantly focused on negative effects of sleep problems along with studies on risk factors, buffers and interventions. This narrative review is accordingly divided into sections on prevalence of sleep problems in the aging, negative effects, risk factors, buffers and interventions. These are followed by sections on potential underlying mechanisms for sleep problems in the aging and methodological limitations of the research.

Sleep Measures

Sleep problems in the aging are typically based on the self-report scale called the Pittsburgh Sleep Quality Index (PSQI) [1].

The seven components of this index include sleep quality, latency, duration, efficiency, disturbances, sleep medications and daytime dysfunction. In this study, 78% reported good sleep quality. Other variables that are based on actigraphy or self-report include wake time after sleep onset, sleep efficiency and total sleep time. In this comparison of sleep assessments, these measures were correlated with the sleep disturbances component of the PSQI but not with the total PSQI score. Others have reported a positive correlation between actigraphy measures and self-report [2]. In their factor analysis, length of wakefulness during sleep, sleep duration and total sleep time were the factors measured. Self-report measures explained 61% of the variance in total sleep time assessed by actigraphy.

In a review on 15 of 133 publications on technology for monitoring sleep, more questionnaire studies were reported than smart phone or wearable technology research [3]. The authors suggested that continuous monitoring is more reliable than self-report measures. Night to night variability has been reported for

Citation: Field T (2023) Sleep Problems in Aging (Ageing) Adults: A Narrative Review. Int J Geriatr Gerontol 6: 149. DOI: 10.29011/2577-0748.100049

sleep EEG, but when it has been averaged over 4 nights, there was decreased variability [4]. These authors concluded that wearable technology was superior to self-report data.

Prevalence of Sleep Problems in the Aging

Given the variability of the measures used in studying sleep problems, it is not surprising that there is variability in prevalence data across countries. The prevalence has ranged from 18% for low sleep efficiency in the UK [5] to more than 50% of people over 65 experiencing sleep problems in China [6]. In between those extremes the U.S. has reported more than 26% for waking in the night and 13% for waking too early [7].

The National Sleep Foundation has recommended 7-9 hours as the ideal sleep duration [8]. Both short sleep (less than 7 hours) and long sleep (greater than 9 hours) have been considered problematic. In several studies the negative effects of both short and long sleep have been referenced as an inverted U function.

The prevalence of long sleep has been increasingly reported as a problem in this literature on sleep problems in aging adults. In a study from China, 44% were reported to have poor sleep with 8% having short sleep less than five hours and 28% having long sleep greater than nine hours [9]. Another example is a study from Africa reporting that 14% were experiencing short sleep and 25% experiencing long sleep [10].

Long sleep propensity has been reported in another study as high napping and high maintenance in 20% of females and 30% of males based on actigraphy [11]. In the same study, adequate sleep was reported in 74% of women and 31% of men. And, inadequate sleep was noted in 6% of women and 30% of men. Inadequate sleep was correlated with mortality risk.

Negative Effects of Sleep Problems on Aging Adults

The recent literature on the negative effects of sleep problems on aging adults has addressed psychological effects including dissatisfaction with life, unhealthy aging and affective/depressive mood states. Physical effects have included elevated blood pressure, reduced functionality, frailty, comorbidity and immune dysfunction. Cognitive impairment has also resulted from sleep problems, and aging brain effects have included shorter telomere length, reduced gray matter volume and earlier mortality.

Psychological Effects of Sleep Problems

Life satisfaction has been directly affected by sleep quality and indirectly affected by depressive symptoms, explaining respectively 84% and 16% of the variance in one study (Banerjee et al, 2022). Functional limitations exacerbated the indirect effect of poor sleep on life satisfaction in this research.

Healthy aging has also been affected by sleep quality which has been measured in different ways. For example, in a longitudinal study, sleep quality and duration were explored as determinants of healthy aging [12]. In that study, highs and lows were determined for sleep quality in a sample who were older than 65 (N= 1226) and the participants were assessed again later for healthy aging.

Thirty-four per cent of the sample was high on sleep quality and high on healthy aging at the follow-up. Greater sleep quality in the high-high group was based on the Pittsburgh Sleep Quality Index. The low-high group comprised 19% of the sample. This group could have gone from low to high as a function of being participants in research that often has therapeutic effects. The low-low group Included 31% of the sample. Sleep duration was inversely associated with being in the high-high group, suggesting an inverted U-curve with both short and long sleep being associated with negative effects.

In another study sleep efficiency was assessed in 65-to-96-year-old adults (N=2468) [13]. Sleep efficiency or the ratio of total sleep time in bed was noted to plummet to 76% in adults greater than 80-years-old. This decrease was associated with greater frailty, poor health and early mortality. In still another study, normal sleep time was associated with greater physical activity and less sedentary behavior which resulted in less unhealthy aging [14]. In contrast, the short sleepers (less than six hours a night) engaged in less physical activity and more sedentary behavior and were later noted to have unhealthy aging.

Negative affect and depressive symptoms have also resulted from inadequate sleep in a study called "Good night-good day? Bidirectional links of daily sleep quality with negative affect and stress reactivity in old age" [15]. In this study, 61- 90-year-old adults (N=325) were assessed for their nighttime sleep and their daytime stress. The data suggested that the older adults could regulate the effects of low sleep quality or negative affect but they had more difficulty down-regulating daytime stress effects on sleep. This study highlights the bidirectionality of sleep and negative affect.

In research based on data from the Health and Aging in Africa Study (N= 3891 adults greater than 40 years), the prevalence of incident depressive symptoms was 26% and the prevalence of persistent depressive symptoms was 31% [10]. The prevalence of very short sleep was 4%, short sleep 10%, normal sleep 61% and long sleep 25%. In this sample, long sleep was associated with both incident depressive symptoms and persistent depressive symptoms but only for men not for women.

In still another sample experiencing depressive symptoms related to sleep disturbances, C-reactive protein (a marker of inflammation) that was assayed in 2012 mediated the effects of sleep disturbances on depressive symptoms that were assessed in 2017 [16]. However, these effects were only noted in women. These results suggested that inflammation mediated the relationship between sleep disturbances and depressive symptoms. The gender differences noted in these two studies are difficult to interpret.

Physical Effects of Sleep Problems

The physical effects of sleep problems in the aging have included abnormal blood pressure, hearing loss, disturbed functionality, frailty, falling and comorbidity. Although sleep deprivation studies have rarely been conducted recently, at least one appeared in this literature [17]. In that study (N= 20, mean

Citation: Field T (2023) Sleep Problems in Aging (Ageing) Adults: A Narrative Review. Int J Geriatr Gerontol 6: 149. DOI: 10.29011/2577-0748.100049

age = 60), blood pressure increased for both males and females following 24 hours of sleep deprivation.

Hearing loss has been associated with sleep problems in the National Health and Nutrition Examination Survey [18]. In this sample (N=632 adults greater than 70-years-old), greater than 8 hours sleep led to poorer perception of high frequency pure tones. The direction of these effects cannot be determined given the cross-sectional nature of these data. However, hearing loss and sleep problems may be bi-directional.

Functional limitations have also been noted to follow from sleep problems in the National Health and Nutrition Examination Survey (N =6020 adults who were older than 65 years) [19]. In this study, those who had short sleep (less than five hours) as well as those with long sleep (greater than nine hours) had inferior performance on 19 functional tasks including basic activities of daily living such as dressing and eating. Other negative effects were noted for instrumental activities of daily living such as shopping and cooking, leisure and social activities, extremity mobility and general physical activity.

Frailty has also been negatively affected by sleep problems in aging adults in at least three studies in this recent literature including one already mentioned where sleep efficiency was associated with frailty (Desjardins et al, 2019). In another study, both short (11%) and long (18%) sleep groups had greater physical frailty (N = 9824, mean age= 74) [20]. Long sleep was a risk factor for frailty in still another study. In this sample (N = 1726 60- to 87-year-old adults), 44% had poor sleep quality including 8% who were experiencing less than five hours and 28% who were experiencing greater than nine hours. Ratings on frailty suggested that 9% were classified as frail and 53% as pre-frail. Poor sleep quality especially long sleep (greater than nine hours) led to greater odds of frailty.

Given the prevalence of frailty, and its relation to long sleep, it is perhaps not surprising that the risk of falling is also associated with long sleep. In this sample (N=902) 2.35 greater odds were noted for long sleep time (greater than 9 hours) contributing to falling.

Comorbidity is surprisingly mentioned in only one study in this recent literature on sleep problems in the aging. In this Canadian longitudinal sample, comorbidity was noted in as many as 30 to 70% of the participants (N= 30,011) Greater odds of comorbidity were noted in those reporting short sleep (less than six hours) or long sleep (greater than eight hours).

Immune function has also been affected by low sleep quality. For example, in a study that documented 15-month trajectories of sleep quality and interleukin-six (IL-6, another marker of inflammation), lower interleukin-six levels were noted in 84% of the sample and higher levels in 16% of the participants [21]. In this study (N= 195, mean age = 74), poor sleep quality led to higher IL-6 levels. Surprisingly, that was the only immune factor explored in this study.

Other immune factors associated with inflammation and immune dysfunction were studied in a sample from the Australian Research Council on Longevity [22]. In this research (N =230 63-to-70 year-old adults), difficulty falling asleep was associated with increased IL –2 and increased IL – 1 beta levels. The selection of specific immune factors has appeared to be arbitrary in these studies.

Cognitive Effects

Cognitive effects are the most frequently addressed in this recent literature (11 studies). In a sample from the World Health Organization Study on Global Aging and Adult Health, adults greater than 50 years of age who slept longer than nine hours on average had cognitive problems [23]. These problems were specified as attention, working memory and executive function. Long sleep has also been a problem for cognitive function in a sample from China [24]. In this sample (N= 9005, mean age =81), long sleep duration plus a greater than two hour increase in sleep time led to mild cognitive impairment.

In a study entitled "Long sleep duration associated with cognitive impairment in Chinese community -dwelling older adults" (N =1591 greater than 60 years), those who were sleeping more than nine hours experienced significant cognitive impairment [25]. On the Mini-mental State Exams, the older elderly (greater than 75-years-old) had low global cognition scores as well as reduced orientation memory, language ability and executive function scores.

Both long and short sleep have been associated with cognitive impairment. In the English Longitudinal Study of Aging, both baseline short and long sleep duration were associated with follow-up cognitive performance [26]. In this sample (N=4877), the inverted U function of both long and short sleep effects, surprisingly, only occurred for male participants which were difficult to interpret. The inverted U-shaped association between sleep duration and cognitive function has also been noted in the Social Isolation, Health and Lifestyle Survey in Singapore on a sample of adults greater than 60-years-old (N=4169) [27]. This association was less pronounced if the participants were married and were experiencing a strong social network.

In still another study, an inverted U-shaped association was noted between sleep problems and cognitive function. In this sample (N=1520 adults greater than 50-years-old), more than 10 hours of sleep was negatively associated with cognitive functions including fluency and delayed recall, and less than five hours sleep was associated with a greater error rate.

The inverted U function of sleep was again noted in the English Longitudinal Study of Ageing (N=28,756 older than 60-year-old adults) [28]. Impaired cognitive function was reported for those who slept less than four hours and those who slept more than 10 hours.

Two other specific cognitive functions that have been affected by sleep include visual paired associates and word

Citation: Field T (2023) Sleep Problems in Aging (Ageing) Adults: A Narrative Review. Int J Geriatr Gerontol 6: 149. DOI: 10.29011/2577-0748.100049

learning [29]. In this sample (N=99 greater than 50-year-old adults), sleep was negatively correlated with those two memory variables. Visual paired associates was negatively correlated with the subjective sleep quality, duration and disturbance components of the Pittsburgh Sleep Quality Index. And word learning was negatively correlated with the subjective sleep quality and efficiency components of that scale.

Better sleep quality has been a mediator for the effects of physical activity on cognitive function [30]. In this sample from the European Longitudinal Study on Aging (N =86,541), better subjective sleep quality partially explained the association between self-reported physical activity and cognitive function. In this sample (N= 86,541) that was seen six times between 2004 and 2017, physical activity affected three cognitive functions including immediate recall, delayed recall and verbal fluency and these relationships were mediated by sleep quality.

Napping has also had negative effects on cognition. In a sample of adults greater than 60-years-old (N=1,740), greater than nine hours sleep at night and greater than 60 minutes napping led to cognitive impairment [31,32]. Similarly, less than seven hours of sleep and no napping had negative effects on cognition. Even worse effects for daytime sleep were noted in a study on brain morphological changes in the eighth decade of life. In this study (N= 457, mean age=76), an increase in weekend daytime sleep led to white matter loss in the brain.

These relationships between poor sleep and impaired cognitive function likely relate to measures of brain aging. Surprisingly, however, most of the former relationships were not measured in the same studies as brain age that tended to focus more on telomere length and diminishing gray and white matter volume based on neuroimaging data.

Brain Age Biomarkers

Telomere length (the DNA-protein structures at both ends of chromosomes protecting the chromosomes) has been an index of brain age associated with poor sleep quality.. In one study, long sleep duration, insomnia and insomnia associated with short objective sleep were independent factors associated with short telomere length [33]. These data suggested an inverted-U function with both long and short sleep being related to short telomere length.

Telomere length has also been called "a marker of cellular aging" [7]. In this sample (N=5268) from the U.S. Health and Retirement Study, 16% never felt rested, 26% had trouble waking up in the night and 13% were waking too early. Those who never felt rested in the morning had shorter telomere length. However, total sleep time was, surprisingly, not related to telomere length.

In an even longer longitudinal study from the Netherlands, sleep was assessed at baseline and telomere length was measured six years later [34]. In this sample (N=2936), delayed sleep onset was, once again, associated with shorter telomere length. And these authors referred to the shortening of telomere length as

a "marker of biological age".

Neuroimaging data have also been assessed for brain age [35]. In this sample (N =50) brain age delta (the difference between chronological age and brain age) was assessed using neuroimaging. The analysis revealed an association between inadequate sleep at baseline and brain age delta two years later.

A reduction in hippocampal volume has also been an indicator of brain aging [36]. In this sample (N = 417, mean age= 69), sleep duration, sleep problems and stress were associated with a reduction in hippocampal volume. A reduction in gray matter volume has also occurred in the right thalamus, the left precuneus and postcentral gyrus of aging adults following sleep restriction [37]. In a study entitled "Sleep and brain morphological changes in the eighth decade of life", weekend daytime sleep increased. In this sample (N=457, mean age=76), an increase in weekday sleep and less efficient nighttime sleep were related to white matter loss. The direction of effects in this sample was difficult to determine given the cross-sectional nature of the study.

Early Mortality

Early mortality has been addressed as the most negative effect of sleep problems on aging adults. In a study on sleep and mortality (N=24,608 65-to-96-year-old adults), for example, sleep efficiency less than 80% was related to several factors including pain, nocturnal sleep, medication use, and awakening from bad dreams [13]. These sleep efficiency factors were not only associated with frailty and poor health but also with early mortality.

In a paper entitled "Sleep lengthening in late adulthood signals an increased risk of mortality", longitudinal data were presented on baseline and follow-up sleep duration [38]. In this sample of 55-to-68-year-olds, long to long, short to short or short to long duration sleep increased the odds of all-cause mortality (caused by any disease but in this case mortality that related to cardiovascular conditions).

In a similar study entitled "Changes in nocturnal and daytime sleep durations predict all-cause mortality", changes were explored in a sample from Singapore (N =2448 adults greater than 60 years) [39]. The results suggested that changes in either direction on nocturnal and nap duration led to early mortality.

In the Sleep Heart Health Study sample (N=4897), a brain age Index was created from calculating brain age minus chronological age (as in brain age delta already mentioned) based on sleep electroencephalography [40]. The data suggested that excess brain age was associated with decreased life expectancy.

In a unique study on centenarians, data were collected from 268 family members [41]. Sleep onset latency along with life satisfaction and attachment closeness were contributors to the number of days lived. These data were based on family member reports as opposed to self-reports, so they may be highly subjective and biased.

Citation: Field T (2023) Sleep Problems in Aging (Ageing) Adults: A Narrative Review. Int J Geriatr Gerontol 6: 149. DOI: 10.29011/2577-0748.100049

Risk Factors/Predictors of Sleep Problems in Aging Adults

Several risk factors have been identified for sleep problems in this recent literature on aging adults. Psychological risk factors have included meta-cognitive beliefs, worrying, loneliness, poor relationships and depression. Physical risk factors have included inactivity, napping and studies in which multiple risk factors have been identified.

Psychological Risk Factors/Predictors

In a study entitled "The influence of metacognitive beliefs on sleep dysfunction", actigraphy recordings were made of sleep across seven days in 50 participants [42]. These objective recordings were not associated with metacognitive activity. However, poor sleepers according to their self-reports had greater metacognitive beliefs about sleep difficulties.

The same research group in a later study entitled "Strategies for controlling sleep-related intrusive thoughts and subjective and objective sleep quality" identified different sleep problems by subjective and objective measures [43]. In this sample (N= 147), more time awake after sleep onset and less efficient sleep were noted on self-report. In contrast, longer sleep onset latency, less total sleep time and less sleep efficiency were revealed by actigraphy.

Loneliness has been identified as a risk factor for sleep problems in older adults in at least three studies. In a sample from the English Longitudinal Study on Ageing (N=5698), loneliness was associated with increased odds of reporting short sleep and long sleep problems at follow-up [44]. In another study, loneliness and isolation were compared (N= 759) [45]. Although a low correlation was noted between loneliness and isolation, both risk factors were associated with more disturbed sleep including waking after sleep onset and percentage sleep time based on 72 hours of actigraphy. Loneliness was associated with more insomnia and shorter sleep, and isolation was associated with more time in bed. This comparison is tentative inasmuch as only three items from the UCLA loneliness scale were used to assess loneliness whereas as many as nine items were used to assess isolation. Nonetheless, the comparison between effects of isolation and loneliness is unusual and the data are suggestive.

In a study entitled "Long time, no sleep", 29% of the sample (N= 71) reported increased sleep problems [46]. Loneliness as well as being a male were risk factors for greater sleep disturbances. In research that addressed the impact of retirement on sleep problems among older workers and their partners, two waves of the longitudinal study from the Netherlands were explored (N= 3726 older Dutch couples) [47]. Increased odds of sleep problems were associated with lower relationship quality and with having a partner who had sleep problems.

In a study entitled "Irregular sleep–wake patterns in older adults with current or remitted depression", the Sleep Regularity Index was used along with actigraphy (N=138) [48]. Sleep-wake fragmentation, sleep instability, sleep onset and offset timing and the number of awakenings were reportedly related to depression.

In another sample from the English Longitudinal Study on Ageing (N =5172 adults greater than 50-years-old) sleep was assessed via self-report and depression by the Center for Epidemiological Studies–Depression Scale [49]. Baseline depression and sleep problems predicted the same problems four years later.

Physical Risk Factors/Predictors

Inactivity, napping and comorbidity are among the physical risk factors/predictor variables in this recent literature on sleep problems in aging adults. In a study already reviewed, sleep-wake fragmentation occurred in older adults who were less active during the day [48].Those adults reported poor quality sleep and less regularity.

In a paper entitled "Analysis of dynamic, bidirectional associations in older adult physical activity and sleep quality", greater physical activity led to greater sleep on the same day [50]. And, surprisingly, long sleep one night led to short sleep the next night.

Napping, not surprisingly, has also been a risk factor for sleep problems in the aging. In a paper that gives its results in its title, "Napping characteristics and restricted participation in valued activities", data were sampled from the National Health and Aging Trends Study (N=1,739 greater than 65-year-old adults) [51]. In this study, each 30-minute increase in the duration of intentional or unintentional napping led to 25% decreased odds of engaging in any valued activity. This, of course, also included less physical activity.

Typically, more daytime sleep leads to less nighttime sleep. In a study entitled "Correlates and influences of taking an afternoon nap on nocturnal sleep ", more napping was associated with decreased sleep duration and increased light sleep as well as a delay of sleep onset at night [31,32]. In this study from China (N=50), the participants averaged 1-to-2 hour naps between 12 and 2 PM. The participants' reasons for napping were "belief in naps", "nothing to do", "low energy level", "compensating for disturbed sleep" and "extreme weather ".

Multiple risk factors have been reported in at least two studies. In one study that was focused on depression and poor sleep, several factors were associated with depression and sleep problems [49]. These included being a female, non-cohabitation, relative poverty, smoking, infrequent physical activity, frequent alcohol use, greater BMI, hypertension, coronary heart disease, diabetes/high glucose levels, pulmonary disease, arthritis and greater fibrinogen and C-reactive protein. Surprisingly, these risk factors were not submitted to a regression analysis or a structural equations analysis to determine their relative significance as predictors of sleep problems.

Similarly, multiple variables were identified in a longitudinal study [4]. In this sample (N=6375), latent class analysis was used to form sub-groups of sleep efficiency that was noted to decrease

Citation: Field T (2023) Sleep Problems in Aging (Ageing) Adults: A Narrative Review. Int J Geriatr Gerontol 6: 149. DOI: 10.29011/2577-0748.100049

19% between the ages of 40 and 100 years. The high efficiency group comprised 32% of the sample, the medium efficiency group included 50% of the sample and the low efficiency group comprised 18% of the sample. The high sleep efficiency group had a lower prevalence of previous hypertension, circulatory problems, general arthritis, breathing problems and recurrent episodes of depression.

The COVID-19 pandemic has also negatively affected sleep quality in at least two studies. For example, research from the U.S. reported a 29% increase in sleep problems of the aging related to the pandemic [46]. And, others have noted that sleep problems have been exacerbated by the pandemic [52]. These findings, however, were confounded by a significant decrease in activity and an increase in depression during the pandemic that were also related to the decrease in sleep quality.

Buffers / Protective Factors for Sleep Problems

Several buffers have been noted as protective of sleep in the aging. These have included retirement, light exercise, consumption of vegetables and melatonin as a sleep medication.

In the study on retirement, two waves of data were analyzed from the Netherlands longitudinal study on older Dutch couples (N=3726) [47]. In this study, retirement was followed by a decreased odds of sleep problems. This may have related to lower levels of work-related stress that no longer existed during retirement.

In a study entitled "Effects of sedentary behavior and activity on sleep quality in older people" sleep was monitored by actigraphy and physical activity by an accelerometer [53]. Replacing 30 minutes of sedentary activity with 30 minutes of light intensity exercise led to improved sleep quality. Surprisingly, vigorous intensity activity did not have the same effects.

In a study that explored the relationships between physical activity, sleep and cognitive function, sleep quality was a mediator between physical activity and cognitive function [54]. In this sample, physical activity attenuated the negative impact of poor sleep on cognition, again suggesting that physical activity had a buffering effect.

Plant-based diets have also had a buffering effect on sleep problems in aging adults. In a study entitled "Sleep duration, vegetable consumption and all–cause mortality among older adults in China", more vegetable consumption led to a 22% lower risk of mortality [55]. In this sample (N=13,441 greater than 65-year-old adults), less than five and greater than nine hours of sleep per night led to a greater mortality risk. Low vegetable consumption exacerbated the risk of mortality for the less than five and greater than nine hours of sleep groups.

Sleep has also been improved by melatonin. However, controlled substances for sleep including z-drugs like zolpidem (ambien) have been associated with falling and injuries [56].

Interventions for Sleep Problems in Aging Adults

Surprisingly, given the prevalence of sleep problems in aging adults, only a few intervention studies could be found in this recent literature. These include Cognitive Behavior Therapy and physical exercise. In a study on insomnia in older adults, sleep medication and medication for psychiatric disorders were noted to increase the risk of insomnia [57]. Cognitive Behavior Therapy including stimulus control, sleep restriction and sleep hygiene was more effective than medication. The positive effects of Cognitive Behavior Therapy were also noted in another study on insomnia [58].

Resistance exercise has reportedly improved all aspects of sleep, but especially sleep quality [59]. In this review of 13 studies, the consistent finding was that chronic resistance exercise protocols improved sleep quality. These data were not surprising given the already summarized research on daily activity as a buffer for sleep problems.

Potential Underlying Mechanisms for Sleep Problems in the Aging

A few potential underlying mechanisms have been suggested for disturbed sleep in aging adults. These include decreased vagal activity, increased connectivity (making disconnecting for sleep difficult), inflammation and orexins (neuropeptides that regulate sleep).

In a review paper on the balance of autonomic nervous system activity, exercise and sleep states in older adults, decreased vagal modulation was noted in several studies due to decreased parasympathetic activity during sleep [60]. Low levels of exercise confounded the effects of low vagal activity or likely contributed to the low vagal activity. As has been noted in research on exercise, the stimulation of pressure receptors under the skin by moving the skin (as in most exercise) increases vagal activity.

In a study entitled "Cerebral functional networks during sleep in young and older individuals", EEG and fMRIs were taken [61]. An increase in connectivity between the frontal regions of various networks during sleep was related to lighter sleep and fragmented sleep in these participants. The authors suggested that increased connectivity likely led to a lesser ability to disconnect during sleep.

In a sample from the Korean Brain Aging Study on 55-to-88 -year-olds (N=238), faster leukocyte telomere shortening was associated with shorter duration and longer latency sleep [62]. Inflammation was also suggested as a potential underlying mechanism for these sleep disturbances. Other mechanisms suggested by these researchers included oxidative stress, increased sympathetic tone and increased cortisol. Chronic inflammation was also related to insufficient sleep in the National Social Life, Health and Aging Project (N=1,124).

In a paper entitled "Physiological role of orexinergic system for health", orexins or hypocretins are defined as excitatory neuropeptides that regulate feeding, sleep and wakefulness, aging and neurodegenerative diseases [63]. These researchers also considered them a promising target for therapeutic approaches to obesity, drug addiction and emotional stress.

Citation: Field T (2023) Sleep Problems in Aging (Ageing) Adults: A Narrative Review. Int J Geriatr Gerontol 6: 149. DOI: 10.29011/2577-0748.100049

In another paper entitled "Sleep, orexins and cognition", orexins were said to regulate the sleep – wake cycle, reward and stress-processing, alertness, vigilance and cognitive function [64]. Alterations in central and peripheral orexins have been linked to narcolepsy, anorexia, age-related cognitive decline and neurodegenerative diseases. Orexin receptor antagonists can promote sleep signals during the night and orexin therapies can increase sleep and memory as well as cognition [65-67].

Methodological Limitations

Several methodological limitations can be noted about these recent studies on sleep problems in aging adults. Significant variability has been reported on the sampling methods, on the sample sizes, and the prevalence and results of the studies. Most of the research has involved self-report surveys which have been notably less reliable than continuous monitoring via actigraphy, although data from the two methods have been significantly correlated.

The key variables have been "pet variables" or those favored by the authors and often as single variables. And the data have frequently been analyzed via logistic regression analysis which controls for confounding variables. Some researchers have studied the controlled variables as risk factors or mediating/moderating variables and they have then been analyzed by mediation/moderation or structural equations analysis.

More studies have appeared on negative effects versus risk factors for sleep problems. Several of the effects that have been noted could also be risk factors, as in bidirectional, reciprocal variables. Directionality cannot be determined as most of the studies are correlational and others that are longitudinal have instead analyzed cross-sectional data. Several of the scales are short, as in the Pittsburgh Sleep Quality Index , or biased as in the number of hours asleep which limits the reliability of these measures. The prevalence of sleep problems, its measures and its effects are sufficiently variable that reviews and meta-analyses have been inconclusive.

Many of the results are relationships between sleep problems and other effects, risk variables or protective factors selected by the researchers. The criteria for aging adults have been arbitrarily selected as being greater than 60 and the greater than 60-year-olds have rarely been compared to younger adults. Gender differences have been infrequently reported and when they have, researchers have expressed difficulty interpreting them.

Only a few potential underlying mechanisms have been studied, for example, decreased vagal activity and inflammation, but measures of potential mechanisms have not been compared. And, the intervention studies in this recent literature have been limited to Cognitive Behavior Therapy and physical exercise. Despite these methodological limitations, the recent literature highlights the relationships between sleep problems and aging, although aging hasn't been associated with more sleep problems necessarily than other stages of life.

Conclusions

Several studies on sleep problems in the aging have appeared in the literature over the last five years. They have typically been assessed by self-report or measured by actigraphy. The cut-off for aging has usually been 60 years of age and the prevalence has ranged from 18% to 50%. Several negative effects have been reported including dissatisfaction with life, unhealthy aging and affective/depressive mood states. More serious effects have included elevated blood pressure, impaired functionality, frailty, comorbidity and immune dysfunction. Cognitive impairment has been associated with aging brain biomarkers including shorter telomere length, reduced gray matter volume and earlier mortality. Risk factors/ predictors have included meta-cognitive beliefs, worrying, loneliness, poor relationships, depression, inactivity, napping and comorbidity. Buffers/protective factors have included retirement, light exercise, consumption of vegetables and melatonin and interventions include Cognitive Behavior Therapy and exercise. Decreased vagal activity, increased connectivity in the brain, inflammation and orexins have been addressed as potential underlying mechanisms for sleep problems in the aging. Despite the limitations of self-report surveys, the data have highlighted the severity of sleep problems for the aging and the need for further research.

References

1. Zitser J, Allen IE, Falgàs N, Le MM, Neylan TC, et al. (2022) Pittsburgh Sleep Quality Index (PSQI) responses are modulated by total sleep time and wake after sleep onset in healthy older adults. PLoS One.17:e0270095.

2. Yeh AY, Pressler SJ, Giordani BJ. (2023) Actigraphic and Self-reported Sleep Measures in Older Adults: Factor Analytic Study. West J Nurs Res.45:4-13.

3. Moreno-Blanco D, Solana-Sánchez J, Sánchez-González P, Oropesa I, Cáceres C, et al. (2019) Technologies for Monitoring Lifestyle Habits Related to Brain Health: A Systematic Review. Sensors (Basel).19:4183.

4. Hogan J, Sun H, Paixao L, Westmeijer M, Sikka P, et al. (2021) Night-to-night variability of sleep electroencephalography-based brain age measurements. Clin Neurophysiol.132:1-12.

5. Didikoglu A, Maharani A, Tampubolon G, Canal MM, Payton A, et al. (2020) Longitudinal sleep efficiency in the elderly and its association with health. J Sleep Res.29:e12898.

6. Fu L, Yu X, Zhang W, Han P, Kang L, et al. (2019) The Relationship Between Sleep Duration, Falls, and Muscle Mass: A Cohort Study in an Elderly Chinese Population. Rejuvenation Res.22:390-398.

7. Iloabuchi C, Innes KE, Sambamoorthi U. (2020) Association of sleep quality with telomere length, a marker of cellular aging: A retrospective cohort study of older adults in the United States. Sleep Health.6:513-521.

8. Paterson JL, Reynolds AC, Dawson D. (2018) Sleep Schedule Regularity Is Associated with Sleep Duration in Older Australian Adults: Implications for Improving the Sleep Health and Wellbeing of Our Aging Population. Clin Gerontol.41:113-122.

Citation: Field T (2023) Sleep Problems in Aging (Ageing) Adults: A Narrative Review. Int J Geriatr Gerontol 6: 149. DOI: 10.29011/2577-0748.100049

9. Sun XH, Ma T, Yao S, Chen ZK, Xu WD, et al. (2020) Associations of sleep quality and sleep duration with frailty and pre-frailty in an elderly population Rugao longevity and ageing study. BMC Geriatr.20:9.

10. Pengpid S, Peltzer K. (2022) Sleep duration and incident and persistent depressive symptoms among a rural ageing population in South Africa. Comprehensive Psychiatry. 119:152354.

11. Wallace ML, Lee S, Stone KL, Hall MH, Smagula SF, et al. (2022) Actigraphy-derived sleep health profiles and mortality in older men and women. Sleep.45:zsac015.

12. Gkotzamanis V, Panagiotakos DB, Yannakoulia M, Kosmidis M, Dardiotis E, et al. (2023) Sleep Quality and Duration as Determinants of Healthy Aging Trajectories: The HELIAD Study. J Frailty Aging.12:16-23.

13. Desjardins S, Lapierre S, Hudon C, Desgagné A. (2019) Factors involved in sleep efficiency: a population-based study of community-dwelling elderly persons. Sleep.42:zsz038.

14. Ortolá R, Garcia-Esquinas E, Cabanas-Sánchez V, Migueles JH, Martínez-Gómez D, et al. (2021) Association of Physical Activity, Sedentary Behavior, and Sleep With Unhealthy Aging: Consistent Results for Device-Measured and Self-reported Behaviors Using Isotemporal Substitution Models. J Gerontol A Biol Sci Med Sci.76:85-94.

15. Lücke AJ, Wrzus C, Gerstorf D, Kunzmann U, Katzorreck M, et al. (2022) Good night-good day? Bidirectional links of daily sleep quality with negative affect and stress reactivity in old age. Psychol Aging.37:876-890.

16. Ballesio A, Zagaria A, Ottaviani C, Steptoe A, Lombardo C. (2022) Sleep disturbance, neuro-immune markers, and depressive symptoms in older age: Conditional process analysis from the English Longitudinal Study of Aging (ELSA). Psychoneuroendocrinology.142:105770.

17. Carter JR, Fonkoue IT, Greenlund IM, Schwartz CE, Mokhlesi B, et al. (2019) Sympathetic neural responsiveness to sleep deprivation in older adults: sex differences. Am J Physiol Heart Circ Physiol.317:H315-H322.

18. Jiang K, Spira AP, Reed NS, Lin FR, Deal JA. (2022) Sleep Characteristics and Hearing Loss in Older Adults: The National Health and Nutrition Examination Survey 2005-2006. J Gerontol A Biol Sci Med Sci.77:632-639.

19. Vincent BM, Johnson N, Tomkinson GR, McGrath R, Clark BC, et al. (2021) Sleeping time is associated with functional limitations in a national sample of older Americans. Aging Clin Exp Res.33:175-182.

20. Nakakubo S, Makizako H, Doi T, Tsutsumimoto K, Hotta R, et al. (2018) Long and Short Sleep Duration and Physical Frailty in Community-Dwelling Older Adults. J Nutr Health Aging.22:1066-1071.

21. Stahl ST, Smagula SF, Rodakowski J, Dew MA, Karp JF, et al. (2021) Subjective Sleep Quality and Trajectories of Interleukin-6 in Older Adults. Am J Geriatr Psychiatry.29:204-208.

22. Petrov KK, Hayley A, Catchlove S, Savage K, Stough C. (2020) Is poor self-rated sleep quality associated with elevated systemic inflammation in healthy older adults? Mech Ageing Dev.192:111388.

23. Gildner TE, Salinas-Rodríguez A, Manrique-Espinoza B, Moreno-Tamayo K, Kowal P. (2019) Does poor sleep impair cognition during aging? Longitudinal associations between changes in sleep duration and cognitive performance among older Mexican adults. Arch Gerontol Geriatr.83:161-168.

24. Wang X, Chen Y, Yue B, Li S, Liu Q, et al. (2021) Association of changes in self-reported sleep duration with mild cognitive impairment in the elderly: a longitudinal study. Aging (Albany NY).13:14816-14828.

25. Zhang H, Ma W, Chen Y, Wang F, Wang J, et al. (2021) Long Sleep Duration Associated With Cognitive Impairment in Chinese Community-Dwelling Older Adults. J Nerv Ment Dis.209:925-932.

26. Jackowska M, Cadar D. (2020) The mediating role of low-grade inflammation on the prospective association between sleep and cognitive function in older men and women: 8-year follow-up from the English Longitudinal Study of Ageing. Arch Gerontol Geriatr.87:103967.

27. Cheng GH, Chan A, Lo JC. (2018) Importance of social relationships in the association between sleep duration and cognitive function: data from community-dwelling older Singaporeans. Int Psychogeriatr.30:893-901.

28. Ma Y, Liang L, Zheng F, Shi L, Zhong B, et al. (2020) Association Between Sleep Duration and Cognitive Decline. JAMA Netw Open.3:e2013573.

29. Cruz T, Garcia L, Álvarez MA, Manzanero AL. (2022) Sleep quality and memory function in healthy ageing. Neurologia (Engl Ed).37:31-37.

30. Cheval B, Maltagliati S, Sieber S, Cullati S, Zou L, et al. (2022) Better Subjective Sleep Quality Partly Explains the Association Between Self-Reported Physical Activity and Better Cognitive Function. J Alzheimers Dis.87:919-931.

31. Lin JF, Li FD, Chen XG, He F, Zhai YJ, et al. (2018) Association of postlunch napping duration and night-time sleep duration with cognitive impairment in Chinese elderly: a cross-sectional study. BMJ Open.8:e023188.

32. Lin JN. (2018) Correlates and influences of taking an afternoon nap on nocturnal sleep in Chinese elderly: A qualitative study. Geriatr Nurs.39:543-547.

33. Tempaku P, Hirotsu C, Mazzotti D, Xavier G, Maurya P, et al. (2018) Long Sleep Duration, Insomnia, and Insomnia With Short Objective Sleep Duration Are Independently Associated With Short Telomere Length. J Clin Sleep Med.14:2037-2045.

34. Wynchank D, Bijlenga D, Penninx BW, Lamers F, Beekman AT, et al. (2019) Delayed sleep-onset and biological age: late sleep-onset is associated with shorter telomere length. Sleep.42:zsz139.

35. Ramduny J, Bastiani M, Huedepohl R, Sotiropoulos SN, Chechlacz M. (2022) The association between inadequate sleep and accelerated brain ageing. Neurobiol Aging.114:1-14.

36. De Looze C, Feeney JC, Scarlett S, Hirst R, Knight SP, et al. (2022) Sleep duration, sleep problems, and perceived stress are associated with hippocampal subfield volumes in later life: findings from The Irish Longitudinal Study on Ageing. Sleep.45:zsab241.

37. Long Z, Cheng F, Lei X. (2020) Age effect on gray matter volume changes after sleep restriction PLoS One.15:e0228473.

38. Soh AZ, Chee MWL, Yuan JM, Koh WP. (2018) Sleep lengthening in late adulthood signals increased risk of mortality. Sleep.41:zsy005.

39. Cheng GH, Malhotra R, Østbye T, Chan A, Ma S, et al. (2018) Changes in nocturnal sleep and daytime nap durations predict all-cause mortality among older adults: the Panel on Health and Ageing of Singaporean Elderly. Sleep.41.

40. Paixao L, Sikka P, Sun H, Jain A, Hogan J, et al. (2020) Excess brain

age in the sleep electroencephalogram predicts reduced life expectancy. Neurobiol Aging.88:150-155.

41. Yorgason JB, Draper TW, Bronson H, Nielson M, Babcock K, et al. (2018) Biological, Psychological, and Social Predictors of Longevity Among Utah Centenarians. Int J Aging Hum Dev.87:225-243.

42. Sella E, Cellini N, Miola L, Sarlo M, Borella E. (2019) The Influence of Metacognitive Beliefs on Sleeping Difficulties in Older Adults. Appl Psychol Health Well Being.11:20-41.

43. Sella E, Borella E. (2021) Strategies for controlling sleep-related intrusive thoughts, and subjective and objective sleep quality: how self-reported poor and good sleepers differ. Aging Ment Health.25:1959-1966.

44. Shankar A. (2020) Loneliness and sleep in older adults. Soc Psychiatry Psychiatr Epidemiol.55:269-272.

45. Benson JA, McSorley VE, Hawkley LC, Lauderdale DS. (2021) Associations of loneliness and social isolation with actigraph and self-reported sleep quality in a national sample of older adults. Sleep.44:zsaa140.

46. Cordeiro CR, Pestana PC, Côrte-Real B, Novais F. (2022) Long Time, No Sleep: Sleep in Older Adults During the COVID-19 Pandemic. Prim Care Companion CNS Disord.24:21m03224.

47. Mutambudzi M, van Solinge H. (2021) Impact of Retirement on Sleep Problems Among Older Workers and Their Partners. Gerontologist.61:1287-1295.

48. Pye J, Phillips AJ, Cain SW, Montazerolghaem M, Mowszowski L, et al. (2021) Irregular sleep-wake patterns in older adults with current or remitted depression. J Affect Disord.281:431-437.

49. Poole L, Jackowska M. (2018) The Epidemiology of Depressive Symptoms and Poor Sleep: Findings from the English Longitudinal Study of Ageing (ELSA). Int J Behav Med.25:151-161.

50. Best JR, Falck RS, Landry GJ, Liu-Ambrose T. (2019) Analysis of dynamic, bidirectional associations in older adult physical activity and sleep quality. J Sleep Res.28:e12769.

51. Owusu JT, Ramsey CM, Tzuang M, Kaufmann CN, Parisi JM, et al. (2018) Napping Characteristics and Restricted Participation in Valued Activities Among Older Adults. J Gerontol A Biol Sci Med Sci.73:367-373.

52. De Pue S, Gillebert C, Dierckx E, Vanderhasselt MA, De Raedt R, et al. (2021) The impact of the COVID-19 pandemic on wellbeing and cognitive functioning of older adults. Sci Rep.11:4636.

53. Seol J, Abe T, Fujii Y, Joho K, Okura T. (2020) Effects of sedentary behavior and physical activity on sleep quality in older people: A cross-sectional study. Nurs Health Sci.22:64-71.

54. Sewell KR, Erickson KI, Rainey-Smith SR, Peiffer JJ, Sohrabi HR, et al. (2021) Relationships between physical activity, sleep and cognitive function: A narrative review. Neurosci Biobehav Rev.130:369-378.

55. Bai C, Guo M, Yao Y, Ji JS, Gu D, et al. (2021) Sleep duration, vegetable consumption and all-cause mortality among older adults in China: a 6-year prospective study. BMC Geriatrics. 21:373.

56. Treves N, Perlman A, Kolenberg Geron L, Asaly A, Matok I. (2018) Z-drugs and risk for falls and fractures in older adults-a systematic review and meta-analysis. Age Ageing.47:201-208.

57. Brewster GS, Riegel B, Gehrman PR. (2018) Insomnia in the Older Adult. Sleep Med Clin.13:13-19.

58. Ebben MR. (2021) Insomnia: Behavioral Treatment in the Elderly. Clin Geriatr Med.37:387-399.

59. Kovacevic A, Mavros Y, Heisz JJ, Fiatarone Singh MA. (2018) The effect of resistance exercise on sleep: A systematic review of randomized controlled trials. Sleep Med Rev.39:52-68.

60. Sato M, Betriana F, Tanioka R, Osaka K, Tanioka T, et al. (2021) Balance of Autonomic Nervous Activity, Exercise, and Sleep Status in Older Adults: A Review of the Literature. Int J Environ Res Public Health.18:12896.

61. Daneault V, Orban P, Martin N, Dansereau C, Godbout J, et al. (2021) Cerebral functional networks during sleep in young and older individuals. Sci Rep.11:4905.

62. Jin JH, Kwon HS, Choi SH, Koh SH, Lee EH, et al. (2020) Association between sleep parameters and longitudinal shortening of telomere length. Aging (Albany NY). 14:2930-2944.

63. Villano I, La Marra M, Di Maio G, Monda V, Chieffi S, et al. (2022) Physiological Role of Orexinergic System for Health. Int J Environ Res Public Health.19:8353.

64. Toor B, Ray LB, Pozzobon A, Fogel SM. (2021) Sleep, Orexin and Cognition. Front Neurol Neurosci.45:38-51.

65. Kamoun A, Hammouda O, Yahia A, Dhari O, Ksentini H, et al. (2019) Effects of Melatonin Ingestion Before Nocturnal Sleep on Postural Balance and Subjective Sleep Quality in Older Adults. J Aging Phys Act.27:316-324.

66. Liu X, Xia X, Hu F, Hao Q, Hou L, et al. (2022) The mediation role of sleep quality in the relationship between cognitive decline and depression. BMC Geriatr.22:178.

67. Scarlett S, Kenny RA, O'Connell MD, Nolan H, de Looze C. (2021) Associations between cognitive function and self-reported sleep in older community-dwelling adults: Findings from the Irish Longitudinal Study on Ageing. Int J Geriatr Psychiatry.36:731-742.

International Journal of Geriatrics and Gerontology

Field T. Int J Geriatr Gerontol 6: 141.

www.doi.org/10.29011/2577-0748.100041

www.gavinpublishers.com

OPEN ACCESS

GAVIN PUBLISHERS

Review Article

Late Life Depression: A Narrative Review

Tiffany Field*

University of Miami/Miller School of Medicine and Fielding Graduate University, USA

*Corresponding author: Field T, University of Miami/Miller School of Medicine and Fielding Graduate University, USA

Citation: Field T (2023) Late Life Depression: A Narrative Review. Int J Geriatr Gerontol 6: 143. DOI: 10.29011/2577-0748.100043

Received Date: 18 January, 2023; Accepted Date: 24 January, 2023; Published Date: 30 January, 2023

Abstract

The recent literature (last five years) on late life depression is predominantly focused on risk factors/predictors of late life depression along with studies on effects, buffers, and interventions. Late life depression has typically been self-reported or diagnosed starting at age 60. The prevalence rates for late life depression were highly variable in this literature, ranging from a low of 7% in Italy to a high of 37% in Chile, a variability that may relate to the year or type of data collection and/or cross-cultural variation. Negative effects have included loneliness, suicidal ideation, cognitive decline, frailty, functional limitations, low heart rate variability, biological aging (short telomere length and white matter lesions) and earlier mortality. Risk factors have included loneliness, aging anxiety, life stressors (marital discord and job strain), physical problems (activities of daily living), physical health (elevated blood pressure), physical weakness (handgrip, frailty, falls and disability) and unhealthy intake (poor diet, excessive alcohol and vitamin D deficiency). Buffers/protective factors have included positive views on aging, resilience, practicing religion, a Mediterranean diet, and remaining active. Interventions have included cognitive training, mindfulness, physical activity and ketamines. Multiple underlying mechanisms have been suggested including dysfunctional connectivity between different networks in the brain. Although the data highlight the severity of late life depression, the recent literature has been based on different measures appearing on self-report surveys that have yielded mixed results across samples.

Prevalence of Late Life Depression

First, some myths about late life depression in a paper entitled "Depression among older adults: A 2-year update on common myths and misconceptions" are worth summarizing [1]. These authors concluded: 1) depression is not more common in older adults; 2) late life depression is not more often caused by psychological factors; 3) those who experience late life depression respond to psychological interventions as well as younger adults, but not to antidepressants; 4) late life depression follows a more chronic course (i.e. a greater rate of relapse); and 5) late life depression is frequently moderated by comorbidity.

Late life depression has typically been measured by self-report scales on surveys in very large sample studies on aging (ageing in the case of European studies). Most frequently, late life depression has been measured by the Geriatric Depression Scale, although occasionally it has been measured by the Center for Epidemiological Studies-Depression Scale or the Hamilton Depression Scale. Diagnostic interviews have rarely been conducted. Late life has been most frequently referred to those over 60 years of age, although some "late life" samples have been as young as 50. In contrast, a sample in a study on centenarians averaged 102 years-old.

The prevalence of late life depression has varied from a low of 7% in Italy (Fanelli et al, 2020) to a high of 37% in Chile [2] (Table 1).

Prevalence	First Authors
7% Italy	Fanelli
8% Ghana	Boima
9% China	Zhang
12% Ireland	Briggs
13% Germany	Qiao
27% France	Qiao
28% Greece	Tsaras
37% Chile	Moreno

Table 1: Prevalence of Late Life Depression.

The prevalence between those lower and upper rates has ranged between lows of 8% for Ghana [3], 9% for China [4], 12% for Ireland (Briggs et al, 2018), and 13% for Germany [5], but significantly higher rates at 27% for France and 28% for Greece [6].

Although prevalence across countries has not been compared in the same study except for the European sample that included Germany and France [5], the variability in prevalence may relate

Citation: Field T (2023) Late Life Depression: A Narrative Review. Int J Geriatr Gerontol 6: 143. DOI: 10.29011/2577-0748.100043

to the different years in which the data were collected and/or cross-cultural variation. Other potential sources of variability have included age, for example in Ghana, where older adults had twice the rate of depression as younger adults (8% versus 5%) [3].

Gender distribution in the samples may also differ across studies. For example, in the Chilean sample of 3,786 older adults, variability was noted across gender with 21% of males (6% major depressive disorder) and, not surprisingly, almost twice as many females (37%), experiencing depression (twice the major depressive disorder diagnosis as the males at 12% versus 6%). In that sample, only 19% of the males and 34% of the females with positive screens had received a clinical diagnosis, suggesting a high proportion of individuals who were undiagnosed. In the case of the female sample, depression occurred in older adults with a lesser probability of a diagnosis.

Although anxiety is often comorbid with depression, anxiety measures were less frequently included in these surveys. In a sample of community-dwelling adults older than 60 in China (N=4103), for example, 9% were noted to have comorbid depression and anxiety [7]. And, treatment resistant depression has been reported in as many as 30% of older patients with depression in another sample from China [8].

Late Life Depression Effects

Studies on late life depression effects have surprisingly appeared less often in this recent literature than risks/predictor variables (Table 2).

Effects		First Authors
	Psychological	
Loneliness		Power, Hsueh
Suicidal ideation		Bickford
	Cognitive	
Decline		Manning, Samir
Dementia		Lee
	Physical	
Frailty		Chang, Borges, Voshaar
Functional limitations		Wassink-Vossen
	Physiological	
Low heart rate variability		Brown
	Quality of Life	
Pro=health status		Han
Insomnia		Tsaras
	Neurological	
DNA methylation patterns		Han

Telomere shortening		Mendes-Silva, Schroder
White and gray matter lesions		Manning, Greene
Inflammation		Van den Berg

Table 2: Effects of Late Life Depression.

Researchers might have been studying the negative effects earlier and have more recently focused on risk/predictor variables. Because most of the studies are cross-sectional, effects and risk/predictor variables have often been reciprocal. They have been treated as risks or effects depending on the interests of the researchers and their selected data analyses. For example, loneliness has been treated as both an effect of depression and as a risk/predictor variable for depression by different research groups. The research on late life depression effects can be categorized as psychological, cognitive, physical, physiological and neurological effects.

Psychological Effects

Psychological effects of late life depression have ranged from loneliness to suicidal ideation. Loneliness as a negative effect of late life depression has been the focus of at least two recent studies. In one study entitled "Depression symptoms predict increased social and emotional loneliness in older adults" (N=373 adults greater than 50-years-old), a cross-lagged approach within a structural equation modelling framework suggested that depression symptoms at baseline predicted emotional and social loneliness, but loneliness at baseline did not predict depression [9]. This finding may have resulted from the direction of the variables entered, as loneliness has been a predictor as well as a mediator variable in other studies. Interestingly, both depression and loneliness were reciprocally related across two years and they both decreased between the two waves of assessments which may have related to their being research effects (i.e. participants receiving support from engaging in research).

In the second study suggesting that loneliness resulted from depression, the paper was called "A longitudinal cross-lagged panel analysis of loneliness and depression" [10]. The data came from the Taiwan Longitudinal Study on Aging (N=3920, Mage=68) noting that depression and loneliness were bidirectional, but the direction was stronger for depression as the initial symptom. This type of data analysis seemed the most appropriate for determining the strongest initial symptom in a bidirectional relationship.

Suicidal ideation and suicide are the most extreme psychological effects that have been cited for late life depression in this recent literature. In a study on suicidal ideation and late life depression (N=88, M= 72-year-old adults with major depressive disorder), the Geriatric Suicide Ideation Scale and the Hamilton Depression Rating Scale were given [11]. Surprisingly, suicidal ideation was independent of depression severity. However, suicidal ideation was correlated with the poorest frailty measures including gait speed and muscle weakness and with functional

Citation: Field T (2023) Late Life Depression: A Narrative Review. Int J Geriatr Gerontol 6: 143. DOI: 10.29011/2577-0748.100043

disability including impaired financial capacity, social interaction and communication skills. The prevalence of suicide has been noted to be 15 in 100,000 in 65–84-year-old adults and 18 per 100,000 in 85-year-old and older adults [12].

Cognitive Decline

Cognitive decline has been noted as a negative effect of late life depression in a few studies. In a study entitled "Cognitive variability, brain aging and cognitive decline in late life depression", dispersion or within person performance variability was noted across cognitive tests [13]. In this study (N=121 adults with late life depression and 39 healthy controls), greater baseline dispersion predicted cognitive decline one year later even when controlling for baseline cognitive function, demographics and clinical confounders. Dispersion was also correlated with white matter brain lesions in those with late life depression as well as with anxiety for both groups. Notably, as in many of these studies, the late life depression and healthy control groups were unequal sample sizes which would affect the reliability of the results.

In another study demonstrating cognitive effects, aging adults with major depressive disorder experienced a decline in cognitive function (Samir et al, 2018). The decline in cognitive function was related to peripheral IL-6 levels that contributed to inflammation that, in turn, negatively affected cognitive function. Late life depression was a correlate of dementia but not necessarily a cause of dementia in a sample of 16,607 adults greater than 65-years-old [14]. While dementia was noted as an effect of late life depression, it could also have been a risk factor for late life depression.

Physical Effects

Physical effects have included frailty, falls, functional limitations and disability. Frailty has been defined as the accumulation of deficits in six dimensions including disease status, sensory dysfunction, balance, functional limitations, health risk behaviors and decreased life satisfaction [15]. In a study entitled "Depression as a determinant of frailty in late life", clinical interviews as well as two screens were given for depression, and frailty was determined by two screens (N=315 geriatric outpatients, mean age=72) [16]. Frailty occurred in 15% of those who had no depression, 47% of those who had subthreshold depression and 65% of those who had major depressive disorder. Thus, there appeared to be a dose–dependent relationship between late life depression and frailty. In an 8-week randomized placebo-controlled trial on 121 greater than 60-year-old adults with major depressive disorder [17]. 63% were considered low frailty while 37% were labeled high frailty risk. In a six-year prospective clinical cohort study on the bidirectional association between frailty and major depressive disorder, greater frailty was related to baseline depression and to less remission from depression [18]. Depression was also associated with biological aging.

Depression has also been a risk factor for incident falls in a study entitled "Risk factors for incident falls in older men and women" from the English Longitudinal Study on Ageing (N=3,298

greater than 60-year-old adults), depression was a risk factor for falling [19]. Additional risk factors were noted for men including greater comorbidity and pain and balance problems

Functional limitations have been noted in the Netherlands Study on Depression in Older Persons (N= 378 adults greater than 60-years-old) [20]. In this study, the depressed adults had greater functional limitations based on growth mixture modeling suggesting two trajectories. 81% had high disability over time and 19% had functional recovery which was predicted by a decrease in depression. Females experienced fewer functional limitations which were related to their greater education, greater gait speed and less depression. One in five depressed older patients experienced functional recovery. Non-remission was related to greater chronic somatic disease, less sense of mastery and greater anxiety.

Depressive symptoms have also been predictive of disability. In a study on 65-88 year-old adults with major depressive disorder (N=78), the Hamilton Depression Rating Scale and the Late Life Function and Disability Instrument were administered (Morin et al, 2020). In a linear regression analysis model, depression accounted for 27% of the variance in disability.

Physiological Effects

Low heart rate variability has been noted as a physiological effect of late life depression. In a meta-analysis on five clinical and six observation studies of adults greater than 60-years-old (N= 550 adults with clinical depression), only low frequency heart rate variability was low in depressed patients [21]. Low heart rate variability as an index of sympathetic activity is notably indicative of depression but not related to anti-depressant use in these samples that were considered heterogeneous.

Quality of Life

Given significant frailty and functional limitations in those with late life depression, it is not surprising that health-related quality of life was also a correlate of depression. In a study on centenarians from China (N=1002, median age =102 years), many covariates were entered into the data analysis on depression and quality of life [22]. 82% of the sample were females, 38% experienced minor depression and 10% major depressive disorder. Poor health status was noted in 45% of the sample. For every one point increase on the Geriatric Depression Scale, there was a 20% increase in poor health state. Surprisingly, there was a negative relationship between depression and the number of comorbidities.

In another quality of life study, depression and insomnia symptoms contributed to quality of life based on the World Health Quality of Life and the Geriatric Depression Scales [6]. In this sample from Greece (N=200 adults who were greater than 60-years-old), 28% experienced depression, 41% had insomnia and 19% had comorbid depression and insomnia. Surprisingly, sleep problems have rarely been mentioned in this literature on late life depression, although a separate literature on sleep problems in the aging involves depression as a variable.

Citation: Field T (2023) Late Life Depression: A Narrative Review. Int J Geriatr Gerontol 6: 143. DOI: 10.29011/2577-0748.100043

Neurological Involvement

The neurological research in this recent literature on late life depression has included studies on biological aging, length of telomeres and white matter lesions. In a study entitled epigenetic aging and major depressive disorder, a sample of 811 depressed adults and 319 control adults were included from the Netherlands Study on Depression and Anxiety [23]. Based on pathway enrollment analysis, greater epigenetic aging occurred in the depressed group including DNA methylation patterns in the blood and brain tissue, suggesting that the depressed group was biologically older than their chronological age. These results are tenuous, however, because of the extremely different sample sizes of the two groups.

Telomere shortening has occurred in late life depression. Telomeres (structures of the extremity of chromosomes that prevent genetic instability) seem to shorten as a hallmark of cellular aging [24]. In this study, telomere length was shorter in a group of adults experiencing late life depression (N=45) versus a no depressed group (N=33) of adults 60-90- years-old. Telomere length was negatively correlated with depression based on the Hamilton Depression Rating Scale as well as medical burden but was not correlated with cognitive performance based on the Mattis Dementia Rating Scale.

In a review on the relationship between telomeres and depression, telomeres were noted to shorten with age and changes in telomerase activity were noted in peripheral blood cells and brain tissues in those with major depressive disorder [25]. Other relevant biological mechanisms were noted in this review including HPA axis activity leading to oxidative stress, inflammation, genetic and epigenetic changes.

As already noted in the study on cognitive decline in adults experiencing late life depression, variability across cognitive tests was correlated with white matter lesions [13]. In a review on neurological changes and depression, structural MRIs were said to reveal both white and gray matter lesions as well as cerebrovascular disease associated with late life depression [12]. Comorbid cognitive effects were also noted including impaired memory recall, executive function and processing speed.

The risk of mortality for late life depression was 2.5 times that of non-depression in the Netherlands Study of Depression in Older Persons (Jeuring et al, 2018). In this sample of 378 depressed and 132 non-depressed adults, the Inventory of Depressed Symptomatology and a diagnostic interview at two and six years suggested the risk of early mortality. Depression was also associated with earlier age onset, greater severity, pain, neuroticism, loneliness and chronic disease.

In a later publication by the same group on the same sample of depressed aging adults, the risk of early mortality was based on a regression adjusting for several potential confounding variables including age, sex, education, smoking, alcohol use, physical activity, medications and somatic comorbidity [26]. The authors suggested that the mortality risk associated with depression

could also relate to inflammation-based sickness, frailty and mild cognitive impairment.

Risk Factors/Predictor Variables

Risk factors/predictor variables for late life depression comprise the majority of the studies in this narrative review (33 of 87 studies). They include 9 studies on psychological risk factors, 6 on lifestyle variables and 18 on physical predictor variables (Table 3)

Risk Factors		First Authors
	Psychological	
Ageism		Bodner, Gum, Segel-Karpas, Protsenko, Li
Loneliness		Domenech-Abella, Yoon, Srivastavan
	Lifestyle Stressors	
Sexual		Willie-Tyndale, Rotter
Marital discord		Whisman
Job strain		Qiao
Retirement		Li
Excessive alcohol		Keyes
Low quality diet		Gomes
	Physical	
Physical health		Tan
Hand grip strength		Muhammed
Activities of daily living		Muhammed
Frailty		Jia

Table 3: Risk Factors/Predictor Variables for Late Life Depression.

Psychological Variables

The psychological risk factors in this recent literature have include ageism (negative perceptions about aging) which has been called subjective aging and "grim" age and loneliness related to spousal loss, social isolation or simply being lonely.

Ageism

Negative perceptions about aging have led to greater depression among Chinese older adults [27]. This relationship resulted from structural equation modeling on a sample of 8,404 older adults. In another study entitled "Day-to-day variability in subjective age and ageism attitudes and their association with depressive symptoms" (N= 134, mean age =70), daily subjective age and ageism attitudes led to depressive symptoms among "old-old" respondents [28]. A time-lagged analysis suggested that ageist

Citation: Field T (2023) Late Life Depression: A Narrative Review. Int J Geriatr Gerontol 6: 143. DOI: 10.29011/2577-0748.100043

attitudes during previous days contributed to feeling older and more depressed but not the reverse. Depression did not precede ageism in this relatively small sample.

In a study on self-perceptions of aging mediating the longitudinal relationship between hopelessness and depressive symptoms, hopelessness in 2008 was an independent predictor of self-perceptions of aging four years later and, in turn, a predictor of depression six years later [29]. Given the age of this study, it's not clear that these results would generalize to self-perceptions of aging today.

In another study on daily fluctuations in subjective age and depressive symptoms (N= 334), daily variation in subjective age was correlated with depressive symptoms [30]. More depressive symptoms occurred on the days when the participants were feeling older. The attitudes towards aging (greater perceptions of loss and low psychological growth) moderated this effect. The moderating effect of loss was greater with age.

"Grim age" has been considered an epigenetic predictor of mortality in major depressive disorder [31]. Based on DNA methylation levels, the authors suggested that a DNA metric was trained on time to death data and outperformed its predecessors in predicting both morbidity and mortality.

Loneliness

Loneliness has been distinguished from social isolation in several studies. An example is a study that reported loneliness and major depressive disorder as being bi-directional two years later [32]. In contrast, the relationship between social isolation and major depressive disorder was unidirectional. This is not surprising as depression has typically led to loneliness but isolating oneself socially would not be an adaptive response to feeling depressed.

In a couple studies, loneliness has been related to spousal loss. For example, in a longitudinal study from Korea (N=685), increased depression was noted following reduced social involvement and increased loneliness in men from 1 to 4 years following the loss [33]. No change in depression or social involvement/loneliness was noted for women, raising the question of the underlying mechanism for this phenomenon. Spousal loss has typically been more difficult for men and has more often led to early mortality for men possibly because of their reduced social involvement and increased loneliness.

In a study from India on the association between widowhood and living alone with depression among older adults, the sample was drawn from the Longitudinal Aging Study in India (N=30,639, 260) [34]. In this sample, 9% were depressed, 10% widowed (8% of those currently married),14% living alone and 8% were co-residing with someone widowed. The widowed were 34% more likely to be depressed, the living alone were 16% more likely to be depressed and the widowed and living alone were 56% more likely to be depressed, suggesting that living alone significantly increases the odds of widowhood leading to depression, as in a moderating variable.

Lifestyle Stressors

Several lifestyle stressors appeared in the recent literature as risk factors for late life depression. These include sexual performance problems, marital discord, job strain, retirement and excessive alcohol.

Sexual performance problems

In a study entitled "Sexual activity and depression problems in late life", aging and sexual activity were discussed in focus groups of adults greater than 50-years-old (N= 557) [35]. The men reportedly engaged in sexual activity more than the women (51 versus 41%) during the last four weeks even though 40% of the men reported erectile dysfunction. The males who engaged in sexual activity had five point lower depression scores, while the females with sexual complaints had two point higher depression scores.

Erectile dysfunction may have related to the testosterone deficiency syndrome which has also been noted in aging men [36]. In this study on 314 men greater than 60-years-old, 49% had testosterone deficiency syndrome and 29% had depressive symptoms. In the testosterone deficiency syndrome group, a significant positive correlation was noted between the syndrome and the metals manganese and chromium. Manganese toxicity is also associated with depression which may be a mediator of the relationship between manganese and testosterone deficiency. Similarly, chromium is associated with mood changes as well as sleep disturbances.

Marital discord

Marital discord is another stressor that has been noted as a risk factor for late life depression [37]. In this Irish Longitudinal Study on Ageing (N =1,445 couples), an actor–partner dependence model was explored. Actor effects of marital discord on depression were greater than for women, likely because men were more often the perpetrators and may have felt guilty. This effect was significant after adjusting for family and friends' discord. It was not clear if adjusting for marital discord, in turn, led to significant effects of discord with family and friends on depression. It was also surprising that the emphasis was on the effects that existed for the actor but not for the partner who is usually the victim of marital discord.

Job strain is still another risk factor for depression. In a sample from the Survey of Health, Aging and Retirement (N=7,879), greater depression was experienced by those aging adults with high physical and psychosocial strain [5]. Job strain at baseline was predictive of depression, although depression at baseline was not associated with subsequent high job strain. This was, surprisingly, not a reciprocal relationship.

Retirement has also been a risk factor for late life depression. In a meta-analysis of 25 longitudinal studies published between 1980 and 2020, retirement was associated with greater depression symptoms [38]. However, retirement as a risk factor for depressive symptoms was specifically for involuntary versus voluntary

Citation: Field T (2023) Late Life Depression: A Narrative Review. Int J Geriatr Gerontol 6: 143. DOI: 10.29011/2577-0748.100043

retirement. And, the association between retirement and depressive symptoms was greater for eastern versus western countries.

Other late life stressors have been mentioned in an extensive review [39-41]. Some that have received less attention include caregiving, financial stress, loss of independence, bereavement, retirement from a low stress job, the loss of role identities (marital, parental, employment) and living in an institution. Having coping resources (meaning and a goal in life) was a moderator for the relationship between interpersonal stressful events on depression in at least one study [14]. In this six-year study on 588 aging adults, coping resources effectively reduced depressive symptoms.

Alcohol consumption has also predicted depressive episodes in late life depression [42]. In this longitudinal sample of older adults in 19 countries (N= 57,276), heavy drinkers had higher depression scores than moderate drinkers. But, surprisingly, long term alcohol abstainers and occasional drinkers also had higher depression scores than moderate drinkers.

Low quality diet has also been a predictor of depressive symptoms in aging adults. In a study from Brazil (N= 1,378), 15% were noted to be depressed [43]. The odds ratio for this reciprocal relationship was 3.8 for males and 2.1 for females. The higher odds ratio for males suggests a greater relationship between poor diet and late life depression for males.

The COVID-19 pandemic has notably affected depression in adults 50 years and older (MacNeil et al, 2022). in a study from Canada (N = 22,622), for example, a logistic regression was used to estimate the odds of depression during COVID. Folks with a history of depression had four times the risk of experiencing depression during COVID. Other factors were being female, having lower savings, health stressors and family conflict.

Physical Risk Factors

A number of physical health risk factors for late life depression have been reported in this literature. These include physical health in general, vitamin D deficiency, hypertension, hand grip strength, activities of daily living, frailty, falling and disabilities.

Physical health. In a meta-analysis on prediction models for depression among older adults, 14 studies were included on 20 different models [44]. In this meta- analysis, physical health was the most common predictor for late life depression. Age and cognitive function were also significant predictors.

Hypertension. Hypertension has also been a risk factor for depression [3]. In this study from Ghana, those aging adults with blood pressure greater than 140/90 had an increased risk of depression. In addition, older adults had twice the depression (8.4 versus 4.5%) as younger folks.

Vitamin D deficiency. This deficiency has also been associated with depressive symptoms in later life (Oliveire et al, 2018). In this study from England (N= 5,607), 9% were depressed. Those women who had less than 30 and less than 50 on their vitamin D levels had

depressive symptoms and for males those with levels less than 30 were depressed. Vitamin D deficiency may have related to frailty-bone loss which has also been a risk factor for depression.

Hand grip strength. In a study from the Longitudinal Ageing Study in India (N= 27,707 adults greater than 60-years-old), less hand grip strength was related to greater depression [45]. Older adults with less hand grip strength, in turn, had greater cognitive impairment.

Activities of daily living. In another study by the same author from the Longitudinal Ageing Study in India, older adults who had difficulty in basic activities of daily living were more depressed [46]. In this study, a greater prevalence of depression occurred in the 9% who were depressed, 15% who had difficulty in basic activities of daily living (like bathing and dressing), 12% who had difficulty in instrumental activities of daily living (like preparing meals and doing laundry), 10% who were unmarried, 10% who were living separately and 10% who were socially inactive.

Physical frailty. Physical frailty has also been a risk factor for major depressive disorder in the aging. In a study from the Irish Longitudinal Study on Ageing (N= 3,671), physical frailty according to five criteria led to greater depression [47]. The physical frailty phenotype (five criteria) was used which defines frailty as fatigue, resistance (difficulty walking up to 10 steps on stairs), ambulation (difficulty walking several hundred yards), illness (five or more of 11 illnesses) and weight loss of greater than 5% total weight within one year. After correcting for several variables including living arrangements, health behavior, common chronic diseases including hypertension, diabetes, cancer, lung disease, heart problems and stroke, a greater incidence of shrinking and exhaustion led to the onset of major depressive disorder over a four-year period.

Frailty based on the Fried Prototype Criteria has been related to depressive symptoms among older adults [4]. In this sample (N =1168), 9% had depressive symptoms, 35% had pre–frailty symptoms and 6 % had frailty symptoms. The percentage of depressive symptoms increased from robust adults (5%) to pre-frail (11%) to frail adults (32%). The odds of having depression for pre-frailty was 1.75 and prevalent frailty had a risk index of 5.64. Depressive symptoms were associated with a 2.79 fold increased risk of three-year incident frailty. Clearly this was a reciprocal relationship where frailty could be considered a risk factor for depression and previous depression could be considered a risk factor for frailty.

In another sample on the comorbidity of depression and frailty among older adults, the West China Health and Aging Trend Study was tapped for participants (N=4,103 community dwelling adults greater than 60-years-old) [7]. In this study, the prevalence of pre-frailty was 47% and frailty was 7% and the prevalence of comorbid depression was 9%.

In at least one study, mortality was associated with frailty and depressive symptoms in older adults [15]. In this longitudinal research from Taiwan, comorbid frailty and depressive symptoms

Citation: Field T (2023) Late Life Depression: A Narrative Review. Int J Geriatr Gerontol 6: 143. DOI: 10.29011/2577-0748.100043

were associated with greater mortality. Depression led to frailty but that was a weaker direction than frailty leading to depression. Unfortunately, these data were collected from 1987 to 2007 which suggests they may not generalize to today's population.

Fear of falling and falling. Frailty may predispose to worrying about falling and experiencing falling. Worrying about falling has been associated with depressive symptoms in aging adults [48]. In this sample (N=3,333 greater than 70-years-old), those with fall worry had more moderate/severe depressive symptoms in 2019 and an increase in fall worrying by 2020. Experiencing falling has also been a risk factor for depression [49]. In this sample (N= 9,355), those who experienced falling had a 1.36 greater risk of becoming depressed.

Chronic illnesses. Chronic illnesses have been a risk factor for depression in the aging. In a study on chronic illness and functional limitations, effects of chronic illness on depression were mediated by functional limitations [23]. Chronic illnesses led to negative self-perceptions that moderated (exacerbated) the effects of illness on depression.

Disability. Disability onset has also been associated with comorbid depression and anxiety [50]. Disability was defined by these authors as receiving help from another person for self-care or mobility activities. They noted a dose-response relationship between disability and onset of depression/anxiety symptoms. Twenty per cent of the sample reported mild or moderate symptoms at baseline while the prevalence of depression rose to 30 to 38% with disability onset.

Buffers against Late Life Depression

Several buffers have been noted for late life depression in the recent literature. These include having a younger subjective age, resilience, religiosity, physical activity, a Mediterranean diet and retirement (Table 4).

Buffers	First Authors
Younger subjective age	Xiao
Resilience	Laird, Reynolds
Religiosity	Foong
Attitudes toward treatment	Nair
Physical activity	Marques, DeSousa
Mediterranean diet	Pagliai
Retirement	Odone

Table 4: Buffers/Protective Factors for Late Life Depression.

Subjective age. Having a younger subjective age has been associated with fewer depressive symptoms among Chinese older adults (N=609) (Xiao et al, 2019). The relationship between subjective age and depressive symptoms may have been partially mediated by perceived control.

Resilience. Resilience has been defined as grit, active coping, accommodative coping, self-efficacy and spirituality [41]. In a study entitled "Promoting resilience and reducing depression in older adults", resilience was defined as the ability to adapt and thrive in the face of adversity [51]. In that study, successful aging was defined as engagement in life, maintenance of high cognitive and physical function and avoidance of disease [51]. In a study on the clinical correlates of resiliency and geriatric depression, the Conners – Davidson Resiliency Scale was given to 337 adults older than 60 years [42]. The definition starting with "grit" was used. In this sample, resilience was negatively associated with depression and white matter integrity. In addition, it was negatively associated with apathy and anxiety and positively associated with quality of life, variables that potentially confounded the relationship between resilience and depression.

A related resilience factor has been called "intrinsic capacity" [52]. In this sample (N=24,136 adults greater than 60), high intrinsic capacity was related to greater activity and yoga and less depression based on a logistic regression analysis.

Several other resilience factors have been discussed in an elaborate review on resilience in late life depression [43]. These include temperament (behavioral inhibition), personality factors such as low extraversion and high neuroticism, and low self-esteem. In addition, the practice of religion and a belief in eternal life were buffers, although greater prayer has been notably associated with greater depression.

Religiosity. Religiosity has decreased the effects of depression in older adults in at least three studies. In the first study entitled "Moderating effects of intrinsic religiosity on the relationship between depression and cognitive function among community-dwelling older adults (N= 2,322 in Malaysia) a hierarchical regression analysis was conducted [53]. Religiosity decreased the negative effects of depression on cognitive function after controlling for demographic variables. In a second study that had one of the lowest rates of depression (Ghana at 8%), participants who had no religion had seven times the rate of depression [3].

In a systematic review of older adults' attitudes toward treatments for depression, 11 studies were included [54]. The participants in the research basically preferred self- management strategies that were aligned with their experience and social image including most prominently prayer and socializing. Thus, praying has had mixed effects across studies.

Physical activity. Physical activity has also been a buffer against late life depression in a study from 14 European countries over a four year follow up from the years 2011 to 2015 [55]. In this Survey of Health, Age and Retirement in Europe (N=32,392), the EURO-D 12-item Scale of Depression (number of symptoms) was used and the intensity and frequency of activity were reported. Moderate and vigorous physical activity at least once per week were negatively correlated with depression after controlling for demographic variables, self-related health and chronic diseases. Although this old database may not generalize to today's adults

Citation: Field T (2023) Late Life Depression: A Narrative Review. Int J Geriatr Gerontol 6: 143. DOI: 10.29011/2577-0748.100043

with late life depression, these results were virtually the same on approximately twice the sample size (N=64,688) by the same authors [55]. In this larger sample, the researchers were looking at the effects of different levels of physical activity on depressive symptoms. Not surprisingly, a dose-response relationship was noted between physical activity and depressive symptoms. The significantly greater number of females in this sample is a limitation of this study, not unlike many other surveys in this literature.

In a systematic review on molecular mechanisms for the positive effects of physical exercise on depression in the elderly, 11 studies met inclusion criteria [56]. Aerobic and resistance training were the most common and on average were moderate intensity exercises of 60 minutes duration, three times a week for 24 weeks. Exercise increased IGF-1 and the expression of BDNF and its receptors in the hippocampus and prefrontal cortex, inhibiting depressive–like behavior.

Mediterranean diet. A Mediterranean diet has also reduced the risk of late life depression in a sample from Florence, Italy on 90 to 99 year-old adults (N=388) [57]. The Mini–Mental State Exam and the Geriatric Depression Scale were included along with the Mediterranean Diet Score. Consumption of more olive oil and fruit was associated with less depression. The sample, however, was limited to depressed participants who were older female widows, limiting the generalizability of the data.

Retirement. In a study entitled "Does retirement trigger depressive symptoms?", a meta-analysis was conducted on 41 studies [58]. As the authors suggested, retirement is a major life transition and existing studies had presented contradictory results. The meta-analysis on 557,811 participants from 60 databases suggested a protective effect of retirement on the risk of depression. Further, studies with the highest quality of longitudinal and validated measures suggested a stronger effect of retirement on depression. Retirement reduced the risk of depression by 20%. Surprisingly, no statistical differences were noted between genders. The results of this meta-analysis were also at odds with the meta-analysis reviewed under risk factors [38]. That meta-analysis, however, included fewer studies (25 versus 41) and the negative effects of retirement appeared to be related to involuntary retirement which would be expected to have negative effects.

Interventions

In the recent late life depression literature, interventions have included education to decrease ageism against older adults. Interventions for those who are depressed have included physical activity, strength training, serious games, mindfulness, and nontraditional interventions like yoga and ketamines (Table 5).

Interventions	First authors
Education to reduce ageism	Burnes
Cognitive training and physical activity	Gunning
Strength and aerobic training	Moraes
Serious games	Kim
Mindfulness meditation	Reangsing
Non-traditional therapies	Laird
Antidepressants	Briggs
Ketamines	Sukhram, Greene
Sleep deprivation	Shanafi

Table 5: Interventions for Late Life Depression.

Decreasing ageism. In a meta-analysis on interventions to decrease ageism against older adults, 63 studies were included (N=6,124) [59]. The meta-analysis revealed that education and intergenerational contact were the most effective interventions for reducing ageism against older adults. Stronger effects were noted for females and younger groups.

Cognitive training and physical activities. Interventions that have been reportedly effective with depressed aging adults include cognitive training and physical activities [60]. Cognitive training has been effective via video games for reducing late life depression. Physical activity is reported ly effective via a number of mechanisms including that it "promotes neurogenesis, upregulates neurotrophic factors and suppresses pro-inflammatory signaling and oxidative damage as well as improves vascular health and increased cerebral blood flow" [60].

Strength training and aerobic training. These two types of training have been compared for their effects on depression in older adults [61]. In this study, 27 aging adults were randomly assigned to strength training or aerobic training. Depression was reduced in 50% of the participants. However, the two exercise groups cannot be compared because different rating scales were used for depression in the two different groups. In addition, the sample size was too small for that comparison.

Serious games. Serious games have been notably effective based on a systematic review and meta-analysis of 17 studies in the recent literature on late life depression (1,280 older adults) [62]. In this meta-analysis games for physical activity and games for both physical activity and cognitive function were noted to decrease late life depression but not cognitive function games alone. No effects were noted for the duration or the number of serious games.

Citation: Field T (2023) Late Life Depression: A Narrative Review. Int J Geriatr Gerontol 6: 143. DOI: 10.29011/2577-0748.100043

Mindfulness meditation. Meta-analysis has also been performed on mindfulness meditation research [63]. In this analysis on 1,076 72-year-old adults, a significant decrease in depression was noted for protocols of less than five weeks of mindfulness meditation. The decrease in depression was greater for the Asians than the Europeans who in turn had a greater decrease in depression than the North Americans. Guided meditation was more effective than non-guided meditation. Some have suggested that nontraditional therapies like meditation, physical activity, or art therapy may be more effective because they are more accepted. Greater acceptance may relate to their being used by non–depressed adults [12].

In a review of the literature on non-traditional therapies, several have been notably effective [39]. These include not only mindfulness meditation but mindfulness-based stress reduction, journaling, yoga, tai chi, kirtans, chanting, a balanced diet and sufficient sleep. Other more medical interventions include cognitive behavior therapy (CBT), ECT biofeedback, heart rate variability feedback and antidepressants [40]. An example of an effective intervention is the peer-led combination of CBT, physical exercise and sleep activities on zoom (14 weeks) leading to decreased depression and stress and increased physical activity, brain health behavior and sleep quality [64]. But this study needs replicating as it is based on a very small sample (N=24 with only 20 completing the intervention).

Participants in at least one study had mixed views on psychotherapy and antidepressants [54]. Antidepressants were frequently used for late life depression until recently. Antidepressants have reportedly only been effective for 30% of those with late life depression likely because of their treatment resistant depression [13]. And, the prevalence of untreated depression has also been increasingly high. For example, in a study on 7,000 adults greater than 50 years old, although 12% were depressed, only 29% of those were on antidepressants in the Irish Longitudinal Study on Ageing.

Ketamines have recently been used more frequently as they are thought to be more immediately effective than antidepressants. In a review entitled "Antidepressant effects of ketamines on inflammation–mediated serotonin dysregulation", ketamine infusions in 5 to 7 studies have notably decreased depression by 50% in 56% of those treated [65]. The effects reputedly involve a reduction in pro-inflammatory cytokines including IL-6 and TNF-1. Rapid treatments have not only included ketamines but also sleep deprivation and acute exercise which have been effective in a few hours to a week [66]. These are reputedly effective due to activation of the endocannabinoid system.

Potential Biomarkers and Underlying Biological Mechanisms

Biomarkers and potential underlying mechanisms have been explored in the recent literature on late life depression. These include cortisol, IL–beta as a marker of inflammation, homocysteine, amyloid, DNA methylation, and disconnected brain networks (Table 6).

Biomarkers and Mechanisms	First authors
>Cortisol, nesfatin-1 and IL-Beta	Wu
>Inflammation	Rozing
>C-reactive protein	Frank
>IL-6 and TNF-alpha leading to <serotonin and BDNF	Kuo
<Functional connectivity in the brain	Laird
>Hippocampal and prefrontal atrophy	Laird
Low low-frequency heart rate variability	Laird

Table 6: Biomarkers and Potential Underlying Mechanisms for Late Life Depression.

Inflammation and its Biomarkers

Serum cortisol, nesfatin-1 and IL-beta have been diagnostic biomarkers in elderly patients with treatment -resistant depression [8]. The stimulation of the HPA axis and over secretion of cortisol contributes to neurodegeneration which is a significant risk for late life depression and cognitive decline [41].

Total plasma homocysteine was also related to depression in a sample of older Hispanic adults after adjusting for age, sex, education, smoking, diabetes, hypertension, alcohol intake, stroke and dementia [67]. After controlling for these many variables in this sample (N=1,418 adults greater than 55 years old), homocysteine explained a significant amount of the variance in the number of depressive symptoms. The authors expressed the concern that excessive homocysteine can damage the interior wall of arteries and increase the chance of forming clots. Amyloid deposition has also been associated with plaques and depression symptoms in the Mayo Clinic Study of Aging (N=1028) [68].

And, late life depression has been associated with greater levels of growth-differentiating factor -15 (GDF-15), a pro-aging mitokine. In this sample (N=393 greater than 70 years old), GDF-15 was associated with increasing chronological age, decreasing telomerase activity and increased early mortality risk. It was also related to a greater incidence of comorbid physical illness and declining executive cognitive function.

Inflammation has been noted as the increase of inflammatory cytokines that interact with neural transmitters, most especially serotonin and dopamine that contribute to mood and cognitive symptoms of depression [38]. Inflammation and its biomarkers have been the focus of a few studies on potential mechanisms underlying late life depression. In a study entitled "Inflammation in older subjects with early and late – onset depression", the Netherlands Study of Depression in Older Persons" was tapped for this database [69]. In this study on 350 persons greater than 60-years-old, 119 had late onset and 231 had early onset depression. C-reactive protein (CRP) levels were more strongly associated with late-onset depression than early onset. The IL-6 levels were

Citation: Field T (2023) Late Life Depression: A Narrative Review. Int J Geriatr Gerontol 6: 143. DOI: 10.29011/2577-0748.100043

significantly lower and declined in depression. Unfortunately, the comparison of these two groups was confounded by the differences in sample size.

CRP levels have distinguished two types of depression in a sample from the English Longitudinal Study on Ageing (N=3,510 adults greater than 50-years-old) (Frank et al, 2021). In this study, CRP levels mediated the relationship between polygenic scores and depressive symptomatology. This finding was specific to somatic symptoms but not cognitive-affective symptoms. These researchers also confirmed the two-factor structure of the CES-D depression scale as being somatic symptoms and cognitive-affective symptoms based on a factor analysis.

Others have also suggested that inflammation and its markers have been the molecular basis for late life depression [70]. They have indicated that the cytokines representing inflammation increase with age and they decrease serotonin. In late life depression, IL-6 and TNF–alpha lead to decreased serotonin and a BDNF (brain-derived neurotrophic factor) decrease which may contribute to the memory impairment and dementia that are seen in late life depression that are reciprocally related to BDNF. The authors suggested that these factors are responsible for the limited treatment response to antidepressants (48%) and a remission rate of only 34%.

Decreased Functional Connectivity

An interesting mechanism has been proposed in a paper entitled "Brain–based mechanisms of late life depression [60]. According to these authors, in late life depression negative cognitive biases and processing happen for both internal and external stimuli which contribute to negative self-referential thoughts, guilt, rumination, self-criticism, feelings of worthlessness and sadness and resistance to traditional antidepressant treatment. This is compounded by apathy which is experienced by one third to one half of those suffering from late life depression. This is related to "decreased extrinsic functional connectivity between the salience network (which is critical for prioritizing stimuli), the executive control network (which is involved in maintaining goal-directed behavior in the face of changing internal and external demands) and the default motor network (which plays a key role in individuals' understanding of their place in the world).". They also mention white matter abnormalities as a hallmark of small vessel disease. They locate the areas of the brain that are involved such as the medial prefrontal cortex, the poster cingulate cortex and the precuneus in the default mode network.

Other Biomarkers

Other biomarkers have been suggested including neuroimaging markers [40]. Neuroimaging markers have included the atrophy that has been shown in the hippocampus and the prefrontal cortex, with fMRI studies suggesting increased activation of the prefrontal cortex and the amygdala during emotion regulation tasks.

Cardiovascular markers have shown an association between depression and cardiovascular disease with two times the risk of developing cardiovascular disease for those who are depressed [41]. This has already been mentioned as being confounded by unhealthy behaviors such as bad diet and physical inactivity. The low low frequency heart rate variability already mentioned reflects both sympathetic and parasympathetic activation. Endocrine changes have included the decreased reproductive hormones. The reproductive hormones that have been emphasized include estrogen which the authors suggest have been "important for brain regions vulnerable to age – related changes including the prefrontal cortex and the hippocampus".

Methodological Limitations

Several methodological limitations can be noted about these recent studies on late life depression. Significant variability has been reported on the sampling methods, on the sample sizes, and the prevalence and results of the studies. Self-report surveys have been the most frequently used method for data collection. Logistic regression analyses have typically been used. They have controlled for confounding variables, for example, gender, socioeconomic status and education that might instead be risk factors or mediating/moderating variables if they had been analyzed by mediation/moderation or structural equations analysis. These confounding variables that might be important for intervention purposes may have been obscured by these analyses.

Several of the effects that have been noted could also be risk factors and risk factors could be effects, as in bidirectional, reciprocal variables, although they have rarely been considered reciprocal. In some studies bidirectional effects have been reported. However, as some have noted, the research has been "methodologically heterogeneous in terms of design, inclusion criteria, measures of multimorbidity and depression and length of follow-up'. Several of the measures are short or dichotomous which limits the reliability of these measures. For example, in a review of the 21 functional assessments that have been used, only two had formal validation data. The direction of effects cannot be determined as most of the studies are correlational and several of the longitudinal studies have focused on cross-sectional data instead of their longitudinal datapoints.

Many of the results are relationships between late life depression and other effects, risk variables or buffers/protective factors selected by the researchers. Rarely has late depression been compared to early onset depression or the depression experienced by younger adults. Surprisingly, sex differences have been rare, although several studies were exclusively male or female, limiting generalizability. The prevalence of late life depression, its measures and its effects are so variable that systematic reviews and meta-analyses have been inconclusive.

Biomarkers and potential underlying mechanisms for late life depression have been suggested in reviews on the topic, although mechanism studies have rarely appeared in the recent literature. And, several of the recent intervention studies have not randomly assigned participants to comparison groups. Despite these methodological limitations, the recent literature highlights the effects and risk variables for late life depression, although it

Citation: Field T (2023) Late Life Depression: A Narrative Review. Int J Geriatr Gerontol 6: 143. DOI: 10.29011/2577-0748.100043

doesn't conclude that aging is associated with more depression necessarily than other stages of life.

Despite all the negative effects reported for aging and depression and the methodological limitations mentioned for this recent literature, at least one research group has suggested that the prevalence of depression has decreased with age [71]. The authors argue that this has related to a bias toward positive information, increased emotion regulation, less regret and greater socioeconomic status. And, they also reported less prediction errors, i.e. that differences between predicted and actual events decreased with age which led to less negative affect and less susceptibility to affective disorders like depression [72].

Conclusions

The recent literature (last five years) on late life depression is predominantly focused on risk factors/predictors of late life depression along with studies on effects, buffers, and interventions. Late life depression has typically been self-reported or diagnosed starting at age 60. The prevalence rates for late life depression were highly variable in this literature, ranging from a low of 7% in Italy to a high of 37% in Chile, a variability that may relate to the year or type of data collection and/or cross-cultural variation. Negative effects have included loneliness, suicidal ideation, cognitive decline, frailty, functional limitations, low heart rate variability, biological aging (short telomere length and white matter lesions) and earlier mortality. Risk factors have included loneliness, aging anxiety, life stressors (marital discord and job strain), physical problems (activities of daily living), physical health (elevated blood pressure), physical weakness (handgrip, frailty, falls and disability) and unhealthy intake (poor diet, excessive alcohol and vitamin D deficiency).

Buffers/protective factors have included positive views on aging, resilience, practicing religion, a Mediterranean diet, and remaining active. Interventions have included cognitive training, mindfulness, physical activity and ketamines. Multiple underlying mechanisms have been suggested including dysfunctional connectivity between different networks in the brain. Although the data highlight the severity of late life depression, the recent literature has been based on different measures appearing on self-report surveys that have yielded mixed results across samples.

References

1. Haigh EAP, Bogucki OE, Sigmon ST, Blazer DG. (2018) Depression Among Older Adults: A 20-Year Update on Five Common Myths and Misconceptions. Am J Geriatr Psychiatry.26:107-122.

2. Moreno X, Gajardo J, Monsalves MJ.(2022) Gender differences in positive screen for depression and diagnosis among older adults in Chile. BMC Geriatr.22:54.

3. Boima V, Tetteh J, Yorke E, Archampong T, Mensah G, et al.(2020) Older adults with hypertension have increased risk of depression compared to their younger counterparts: Evidence from the World Health Organization study of Global Ageing and Adult Health Wave 2 in Ghana. J Affect Disord.277:329-336.

4. Zhang N, Shi GP, Wang Y, Chu XF, Wang ZD, et al. (2020) Depressive symptoms are associated with incident frailty in a Chinese population: the Rugao Longevity and Aging Study. Aging Clin Exp Res 32: 2297-2302.

5. Qiao YM, Lu YK, Yan Z, Yao W, Pei JJ, et al. (2019) Reciprocal associations between job strain and depression: A 2-year follow-up study from the Survey of Health, Ageing and Retirement in Europe. Brain Behav 9: e01381.

6. Tsaras K, Tsiantoula M, Papagiannis D, Papathanasiou IV, Chatzi M, et al. (2022) The Effect of Depressive and Insomnia Symptoms in Quality of Life among Community-Dwelling Older Adults. Int J Environ Res Public Health 19: 13704.

7. Zhao W, Zhang Y, Liu X, Yue J, Hou L,et al. (2020) Comorbid depressive and anxiety symptoms and frailty among older adults: Findings from the West China health and aging trend study. J Affect Disord 277: 970-976.

8. Wu X, Dai B, Yan F, Chen Y, Xu Y, et al. (2022) Serum Cortisol, Nesfatin-1, and IL-1β: Potential Diagnostic Biomarkers in Elderly Patients with Treatment-Resistant Depression. Clin Interv Aging 17: 567-576.

9. McHugh Power J, Hannigan C, Hyland P, Brennan S, Kee F, et al.(2020) Depressive symptoms predict increased social and emotional loneliness in older adults. Aging Ment Health.24:110-118.

10. Hsueh YC, Chen CY, Hsiao YC, Lin CC.(2019) A longitudinal, cross-lagged panel analysis of loneliness and depression among community-based older adults. J Elder Abuse Negl.31:281-293.

11. Bickford D, Morin RT, Woodworth C, Verduzco E, Khan M, et al. (2021) The relationship of frailty and disability with suicidal ideation in late life depression. Aging Ment Health.25:439-444.

12. Greene RD, Cook A, Nowaskie D, Wang S.(2020) Neurological Changes and Depression: 2020 Update. Clin Geriatr Med.36:297-313.

13. Manning KJ, Preciado-Pina J, Wang L, Fitzgibbon K, Chan G, et al.(2021) Cognitive variability, brain aging, and cognitive decline in late-life major depression. Int J Geriatr Psychiatry.36:665-676.

14. Lee ATC, Fung AWT, Richards M, Chan WC, Chiu HFK, et al.(2021) Risk of incident dementia varies with different onset and courses of depression. J Affect Disord.282:915-920.

15. Chang HY, Fang HL, Ting TT, Liang J, Chuang SY, et al.(2019) The Co-Occurrence Of Frailty (Accumulation Of Functional Deficits) And Depressive Symptoms, And Its Effect On Mortality In Older Adults: A Longitudinal Study. Clin Interv Aging.14:1671-1680.

16. Borges MK, Aprahamian I, Romanini CV, Oliveira FM, Mingardi SVB, et al.(2021) Depression as a determinant of frailty in late life. Aging Ment Health.25:2279-2285.

17. Brown PJ, Ciarleglio A, Roose SP, Montes Garcia C, Chung S, et al.(2022) Frailty and Depression in Late Life: A High-Risk Comorbidity With Distinctive Clinical Presentation and Poor Antidepressant Response. J Gerontol A Biol Sci Med Sci.77:1055-1062.

18. Oude Voshaar RC, Dimitriadis M, vandenBrink RHS, Aprahamian I, Borges MK, et al.(2021) A 6-year prospective clinical cohort study on the bidirectional association between frailty and depressive disorder. Int J Geriatr Psychiatry.36:1699-1707.

19. Gale CR, Westbury LD, Cooper C, Dennison EM.(2018) Risk factors for incident falls in older men and women: the English longitudinal study of ageing. BMC Geriatr.18:117.

Citation: Field T (2023) Late Life Depression: A Narrative Review. Int J Geriatr Gerontol 6: 143. DOI: 10.29011/2577-0748.100043

20. Wassink-Vossen S, Collard RM, Wardenaar KJ, Verhaak PFM, Rhebergen D, et al. (2019) Trajectories and determinants of functional limitations in late-life depression: A 2-year prospective cohort study. Eur Psychiatry 62: 90-96.

21. Brown L, Karmakar C, Gray R, Jindal R, Lim T, et al.(2018) Heart rate variability alterations in late life depression: A meta-analysis. J Affect Disord.235:456-466.

22. Han K, Yang S, Jia W, Wang S, Song Y, et al.(2020) Health-Related Quality of Life and Its Correlation With Depression Among Chinese Centenarians. Front Public Health.8:580757.

23. Han LKM, Aghajani M, Clark SL, Chan RF, Hattab MW, et al.(2018) Epigenetic Aging in Major Depressive Disorder. Am J Psychiatry.175:774-782.

24. Mendes-Silva AP, Vieira ELM, Xavier G, Barroso LSS, Bertola L, et al. (2021)Telomere shortening in late-life depression: A potential marker of depression severity. Brain Behav.11:e2255.

25. Schroder JD, de Araújo JB, de Oliveira T, de Moura AB, Fries GR, et al. (2021) Telomeres: the role of shortening and senescence in major depressive disorder and its therapeutic implications. Rev Neurosci 33: 227-255.

26. van den Berg KS, Wiersema C, Hegeman JM, van den Brink RHS, Rhebergen D, et al. (2021) Clinical characteristics of late-life depression predicting mortality. Aging Ment Health 25: 476-483.

27. Li Y, Chan WCH, Chen H, Ran M.(2022)Widowhood and depression among Chinese older adults: examining coping styles and perceptions of aging as mediators and moderators. Aging Ment Health.26:1161-1169.

28. Bodner E, Shrira A, Hoffman Y, Bergman YS.(2021) Day-to-Day Variability in Subjective Age and Ageist Attitudes and Their Association With Depressive Symptoms. J Gerontol B Psychol Sci Soc Sci.76:836-844.

29. Gum AM, Ayalon L.(2018) Self-perceptions of aging mediate the longitudinal relationship of hopelessness and depressive symptoms. Int J Geriatr Psychiatry.33:591-597.

30. Segel-Karpas D, Shrira A, Cohn-Schwartz E, Bodner E (2022) Daily fluctuations in subjective age and depressive symptoms: the roles of attitudes to ageing and chronological age. Eur J Ageing 19: 741-751.

31. Protsenko E, Yang R, Nier B, Reus V, Hammamieh R, et al. (2021) "GrimAge," an epigenetic predictor of mortality, is accelerated in major depressive disorder. Transl Psychiatry 11: 193.

32. Domènech-Abella J, Mundó J, Haro JM, Rubio-Valera M.(2018) Anxiety, depression, loneliness and social network in the elderly: Longitudinal associations from The Irish Longitudinal Study on Ageing (TILDA). J Affect Disord.246:82-88.

33. Yoon H, Park GR, Kim J (2022) Psychosocial trajectories before and after spousal loss: Does gender matter? Soc Sci Med 294: 114701.

34. Srivastava S, Debnath P, Shri N, Muhammad T (2021) The association of widowhood and living alone with depression among older adults in India. Sci Rep 11: 21641.

35. Willie-Tyndale D, Donaldson-Davis K, Ashby-Mitchell K, McKoy Davis J, Aiken WD,et al. (2021) Sexual Activity and Depressive Symptoms in Later Life: Insights from Jamaica. Clin Gerontol 44: 316-330.

36. Rotter I, Wiatrak A, Ryl A, Kotfis K, Ciosek Ż, et al. (2020) The Relationship between Selected Bioelements and Depressiveness Associated with Testosterone Deficiency Syndrome in Aging Men. Medicina (Kaunas) 56: 125.

37. Whisman MA, Robustelli BL, Labrecque LT (2018) Specificity of the Association between Marital Discord and Longitudinal Changes in Symptoms of Depression and Generalized Anxiety Disorder in the Irish Longitudinal Study on Ageing. Fam Process 57: 649-661.

38. Li W, Ye X, Zhu D, He P.(2021) The Longitudinal Association Between Retirement and Depression: A Systematic Review and Meta-Analysis. Am J Epidemiol.190:2220-2230.

39. Laird KT, Krause B, Funes C, Lavretsky H.(2019) Psychobiological factors of resilience and depression in late life. Transl Psychiatry.9:88.

40. Laird KT, Lavretsky H, Paholpak P, Vlasova RM, Roman M, et al.(2019) Clinical correlates of resilience factors in geriatric depression. Int Psychogeriatr.31:193-202.

41. Laird KT, Lavretsky H, Wu P, Krause B, Siddarth P.(2019) Neurocognitive Correlates of Resilience in Late-Life Depression. Am J Geriatr Psychiatry.27:12-17.

42. Keyes KM, Allel K, Staudinger UM, Ornstein KA, Calvo E.(2019) Alcohol consumption predicts incidence of depressive episodes across 10 years among older adults in 19 countries. Int Rev Neurobiol.148:1-38.

43. Gomes AP, Oliveira Bierhals I, Gonçalves Soares AL, Hellwig N, Tomasi E, et al.(2018) Interrelatioship between Diet Quality and Depressive Symptoms in Elderly. J Nutr Health Aging.22:387-392.

44. Tan J, Ma C, Zhu C, Wang Y, Zou X, et al. (2023) Prediction models for depression risk among older adults: systematic review and critical appraisal. Ageing Res Rev 83: 101803.

45. Muhammad T, Maurya P.(2022) Social support moderates the association of functional difficulty with major depression among community-dwelling older adults: evidence from LASI, 2017-18. BMC Psychiatry.22:317.

46. Muhammad T, Hossain B, Das A, Rashid M.(2022) Relationship between handgrip strength and self-reported functional difficulties among older Indian adults: The role of self-rated health. Exp Gerontol.165:111833.

47. Jia F, Shi X, Li X, Wang B, Liu F, et al.(2020) Physical frailty and the risk of major depressive disorder: The Irish Longitudinal Study on Ageing. J Psychiatr Res.125:91-95.

48. Choi NG, Zhou Y, Marti CN, Kunik ME.(2022) Associations Between Changes in Depression/Anxiety Symptoms and Fall Worry Among Community-Dwelling Older Adults. J Appl Gerontol. 41:2520-2531.

49. Kim JH.(2021) Experiences of falling and depression: Results from the Korean Longitudinal Study of Ageing. J Affect Disord.281:174-182.

50. Dong L, Freedman VA, Mendes de Leon CF.(2020) The Association of Comorbid Depression and Anxiety Symptoms With Disability Onset in Older Adults. Psychosom Med.82:158-164.

51. Reynolds CF (2019) Promoting resilience, reducing depression in older adults. Int Psychogeriatr 31: 169-171.

52. Muneera K, Muhammad T, Althaf S.(2022) Socio-demographic and lifestyle factors associated with intrinsic capacity among older adults: evidence from India. BMC Geriatr.22:851.

53. Foong HF, Hamid TA, Ibrahim R, Haron SA.(2018) Moderating effect of intrinsic religiosity on the relationship between depression and cog-

nitive function among community-dwelling older adults. Aging Ment Health.22:483-488.

54. Nair P, Bhanu C, Frost R, Buszewicz M, Walters KR.(2020) A Systematic Review of Older Adults' Attitudes Towards Depression and Its Treatment. Gerontologist.60:e93-e104.

55. Marques A, Bordado J, Peralta M, Gouveia ER, Tesler R, et al.(2020) Cross-sectional and prospective relationship between physical activity and depression symptoms. Sci Rep.10:16114.

56. De Sousa RAL, Rocha-Dias I, de Oliveira LRS, Improta-Caria AC, Monteiro-Junior RS, et al.(2021) Molecular mechanisms of physical exercise on depression in the elderly: a systematic review. Mol Biol Rep.48:3853-3862.

57. Pagliai G, Sofi F, Vannetti F, Caiani S, Pasquini G, et al.(2018) Mediterranean Diet, Food Consumption and Risk of Late-Life Depression: The Mugello Study. J Nutr Health Aging.22:569-574.

58. Odone A, Gianfredi V, Vigezzi GP, Amerio A, Ardito C, et al. (2021); Italian Working Group on Retirement and Health. Does retirement trigger depressive symptoms? A systematic review and meta-analysis. Epidemiol Psychiatr Sci.30:e77.

59. Burnes D, Sheppard C, Henderson CR Jr, Wassel M, Cope R, et al.(2019) Interventions to Reduce Ageism Against Older Adults: A Systematic Review and Meta-Analysis. Am J Public Health.109:e1-e9.

60. Gunning FM, Oberlin LE, Schier M, Victoria LW.(2021) Brain-based mechanisms of late-life depression: Implications for novel interventions. Semin Cell Dev Biol.116:169-179.

61. Moraes HS, Silveira HS, Oliveira NA, Matta Mello Portugal E, Araújo NB, et al.(2020) Is Strength Training as Effective as Aerobic Training for Depression in Older Adults? A Randomized Controlled Trial. Neuropsychobiology.79:141-149.

62. Kim Y, Hong S, Choi M.(2022) Effects of Serious Games on Depression in Older Adults: Systematic Review and Meta-analysis of Randomized Controlled Trials. J Med Internet Res.24:e37753.

63. Reangsing C, Lauderman C, Schneider JK (2022) Effects of Mindfulness Meditation Intervention on Depressive Symptoms in Emerging Adults: A Systematic Review and Meta-Analysis. J Integr Complement Med 28: 6-24.

64. Roberts JS, Ferber RA, Funk CN, Harrington AW, Maixner SM, et al. (2022) Mood Lifters for Seniors: Development and Evaluation of an Online, Peer-Led Mental Health Program for Older Adults. Gerontol Geriatr Med 8: 23337214221117431.

65. Sukhram SD, Yilmaz G, Gu J (2022) Antidepressant Effect of Ketamine on Inflammation-Mediated Cytokine Dysregulation in Adults with Treatment-Resistant Depression: Rapid Systematic Review. Oxid Med Cell Longev 2022: 1061274.

66. Sharafi A, Pakkhesal S, Fakhari A, Khajehnasiri N, Ahmadalipour A (2022) Rapid treatments for depression: Endocannabinoid system as a therapeutic target. Neurosci Biobehav Rev 137: 104635.

67. Castro F, Melgarejo J, Chavez CA, de Erausquin GA, Terwilliger JD, et al.(2021) Total Plasma Homocysteine and Depressive Symptoms in Older Hispanics J Alzheimers Dis.82:S263-S269.

68. Krell-Roesch J, Lowe VJ, Neureiter J, Pink A, Roberts RO, et al.(2018) Depressive and anxiety symptoms and cortical amyloid deposition among cognitively normal elderly persons: the Mayo Clinic Study of Aging. Int Psychogeriatr.30:245-251.

69. Rozing MP, Veerhuis R, Westendorp RGJ, Eikelenboom P, Stek M, et al. (2019) Inflammation in older subjects with early- and late-onset depression in the NESDO study: a cross-sectional and longitudinal case-only design. Psychoneuroendocrinology 99: 20-27.

70. Kuo CY, Lin CH, Lane HY.(2021) Molecular Basis of Late-Life Depression. Int J Mol Sci.22:7421.

71. Trapp S, Guitart-Masip M, Schröger E (2022) A link between age, affect, and predictions? Eur J Ageing 19: 945-952.

72. Ali NS, Hashem AHH, Hassan AM, Saleh AA, El-Baz HN.(2018) Serum interleukin-6 is related to lower cognitive functioning in elderly patients with major depression .Aging Ment Health.22:655-661.

Review Article   AJPRR (2023) x:xx

American Journal of Psychiatric Research and Reviews
(ISSN:2637-479X)

Late Life Suicidality: A Narrative Review

Tiffany Field, PhD

University of Miami/Miller School of Medicine and Fielding Graduate University

ABSTRACT

This review summarizes research on late life suicidality found in the recent literature (last five years). The prevalence has widely ranged from 5-56% for suicidality in late life. The research has focused primarily on predictors/risk factors for suicidality. Social factors have included bereavement, isolation and loneliness. Psychological problems have included anxiety, depression, cognitive impairment, sleep disturbances and prior suicide attempts. Physical conditions have included functional disability, inflammation, chronic illness and drug misuse. Interventions have focused primarily on exercise and increasing physical activity. The interpersonal theory of suicide (thwarted belongingness and perceived burdensomeness), inflammation and immune dysfunction have been considered potential underlying mechanisms for late life suicidality. This research is limited to self-report, cross-sectional studies that typically involve several variables, although the relative significance of the different variables is frequently not reported.

*Correspondence to Author:
Tiffany Field, PhD
University of Miami/Miller School of Medicine and Fielding Graduate University

How to cite this article:
Tiffany Field. Late Life Suicidality: A Narrative Review. American Journal of Psychiatric Research and Reviews, 2023; x:xx

eSciPub LLC, USA.
Website: https://escipub.com/

This narrative review involved entering the terms suicidality and aging (ageing) into PubMed and PsycINFO. The search yielded 162 papers for the last five years. However, following exclusion criteria including case studies and non-English language papers, this review is a summary of the research reported in 39 papers. This recent literature on suicidality (usually defined as the risk for suicide indicated by suicidal ideation) is predominantly focused on predictors/risk factors for suicidality in aging adults along with studies on prevalence, interventions and potential underlying mechanisms. This narrative review is accordingly divided into sections on prevalence, predictors/risk factors, interventions and potential underlying mechanisms. These are followed by a section on methodological limitations of the research.

Prevalence

The prevalence of suicidality has varied widely from the "wish to die" at 5% to as many as 56% expressing suicidal thoughts when several studies are combined in a review (see table 1). In a paper entitled "Social interactions among older adults who "wish for death" (N =2787 French adults, mean age= 74), the sample from the Seniors Health Survey suggested that 5% expressed the "wish to die" (Bernier et al, 2020).

In a study on older adults in Brazil called the Global Burden of Disease Study, the mortality from suicide varied from 7% to 26% across 15 states (Pires et al, 2022). The mortality rate for men in this sample was 3 to 4 times greater than for women. The variation of mortality across the 15 states is difficult to interpret and highlights the need for more demographic data that might reveal a risk profile.

In an epidemiological study on suicide in older adults, the rate was 47% higher in older adults than in the general population (Santos et al, 2021). And the highest rates were in the adults who were older than 80 years.

In a review on older adults with major depression disorder, the prevalence of suicidality ranged from 5% to 56% (Donkor et al, 2021). The older

women were more depressed and the older men more successfully suicided. In this review, hanging was the most common form of suicide, although the women preferred poisoning and the men preferred firearms. In another study, hanging was the most popular form of suicide by 68% of the participants (Santos et al, 2021). Firearms were used by under11%, self-intoxication by 9%, falling from a high place by 5% and "undetermined" by 6%.

In some countries, the prevalence of suicide has been decreasing. For example, starting in 1985, the prevalence of late life suicide in Italy started decreasing, especially in older adults and females (DeLeo et al, 2020). This was attributed to increased health care assistance and quality of life.

Clearly, the prevalence of suicidality in late life has varied across countries, within countries, by gender and by severity from suicidal thoughts to suicidal mortality. The suicidality rates may be underestimated due to "faking good" or reluctance to express suicidal thoughts even on anonymous surveys. However, the decreasing rate of death by suicide in Italy is a promising trend.

Predictors/Risk Factors

This recent literature on suicidality in aging adults is focused primarily on predictors/risk factors (see table 2). These include social factors, psychological problems, physical conditions, and drug misuse. Most of the studies have included several of these factors, which may be confounded, and which often are not assessed for the relative variance they explain in suicidality.

Social Factors

The social factors that have been problematic include bereavement, isolation, and loneliness.

Divorce and widowhood have been risk factors for suicidal thoughts in older adults. In a sample from the Swedish National Study on Aging and Care, being widowed or divorced were risk factors for suicidal thoughts (N=7,913 adults greater than 60 years-old) (Tuvesson et al,

2018). This may relate to bereavement over the loss of the relationships. Bereavement has been a specific risk factor in a systematic review on suicide behavior in older age adults (Beghi et al, 2021). In this review, related risk factors were living alone, depression, psychotropic drugs, being male, and being in poor medical condition.

Isolation and loneliness have often resulted from the loss of relationships by divorce and widowhood. The prevalence of loneliness in aging adults has varied from a low of 11% in Norway to a high of 76% in SanDiego (Field, 2023). In a study on social interactions among older adults who "wished to die" (N=2,787 French adults, mean age=74), three social variables predicted the "wish to die" including dissatisfaction with social life, being distant toward others and lack of participation in organizations. (Bernier et al, 2020). The authors interpreted their results as providing support for the Interpersonal Theory of Suicide that cites "thwarted belongingness" as a major risk factor.

Psychological Problems

The psychological problems that have been addressed in this literature include anxiety, depression, cognitive impairment, food insecurity, sleep disturbances and prior suicide attempts.

Anxiety has typically been comorbid with depression. For example, in a study, entitled "Anxiety symptoms in older adults with depression", anxiety was associated with both depression and suicidality (N=218, mean age=76-years-old) (Bendixen et al, 2018). In that study, older adults experienced anxiety based on the Geriatric Anxiety Inventory. In another study on depressed adults (N=52), suicide ideation was associated with anxiety disorder, but also with being female, having pain and experiencing a number of lifetime events (Caceda et al, 2018).

Depression has rarely been the primary focus in these studies on suicidality in aging adults. This is surprising given the high incidence of late life depression ranging as high as 28% in Greece and the association between late life depression and late life suicidality (Field, 2023). Despite the lack of focus on depression, several samples in suicidality research have been exclusively older adults with depression. And depression often appears in a collection of variables, or as a mediator variable. For example, in a study on mental disorders as potential mediators of the association between chronic physical conditions and suicidal ideation (N=1,533 adults older than 65-years-old), the Quebec Health Survey on Services was sampled (Vasiliadis et al, 2022). In a path analysis, depression mediated the association between chronic physical conditions and suicidal ideation, although post-traumatic stress syndrome and functional disability were also mediators. In contrast, pain and anxiety were not mediators.

In another study entitled "Bridging late-life depression and chronic somatic diseases" (N=2,860 older than 60 years-old), the Swedish National Study on Aging and Care was sampled (Triolo et al, 2021). The diseases in the study included cardiovascular, neurological, gastrointestinal, metabolic, musculoskeletal, respiratory, sensory and unclassified. Depressive symptoms along with these disease clusters were associated with suicidal thoughts. But they were also associated with pessimism, anxiety, reduced appetite and cognitive difficulties.

In data from the CDC, depression and mood problems were the most common risk factors for suicide (Schwab-Reese et al, 2021). And, in a review on mental health conditions and suicidal thoughts, depression was a predictor of suicidal thoughts (Obuobi-Donker et al, 2021). Other variables that were risk factors in this review included physical illness, financial constraints, sexual dysfunction and living alone.

In a review of 23 papers on "rational suicide" in late life, which was defined as a well-thought-out decision by mentally competent adults, depression was a major risk factor. (Gramaglia et al, 2019). Ageism, and what was termed "the slippery slope" ("the right to die leading to the social obligation to die") were also significant predictors.

Assisted suicide may be relevant for those who experience rational suicide. In a study entitled "Social, cultural and experiential patterning of attitudes and behavior toward assisted suicide in Switzerland" (N=2,015 55+ year-old adults), the Survey of Health, Aging and Retirement in Europe was examined for attitudes about assisted suicide (Vilpert et al, 2020). Positive attitudes toward assisted suicide were held by 82% and 28% were already involved and 61% considered asking for it. More negative attitudes were expressed among the religious and among those in the 75 and older group.

Cognitive impairment is another psychological variable that has an extensive literature of its own regarding aging problems. However, it rarely appears as a single variable contributing to suicide. An exception is a study entitled "Risk of suicide attempts and patients with a recent diagnosis of mild cognitive impairment or dementia" (N=147,595, mean age=75) (Gunak et al, 2021). In this study, those with recent mild cognitive impairment or dementia were at greater risk for suicide. However, this sample was drawn from VA medical centers resulting in 97% of the sample being men and 86% being non-Hispanic white which limits the generalizability of these findings.

Food insecurity was assessed in a study entitled "Association of food insecurity with suicidal ideation and suicide attempts" by two questions including "the frequency of eating less" and "hunger due to lack of food" (N=34,129, mean age=62) (Smith et al, 2022). Severe food insecurity led to five times greater odds for suicide attempts. The self-reported "wish to die" was the measure of suicide ideation, but was only assessed for those who were depressed.

Sleep disturbances have also rarely been the focus of studies on late life suicidality. This is surprising given the high prevalence of sleep disturbances in aging adults ranging from 18% in the UK to greater than 50% in China (Field,

2023). Two studies on the relationship between sleep disturbances and suicidal ideation and attempts have appeared in the recent literature on late life suicidality. In one study, entitled "Association of sleep characteristics and suicidal ideation and suicide attempts among adults greater than 50 with depressive symptoms", the sample was drawn from the WHO study (N= 2040) (Owusu et al, 2020). Sleep quality, which was defined as less than seven hours per night or greater than nine hours per night, was associated with suicidal ideation and suicidal attempts.

In a study entitled "Physical multi-morbidity, suicidal ideation and suicide attempts among adults", the Study on Global Aging and Adult Health was sampled (N =34,129, mean age=62 and maximum age was 114) (Smith et al, 2023). In this study, physical multi-morbidity was associated with increased odds of suicidal ideation (odds ratio =2.99) and attempts (odds ratio = 2.79). These were mediated by sleep/energy limitations (28–34%) but also by mobility limitations (26–35%) and pain/discomfort (33–44%).

Previous attempts at suicide, surprisingly, have only appeared among a series of risk factors in a couple review papers. In one review, previous attempts were listed along with depression, physical illness, substance use, loneliness, marital status and low social support (Chatton et al, 2022). In another review, previous suicidal attempts were listed as a risk factor for future suicides along with mood disorders, physical health and social isolation (Shan et al, 2022).

Physical Conditions

Physical conditions have included functional disabilities, pain, inflammation, and disease. These problems have typically been studied along with other risk factors, and it is often unclear which of the risk factors is most related to suicidality.

Functional disability has been related to suicidal behavior in older adults (Lutz et al, 2018).

In this sample, depression was a mediator for the relationship between functional disability and suicide attempts, although depression has rarely been treated as a mediator in the studies of this literature. In a study entitled "The relationship of frailty and disability with suicidal ideation in late life depression", poor performance was noted on frailty measures of gait speed and muscle weakness (N=72 adults with depression) (Bickford et al, 2021). These frailty measures were associated with greater suicidal ideation, independent of depression severity and demographics. Functional disability in this study was uniquely defined as impairment in financial capacity, social interaction, and communication skills all of which were associated with suicidal ideation.

Pain has surprisingly been rarely mentioned in this literature. In a review on suicide in older adults, it was one among many predictor variables (Conejero et al, 2018). Other risk factors included psychological and neurological disorders, social exclusion, bereavement, cognitive impairment, difficult decision-making, cognitive inhibition, physical illness, and psychological problems.

Inflammation was the focus of a study entitled "A probe in the connection between inflammation, cognition and suicide" (Caceda et al, 2018). C-reactive protein, as an inflammation marker, was associated with suicide attempts, but, surprisingly, not with ideation (N=52 depressed adults). Suicide attempts were also associated with age, BMI, interleukin–6 (another inflammation biomarker) and pain. And, suicidal ideation was associated with pain and lifetime events as well as being female and having an anxiety disorder.

C-reactive protein was also related to depression and risk for suicide in a study that compared aging adults who were depressed, non-depressed, and those with treatment–resistant depression (Wu et al, 2022). The pro-inflammatory markers including CRP, TNF-alpha and IL–6 levels were greater in depressed versus non-depressed individuals, as might be expected. However, surprisingly, they were also greater in depressed adults who responded to anti-depressants. Those with treatment-resistant depression were at greater risk for suicide. These results are limited by the small sample (N=30 each group) and its cross-sectional design. And, the sampling for inflammation markers was conducted at only one time point.

Chronic illness is another variable that has been listed among many others as being risk conditions for suicidal ideation and attempts in older people. For example, in a large sample study (N= 52,150), chronic health conditions were considered a risk factor for suicidal ideation and attempts (Cabello et al, 2020). In that study, other risk factors included being greater than 65-years-old, being from a high-income country, having more negative affect, disability and food insecurity, and being isolated.

Drug Misuse

Drug misuse has been highlighted in a few studies. In a paper entitled "Prescription opioid and benzodiazepine misuse is associated with suicidal ideation in older adults" (N =17,608 adults greater than 50 years), a sample was taken from the U.S. National Survey of Drug Use and Health (Schepis et al, 2019). Drug use in the past year but without misuse was associated with suicidal ideation. Only 2% of adults not engaged in misuse had suicidal ideation, while as many as 25% of those who misused drugs endorsed suicidality.

In a study on co-ingestion of prescription drugs and alcohol in U.S. adults greater than 50-years-old, the U.S. National Survey on Drug Use and Health was again used (N=35,190) by the same author on twice the sample size (Schepis et al, 2021). In this sample, prescription opioid, tranquilizer/sedative and stimulant misuse occurred while "drinking or within a couple hours of drinking". As many as 27% of the sample engaged in past month co-ingestion. The risk for suicidal ideation was 506% greater in those with co-ingestion than those with past year prescription drug misuse.

Table 1. Prevalence of late life suicidality

Prevalence	First Author
France- 5% "wish to die"	Bernier
Brazil- 7-26% mortality	Pires
Major depressive disorder- 5-56%	Donker
47% greater in very old vs. general population	Santos
Decreasing in Italy	DeLeo

Table 2. Risk factors for late life suicidality

Risk Factor	First Author
Social Factors	
Widowhood/divorce	Tuvesson
Bereavement	Beghi
Isolation	Bernier
Loneliness	Bernier
Psychological Problems	
Anxiety	Bendixen, Caceda
Depression	Vasiliadis, Triolo, Schwab-Reese, Obuobi-Danker, Gramaglia
Cognitive impairment	Gumak
Food insecurity	Smith (22)
Sleep disturbances	Owusu, Smith (23)
Previous suicide attempts	Chatton, Shan
Physical Conditions	
Functional disability	Lutz
Frailty	Bickford
Pain	Conejero
Inflammation	Caceda
C-reactive protein	Wu
Chronic illness	Cabello
Drug Misuse	
25% misused	Schepis (19)
17% co-ingestion prescription drugs and alcohol	Schepis (21)
Overdose or suicide	Lundgren

Table 3. Interventions for late life suicidality

Interventions	First Author
Emotion regulation	Kiosses
Physical exercise	Shan, Laflamme

Table 4. Potential underlying mechanisms for late life suicide

Mechanisms	First Author
Interpersonal Theory of Suicide	Sheffler
Perceived burdensomeness	Odam, Troya
Thwarted belonginess	Bernier
Inflammation	Xiao
C-reactive protein	Caceda
Lower natural killer cell number	Schiweck
Higher natural killer cell number	Okazaki

The Cause of Death Registry from the Swedish National Board of Health and Welfare has been studied for opioid use and death due to an overdose or suicide (N=1500 with N=136 adults who committed suicide and N=405 who experienced death due to suicide from an overdose) (Lundgren et al, 2022). The risk factors for death due to suicide included elevated mental health scores, previous suicide attempts, non-medical opioids one to two times per week for a year, history of drug use and early onset drug use. The risk factors for deaths due to accidental overdose included again elevated mental health scores, recency of non-medical opioids as well as frequency of that use.

Interventions

Surprisingly, only a few intervention studies have appeared in this literature (see table 3). These include an application for emotion regulation, physical activity programs and exercise interventions.

In a study entitled "An emotion regulation app for middle age and older adults at high suicide risk", a tablet app that helps suicide risk patients regulate their emotions outside of therapy sessions was developed (Kiosses et al, 2022). The intervention was called wellPATH.

In a mini-review and synthesis of literature, several different interventions were reviewed including diet, psychosocial programs, and depression medication (Shan et al, 2022). In this review, physical exercise was the most effective intervention. In a systematic review of reviews, physical activity was again the most effective intervention in contrast to antidepressant data that were inconclusive (Laflamme et al,2022). Surprisingly, these two reviews suggested that activity/exercise was the most effective intervention, although no studies appeared in this literature suggesting that inactivity was a risk factor for suicidality. There is, however, an extensive separate literature on inactivity in aging adults suggesting a prevalence ranging from 21% in Malaysia to as high as 79% in European countries (Field, 2023). These data highlight the need for activity interventions.

Potential Underlying Mechanisms

Potential underlying mechanisms for late life suicidality have appeared in this literature (see table 4). They include the Interpersonal Theory of Suicide, inflammation and immune variables.

The interpersonal theory of suicide includes three main components. These are thwarted belongingness, perceived burdensomeness, and capability for suicide (Sheffler et al, 2021). Some research groups have interpreted their findings as support for thwarted belongingness, and others for perceived burdensomeness. In a study entitled "Validating the interpersonal theory of suicide among older adults, pre and peri– Covid–19 Pandemic", 208 older Australians were surveyed face-to-face pre-pandemic or online peri- pandemic (Okan et al, 2022). Perceived burdensomeness was a greater predictor than depression or thwarted belongingness of suicidal ideation. Suicidal ideation and perceived burdensomeness were greater in men and the interaction of perceived burdensomeness and thwarted belongingness added to the variance.

Perceived burdensomeness was also highlighted in another review on 40 articles (62,755) (Troya et al, 2019). I% this review, perceived burdensomeness was the most frequent predictor variable of late life suicidality along with comorbid, physical problems, loss of control and increased loneliness. Self- poisoning was the most common method.

In contrast, in the French study on the Seniors Health Survey, the authors found that suicidality was more prevalent in those who are distant toward others (Bernier et al, 2020). They interpreted these findings as support for the thwarted belongingness component of the Interpersonal Theory of Suicide.

Inflammation and immune dysfunction have also been noted as potential underlying mechanisms for late life suicidality. In a paper, entitled "Association of dietary inflammatory index with depression and suicidal ideation in older adults", the high dietary, inflammatory index group had more prevalent depression (9% versus 7%) and suicidal ideation (9% versus 3%) (Xiao et al, 2022). In a small-sample study on inflammation and suicide, the inflammatory marker C- reactive protein was surprisingly associated with the number of lifetime suicide attempts, but not with suicidal ideation (Caceda et al, 2018).

Mixed findings have been reported for natural killer cell number. In one study (N=306 older adults with major depressive disorder and control participants), natural killer cell number was lower in those with depression and suicidality suggesting immune dysfunction (Schiweck et al, 2020). In contrast, in a study, in which suicide completers as compared to non-psychiatric patients (N=56 per group), a higher natural killer number was noted in the completers group, suggesting that natural killer cells may be a biomarker for suicide completion (Okazaki et al, 2020). The authors of this study referred to their results as "accelerated extrinsic epigenetic aging" which they say involved "immunosenescence in blood cell composition".

Methodological Limitations

Several methodological limitations can be noted about these recent studies on late life suicidality. Significant variability has been reported on the prevalence data which likely relates to variability on sampling methods and on the sample sizes. And, the variable prevalence may relate even more to some of the studies being based on suicidal thoughts while others are on suicidal attempts and still others on suicide completers.

Self-report surveys have been the most frequently used method for data collection for suicidal ideation which has its limitations especially for as sensitive a topic as suicidal thoughts unless participants are assured of anonymity of their report. Death records have been used for completed suicides which make those studies cross-sectional by nature as they cannot retrospectively determine risk factors.

Most of the studies have focused on multiple risk factors but regression analyses have rarely been conducted to determine the relative variance explained by the different risk factors. Profile analyses would be very useful for identifying those who might have a risk profile for late life suicidal thoughts to inform intervention efforts. Surprisingly, very few studies in this recent literature have reported medical problems, frailty and/or cognitive deficits as being risk factors for suicidality. Additional risk factors that have been rarely considered include socioeconomic status and education that might be risk factors or mediating/ moderating variables if they had been analyzed by mediation/ moderation or structural equations analysis.

Late life suicidality has rarely been compared to suicidality by younger adults. Surprisingly, sex differences have been rare, although several studies were exclusively male or female, limiting generalizability. The prevalence of late life suicidality and its risk factors are so variable that systematic reviews are inconclusive and meta-analyses have not been conducted. Biomarkers and potential underlying mechanisms for late life suicidality have been suggested in reviews on the topic, although mechanism studies have rarely appeared in the recent literature. And, several of the recent intervention studies have not randomly assigned participants to comparison groups. Despite these methodological limitations, the recent literature on late life suicidality highlights the significant problem of identifying a risk profile that informs prevention programs.

References

[1]. Beghin M, Butera E, Cerri CG, Cornaggia CM, Febbo F, Mollica A, Berardino G, Piscitelli D, Resta E, Logroscino G, Daniele A, Altamura M, Bellomo A, Panza F, Lozupone M. Suicidal behaviour in older age: A systematic review of risk factors associated to suicide attempts and completed suicides. Neurosci Biobehav Rev. 2021 Aug;127:193-211. doi: 10.1016/j.neubiorev.2021.04.011. Epub 2021 Apr 18. PMID: 33878336.

[2]. Bendixen, A.B., Engedal, K., Selbaek, G , Hartberg, B. Anxiety symptoms in older adults with depression are associated with suicidality. Dement Geriatr Cogn Disorder. 2018, 453-4): 180-189.doi.org/10.1159/000488480.

[3]. Bernier S, Lapierre S, Desjardins S. Social Interactions among Older Adults Who Wish for Death. Clin Gerontol. 2020 Jan-Feb;43(1):4-16. doi: 10.1080/07317115.2019.1672846. Epub 2019 Oct 15. PMID: 31615349.

[4]. Bickford D, Morin RT, Woodworth C, Verduzco E, Khan M, Burns E, Nelson JC, Mackin RS. The relationship of frailty and disability with suicidal ideation in late life depression. Aging Ment Health. 2021 Mar;25(3):439-444. doi: 10.1080/13607863.2019.1698514. Epub 2019 Dec 6. PMID: 31809584; PMCID: PMC8931702.

[5]. Cabello M, Miret M, Ayuso-Mateos JL, Caballero FF, Chatterji S, Tobiasz-Adamczyk B, Haro JM, Koskinen S, Leonardi M, Borges G. Cross-national prevalence and factors associated with suicide ideation and attempts in older and young-and-middle age people. Aging Ment Health. 2020 Sep;24(9):1533-1542. doi: 10.1080/13607863.2019.1603284. Epub 2019 Apr 16. PMID: 30990056.

[6]. Cáceda R, Griffin WST, Delgado PL. A probe in the connection between inflammation, cognition and suicide. J Psychopharmacol. 2018 Apr;32(4):482-488. doi: 10.1177/02698811187640. PMID: 29552947; PMCID: PMC9230995.

[7]. Chattun MR, Amdanee N, Zhang X, Yao Z. Suicidality in the geriatric population. Asian J Psychiatr. 2022 Sep;75:103213. doi: 10.1016/j.ajp.2022.103213. Epub 2022 Jul 16. PMID: 35917739.

[8]. Conejero I, Olié E, Courtet P, Calati R. Suicide in older adults: current perspectives. Clin Interv Aging. 2018 Apr 20;13:691-699. doi: 10.2147/CIA.S130670. PMID: 29719381; PMCID: PMC5916258.

[9]. De Leo D, Vichi M, Kolves K, Pompili M. Late life suicide in Italy, 1980-2015. Aging Clin Exp Res. 2020 Mar;32(3):465-474. doi: 10.1007/s40520-019-01431-z. Epub 2019 Dec 2. PMID: 31792764.

[10]. Field, T. Loneliness in aging adults:A narrative review. 2023. International Journal of Psychological Research and Reviews, ISSN:2639-6041

[11]. Field, T. Late life depression: A narrative review. 2023. International Journal of Geriatrics and Gerontology, 6, 141. Doi.org/10.29011/2577-0748.

[12]. Field, T. Sleep problems in aging adults: A narrative review.2023. International Journal of Geriatrics and Gerontology 6: 149. www.doi.org/10.29011/2577-0748.100049

[13]. Field, T. Late life inactivity: A narrative review. 2023. Unpublished manuscript.

[14]. Gramaglia C, Calati R, Zeppegno P. Rational Suicide in Late Life: A Systematic Review of the Literature. Medicina (Kaunas). 2019 Sep 29;55(10):656. doi: 10.3390/medicina55100656. PMID: 31569542; PMCID: PMC6843265.

[15]. Günak MM, Barnes DE, Yaffe K, Li Y, Byers AL. Risk of Suicide Attempt in Patients With Recent Diagnosis of Mild Cognitive Impairment or Dementia. JAMA Psychiatry. 2021 Jun 1;78(6):659-666. doi: 10.1001/jamapsychiatry.2021.0150. PMID: 33760039; PMCID: PMC7992018.

[16]. Kiosses DN, Monkovic J, Stern A, Czaja SJ, Alexopoulos G, Arslanoglou E, Ebo T, Pantelides J, Yu H, Dunefsky J, Smeragliuolo A, Putrino D. An Emotion Regulation Tablet App for Middle-Aged and Older Adults at High Suicide Risk: Feasibility, Acceptability, and Two Case Studies. Am J Geriatr Psychiatry. 2022 May;30(5):575-584. doi: 10.1016/j.jagp.2021.08.015. Epub 2021 Sep 8. PMID: 34656396.

[17]. Laflamme L, Vaez M, Lundin K, Sengoelge M. Prevention of suicidal behavior in older people: A systematic review of reviews. PLoS One. 2022 Jan 25;17(1):e0262889. doi: 10.1371/journal.pone.0262889. PMID: 35077476; PMCID: PMC8789110.

[18]. Lissemore JI, Bhandari A, Mulsant BH, Lenze EJ, Reynolds CF 3rd, Karp JF, Rajji TK, Noda Y, Zomorrodi R, Sibille E, Daskalakis ZJ, Blumberger DM. Reduced GABAergic cortical inhibition in aging and depression. Neuropsychopharmacology. 2018 Oct;43(11):2277-2284. doi: 10.1038/s41386-018-0093-x. Epub 2018 May 17. PMID: 29849055; PMCID: PMC6135847.

[19]. Lundgren L, Padyab M, Sandlund M, McCarty D. Frequency and recency of non-medical opioid use and death due to overdose or suicide among individuals assessed for risky substance use: A national registry study in Sweden. J Subst Abuse Treat. 2022 Mar;134:108567. doi: 10.1016/j.jsat.2021.108567. Epub 2021 Jul 21. PMID: 34340844.

[20]. Lutz J, Fiske A. Functional disability and suicidal behavior in middle-aged and older adults: A systematic critical review. J Affect Disord. 2018 Feb;227:260-271. doi: 10.1016/j.jad.2017.10.043. Epub 2017 Oct 31. PMID: 29107819.

[21]. Obuobi-Donkor G, Nkire N, Agyapong VIO. Prevalence of Major Depressive Disorder and Correlates of Thoughts of Death, Suicidal Behaviour, and Death by Suicide in the Geriatric

Population-A General Review of Literature. Behav Sci (Basel). 2021 Oct 21;11(11):142. doi: 10.3390/bs11110142. PMID: 34821603; PMCID: PMC8614881.

[22]. Okan C, Bilson L, Zhong D, Weidemann G, Bailey PE. Validating the interpersonal theory of suicide among older adultspre- and peri-COVID-19 pandemic. Aging Ment Health. 2022 Sep 2:1-7. doi: 10.1080/13607863.2022.2116402. Epub ahead of print. PMID: 36052977.

[23]. Okazaki S, Otsuka I, Horai T, Hirata T, Takahashi M, Ueno Y, Boku S, Sora I, Hishimoto A. Accelerated extrinsic epigenetic aging and increased natural killer cells in blood of suicide completers. Prog Neuropsychopharmacol Biol Psychiatry. 2020 Mar 2;98:109805. doi: 10.1016/j.pnpbp.2019.109805. Epub 2019 Nov 7. PMID: 31707091.

[24]. Owusu JT, Doty SB, Adjaye-Gbewonyo D, Bass JK, Wilcox HC, Gallo JJ, Spira AP. Association of sleep characteristics with suicidal ideation and suicide attempt among adults aged 50 and older with depressive symptoms in low- and middle-income countries. Sleep Health

[25]. Pires AM, Reis JGM, Garcia FM, Veloso GA, Melo APS, Naghavi M, Passos VMA. Suicide mortality among older adults in Brazil between 2000 and 2019 - estimates from the Global Burden of Disease Study 2019. Rev Soc Bras Med Trop. 2022 Jan 28;55(suppl 1):e0322. doi: 10.1590/0037-8682-0322-2021. PMID: 35107540; PMCID: PMC9009432.

[26]. Pisanu C, Tsermpini EE, Skokou M, Kordou Z, Gourzis P, Assimakopoulos K, Congiu D, Meloni A, Balasopoulos D, Patrinos GP, Squassina A. Leukocyte telomere length is reduced in patients with major depressive disorder. Drug Dev Res. 2020 May;81(3):268-273. doi: 10.1002/ddr.21612. Epub 2019 Nov 1. PMID: 31675136.

[27]. Santos MCLD, Giusti BB, Yamamoto CA, Ciosak SI, Szylit R. Suicide in the elderly: an epidemiologic study. Rev Esc Enferm USP. 2021 May 31;55:e03694. English, Portuguese. doi: 10.1590/S1980-220X2019026603694. PMID: 34076149.

[28]. Schepis TS, Ford JA, McCabe SE. Co-ingestion of prescription drugs and alcohol in US adults aged 50 years or older. Hum Psychopharmacol. 2021 Nov;36(6):e2803. doi: 10.1002/hup.2803. Epub 2021 Jul 8. PMID: 34237180; PMCID: PMC9254454.

[29]. Schepis TS, Simoni-Wastila L, McCabe SE. Prescription opioid and benzodiazepine misuse is associated with suicidal ideation in older adults. Int J Geriatr Psychiatry. 2019 Jan;34(1):122-129. doi: 10.1002/gps.4999. Epub 2018 Oct 16. PMID: 30328160; PMCID: PMC6445380.

[30]. Schiweck C, Valles-Colomer M, Arolt V, Müller N, Raes J, Wijkhuijs A, Claes S, Drexhage H, Vrieze E. Depression and suicidality: A link to premature T helper cell aging and increased Th17 cells. Brain Behav Immun. 2020 Jul;87:603-609. doi: 10.1016/j.bbi.2020.02.005. Epub 2020 Feb 14. PMID: 32061905.

[31]. Schwab-Reese LM, Murfree L, Coppola EC, Liu PJ, Hunter AA. Homicide-suicide across the lifespan: a mixed methods examination of factors contributing to older adult perpetration. Aging Ment Health. 2021 Sep;25(9):1750-1758. doi: 10.1080/13607863.2020.1795620. Epub 2020 Jul 20. PMID: 32686960.

[32]. Shah J, Kandil OA, Mortagy M, Abdelhameed A, Shah A, Kuron M, Abdellatif YO. Frailty and Suicidality in Older Adults: A Mini-Review and Synthesis. Gerontology. 2022;68(5):571-577. doi: 10.1159/000523789. Epub 2022 Apr 13. PMID: 35417914.

[33]. Sheffler JL, Joiner TE, Sachs-Ericsson NJ. The Interpersonal and Psychological Impacts of COVID-19 on Risk for Late-Life Suicide. Gerontologist. 2021 Jan 21;61(1):23-29. doi: 10.1093/geront/gnaa103. Erratum in: Gerontologist. 2021 Feb 23;61(2):293. PMID: 32959869; PMCID: PMC7454594.

[34]. Smith L, Shin JI, Carmichael C, Jacob L, Kostev K, Grabovac I, Barnett Y, Butler L, Lindsay RK, Pizzol D, Veronese N, Soysal P, Koyanagi A. Association of food insecurity with suicidal ideation and suicide attempts in adults aged ≥50 years from low- and middle-income countries. J Affect Disord. 2022 Jul 15;309:446-452. doi: 10.1016/j.jad.2022.04.109. Epub 2022 Apr 21. PMID: 35461821.

[35]. Smith L, Shin JI, López Sánchez GF, Kostev K, Jacob L, Tully MA, Butler L, Barnett Y, Veronese N, Soysal P, Abduljabbar AS, Haro JM, Koyanagi A. Physical multimorbidity, suicidal ideation, and suicide attempts among adults aged ≥50 years from low- and middle-income countries. Int J Geriatr Psychiatry. 2023 Jan;38(1):e5873. doi: 10.1002/gps.5873. PMID: 36683020; PMCID: PMC10108020.

[36]. Triolo F, Belvederi Murri M, Calderón-Larrañaga A, Vetrano DL, Sjöberg L, Fratiglioni L, Dekhtyar S. Bridging late-life depression and chronic somatic diseases: a network analysis. Transl Psychiatry. 2021 Oct 30;11(1):557. doi: 10.1038/s41398-021-01686-z. PMID: 34718326; PMCID: PMC8557204.

[37]. Troya MI, Babatunde O, Polidano K, Bartlam B, McCloskey E, Dikomitis L, Chew-Graham CA. Self-harm in older adults: systematic review. Br J Psychiatry. 2019 Apr;214(4):186-200. doi: 10.1192/bjp.2019.11. Epub 2019 Feb 21. PMID: 30789112.

[38]. Tuvesson H, Hellström A, Sjöberg L, Sjölund BM, Nordell E, Fagerström C. Life weariness and suicidal thoughts in late life: a national study in Sweden. Aging Ment Health. 2018 Oct;22(10):1365-1371. doi: 10.1080/13607863.2017.1348484. Epub 2017 Jul 7. PMID: 28685600.

[39]. Vasiliadis HM, D'Aiuto C, Lamoureux-Lamarche C, Pitrou I, Gontijo Guerra S, Berbiche D. Pain, functional disability and mental disorders as potential mediators of the association between chronic physical conditions and suicidal ideation in community living older adults. Aging Ment Health. 2022 Apr;26(4):791-802. doi: 10.1080/13607863.2021.1913478. Epub 2021 Apr 23. PMID: 33890523.

[40]. Vilpert S, Bolliger E, Borrat-Besson C, Borasio GD, Maurer J. Social, cultural and experiential patterning of attitudes and behaviour towards assisted suicide in Switzerland: evidence from a national population-based study. Swiss Med Wkly. 2020 Jul 1;150:w20275. doi: 10.4414/smw.2020.20275. PMID: 32657420.

[41]. Wand APF, Peisah C, Draper B, Brodaty H. Understanding self-harm in older people: a systematic review of qualitative studies. Aging Ment Health. 2018 Mar;22(3):289-298. doi: 10.1080/13607863.2017.1304522. Epub 2017 Mar 22. PMID: 28326821.

[42]. Wu X, Dai B, Yan F, Chen Y, Xu Y, Xia Q, Zhang X. Serum Cortisol, Nesfatin-1, and IL-1β: Potential Diagnostic Biomarkers in Elderly Patients with Treatment-Resistant Depression. Clin Interv Aging. 2022 Apr 21;17:567-576. doi: 10.2147/CIA.S361459. PMID: 35480963; PMCID: PMC9038158.

[43]. Xiao Y, Huang W. Association of Dietary Inflammatory Index With Depression and Suicidal Ideation in Older Adult: Results From the National Health and Nutrition Examination Surveys 2005-2018. Front Psychiatry. 2022 Jul 5;13:944154. doi: 10.3389/fpsyt.2022.944154. PMID: 35865298; PMCID: PMC9294216.

International Journal of Psychological Research and Reviews
(ISSN:2639-6041)

Elderly Problems During COVID-19: A Narrative Review

Tiffany Field, PhD

University of Miami/Miller School of Medicine and Fielding Graduate University

ABSTRACT

This narrative review summarizes published research on psychological problems of the elderly during COVID-19. This includes brief reviews of 54 studies that have focused on loneliness, anxiety, depression and/or sleep problems and their comorbidities. Risk factors for these problems have included pre-existing conditions, infection, inactivity, fear of COVID, fear of death, and lack of social media skills. Buffers for the problems have included exercise, cognitive behavior therapy, acupuncture and melatonin. Limitations of this literature are that the studies are typically surveys, they focus on infections or psychological problems but rarely on the combination of those problems, and they are highly variable on recruitment during lockdown and non-lockdown periods as well as varying on their measures, precluding the use of meta-analyses.

Keywords: Elderly, COVID, anxiety, depression, sleep problems, inactivity

*Correspondence to Author:
Tiffany Field, PhD
University of Miami/Miller School of Medicine and Fielding Graduate University

How to cite this article:
Tiffany Field. Elderly Problems During COVID-19: A Narrative Review. International Journal of Psychological Research and Reviews, 2022, x:xx

eSciPub LLC, Houston, TX USA.
Website: https://escipub.com/

This narrative review is based on studies on problems of the elderly during COVID-19 that have appeared on PubMed for the years 2019-2022. The terms elderly and COVID-19 were entered into the advanced search which yielded 586 papers. Inclusion criteria were peer-reviewed studies and exclusion criteria were case reports, non-English papers and research that was exclusively focused on the COVID infection. Following these criteria, 54 papers were selected for this review. Following a brief section on COVID infection studies, the review is organized around the primary psychological problems of the elderly in the COVID literature including loneliness, anxiety, depression and sleep problems. These are followed by sections on risk factors including inactivity, fear of COVID and death, and lacking social media skills. Buffers are discussed including exercise, cognitive behavior therapy, acupuncture and melatonin. And the review concludes with limitations of the literature and suggested future directions.

Comparisons of Effects of COVID Infection on the Elderly and Younger Adults

Most of the COVID literature on the elderly is focused on the infection. Only a few of those studies have also highlighted psychological problems. The studies that are focused on the elderly contrast elderly groups, typically greater than 60-years-old, with groups that are younger than 60-years-old. And, in most studies infection is more prevalent in the older group. In a comparison of the young and elderly (N=187), for example, more asymptomatic and severe cases were seen in the elderly and those numbers increased across 10-year age groups (Mori et al, 2021) And, a correlation was noted between age group and duration of COVID disease. In a study from Wuhan (N=273), the older group surprisingly showed decreased C-reactive protein (CRP) while the younger group showed increased CRP (Liu et al, 2020). This was surprising inasmuch as CRP is a marker for inflammation that is typically seen in COVID-19 infection. It is possible that because the elderly

are typically asymptomatic or severely ill, grouping those two extremes resulted in lower CRP levels than those noted for the younger group. In any case, the younger group was given an inflammatory corticosteroid while cardiovascular protection was provided for the older group.

In another elderly/young group comparison, also from Wuhan (N=222), a 28-day follow-up of those who had been hospitalized showed that the greater than 70-year-old group had more dyspnea, chronic cardiovascular disease, diabetes, a greater death rate, a longer hospital stay and they were lower socioeconomic status (Zhang et al, 2020). The death rate in the greater than 70 group was related to dyspnea, muscle ache, increased myocardial enzymes and elevated C3. Not surprisingly, the same predictors of hospitalization for the elderly were the predictors of death for the elderly. Likely, the severity of symptoms was just greater in the case of death. Similarly, in a sample of 204 elderly folks, the risk factors that were independently associated with death again included not only older age but also dyspnea, neutrophilia and cardiac troponin (Song et al, 2020). And, the comorbidities that were reported for this sample were similar to those of other samples including hypertension, cardiovascular disease and COPD, although, again, the data were not analyzed for the relative contribution these variables made to the disease severity and mortality outcomes.

In a study from South Korea (N=488) on severe COVID cases, a comparison again between the old and the young suggested that the old group had more severe COVID, underlying disease and a greater mortality rate (Seong et al, 2021). The risk factors for COVID severity were again the same as those for mortality including not only age but also acute physiology, diabetes, COPD, high white blood cell count, low neutrophil-lymphocyte ratio, a "do not resuscitate" order and invasive mechanical ventilation. In a significantly larger sample (N= 5746) from the International Hope- COVID-19 Registry

Multicenter, the mortality rate was 32% for the greater than 65-year-old group and 7% for the less than 65-year-old group (Pepe et al, 2021). In this sample, the therapeutic approaches for the elderly were more conservative.

Most of the COVID-19 infection studies were focused on prognostic factors for mortality. In a study from South Korea, activities of daily living impairment, comorbidity, fever and increased CRP were associated with death (Hwang et al, 2020). In this sample (N=340), 35% had severe pneumonia which was associated with impairment of activities of daily living, fever, infiltration of the chest, and increased CRP. Fifteen percent of the sample died. In another study on risk factors, a nonogram was formed from the combination of risk factors for severe versus non-severe COVID infection (Zeng et al, 2020). The risk factors included albumin, d-dimer and onset to hospitalization time. The decision curve analysis confirmed this nonogram.

It is perhaps not surprising that Long COVID has rarely appeared in this literature on the elderly given that as many as 80% of those older than 65 in some samples have been noted to die (Lee et al, 2020). In one review on Long COVID, the long-term effects included polyneuropathy, cerebrovascular disease, CNS infection, cognitive deficits and fatigue (Krupp et al, 2021). These symptoms are very similar to those that have been noted for chronic fatigue syndrome prior to COVID-19 (Aly et al, 2021). According to the review paper, the neurocognitive symptoms of Long COVID have been correlated not only with older age but also with severity of the disease, hypertension and renal failure. Underlying mechanisms were also addressed including hypoxic-ischemic brain injury and immunopathological mechanisms.

Some have argued that focusing health resources on COVID emergencies of the elderly has left major elderly medical areas uncovered including oncology and time-dependent and degenerative diseases (Iodice et al, 2021). Further, these authors suggested that larger numbers have psychological problems that need to be evaluated for their cognitive and behavioral effects.

Psychological Problems of Infected Elderly

Daily COVID deaths have been correlated with depression (.36), anxiety (.50), suicide (.10) and insomnia (.10) (Rana, 2020). And, in that sample from India, mental health issues increased by 40% during the lockdown. The prevalence of psychological problems in elderly survivors of COVID infection has also been high in a sample that was collected two weeks post discharge (N= 69) (Mowla et al, 2022). The Geriatric Anxiety Scale and the Geriatric Depression Scale were administered in that study. The high prevalence being reported may relate to greater sensitivity of these scales that were specifically designed for the elderly. They may be more reliable for identifying these problems in the elderly than the more traditional anxiety and depression scales.

When an elderly group of survivors (65 years plus) was compared to an age-matched control group, those who were survivors, not surprisingly, had higher anxiety and depression scale scores (Mowla et al, 2022). Ninety-three per cent of the survivor group reported anxiety versus 60% of the age- matched control group and 87% reported depression versus 47% of the control group. The high rates of psychological problems in these studies highlight the prevalence of anxiety and depression not only in survivors of the infection but also in the non-infected folks who were experiencing the pandemic. In another study on COVID survivors (N =402), several psychological problems were reported in addition to anxiety (42%), and depression (31%) including insomnia (40%), post-traumatic stress disorder (32%) and obsessive-compulsive disorder (20%) (Mazza et al 2021). Females were noted to have more depression and anxiety despite their lower inflammatory markers which might relate to the typical two to one ratio of females to males reporting depression. In addition to having a previous psychiatric history, inflammatory markers were also predictors of depression and anxiety at the follow-up assessment of this sample, but gender was not.

As some have noted, psychological/psychiatric disorders in the elderly accentuate the inflammatory state or in themselves are considered persistent inflammatory states that have been labeled immunosenescence (Grolli et al, 2021). Examples, including dementia, major depressive disorder and anxiety are notably more prevalent in the elderly. The immune and psychological problems are likely reciprocal/bidirectional.

Psychological Effects of the Pandemic on Non-Infected Elderly

Some have suggested that the number of those psychologically affected by the pandermic exceeds those physically affected by the infection during COVID (Lee et al, 2020). According to those authors, more than 20% of those older than 60 in the world have psychological problems. Nonetheless, the literature on psychological problems of the elderly comprises less than 10% of the published COVID-19 research. The most commonly researched psychological problems have included loneliness, fear of COVID, fear of death, anxiety, depression and sleep disturbances.

Loneliness

A study from Poland on the elderly suggested that as many as 59% were experiencing loneliness (Dziedzic et al, 2021). In this sample, significantly fewer people (19%) were experiencing depression. However, loneliness and depression were significantly correlated, as were loneliness and anxiety, which are frequently comorbid problems in this literature. Loneliness may have been reported more frequently not only because it is less severe than depression but also because it is less stigmatic than depression. And, the elderly who are often living alone and socially isolated might expect to be lonely and report it accordingly.

In a cross-sectional study from China (N=568), 34% reported being lonely and 16% severely lonely (Ju et al, 2022). The risk factors for loneliness in this study were poor quality sleep, inactivity and low socioeconomic status, although the relative variance of these was not reported. And, a comparison between the lonely and the non-lonely groups on these variables would have been informative.

In contrast to the high rates of loneliness in the previous samples, as many as 75% reported low loneliness in a phone survey from Austria (N=521) (Heidinger et al, 2020). In this longitudinal study that included pre-pandemic and during the pandemic assessments, loneliness slightly increased, although it remained rather low. Surprisingly, loneliness increased for folks living with someone else but not for those living alone. Conceivably, folks who were living alone were used to being alone and did not report being lonely or were not lonely because they were more frequently contacted during the lockdown because they were alone. These findings are seemingly inconsistent with several elderly loneliness studies in the literature, although at least one other comparison between loneliness in the young (20-40 years-old) and old (60-80 years-old) reported that the young living alone were more lonely than the old living alone (Field et al, 2020). And, loneliness increased across the course of the lockdown, as was predicted.

Loneliness has also been related to death anxiety. In a study from Turkey, the Loneliness Scale for the Elderly and The Death Anxiety Scale were administered to 354 participants (Guner et al, 2021). Moderate levels of loneliness and death anxiety were reported with as many as 75% experiencing increased levels of worry during COVID. Other data from this study suggested that those who were single and those with chronic conditions had higher loneliness scale scores. In addition, the authors reported that 46% had sufficient knowledge of COVID, 69% communicated with relatives and 49% had no hobby at home, factors that might have contributed to their loneliness, death anxiety and increased levels of worry. The high levels of loneliness may have related to the Loneliness Scale for the Elderly being more sensitive to elderly reports and the high levels of worry would certainly relate to death anxiety given the prevalence of death in the elderly who have been infected. And death anxiety may be greater in those who live alone and are lonely because they do not want to die alone.

Loneliness has been a significant predictor of other problems as well. For example, in a study on sleep, loneliness was noted in 50% of older adults and, not surprisingly, mental health comorbidities overlapped (Parveen et al, 2021). In this study, loneliness was said to contribute to sleep problems, although this relationship was likely bidirectional. In another study from Turkey, the UCLA Loneliness Scale and the Insomnia Severity Index were administered (N=412) (45). The results suggested that loneliness and insomnia were significantly correlated, again a likely bidirectional relationship.

In a study from Hungary (N=589), both loneliness and intolerance of uncertainty led to mental health problems (Labadi et al, 2021). The relationship between Intolerance of uncertainty and fear of COVID would have been an interesting question to address in this study. Loneliness was the primary problem in a review of seven studies on the elderly during COVID (Kasar & Karaman, 2021). The authors concluded that technological opportunities and cognitive behavior therapies were needed for loneliness prevention. Although technology education would seemingly be more cost-effective than cognitive behavior therapies, that issue was not addressed in this review.

Fear of COVID and Fear of Death

Fear of Covid and fear of death are significant psychological problems that have been experienced during COVID–19. The prevalence warranted the development of a 7-item scale called The Scale of Fear of COVID-19 Infection. In a study from Poland (N = 500), elderly with higher anxiety levels scored higher on the fear scale (Agrawal et al, 2021). In addition, females and patients taking anticoagulants were higher-scoring. The question arises as to how much fear of COVID infection predicts the fear of death in the elderly, although this was not addressed in this study.

In another study using the Scale of Fear of COVID-19, pre-existing conditions were negatively correlated with scores on the scale (Yadav et al, 2021). In this study from Nepal (N=847), those who had pre-existing conditions may have been more worried about their pre-existing conditions than about COVID infection. Not surprisingly, remoteness of a health facility was positively related to the fear of COVID infection. In still a third study using the Fear of COVID Scale, older isolated adults in Bangladesh who had friends or relatives who had been infected were more fearful which was not surprising (Mistry et al, 2021). A surprising finding for the COVID fear scale was that as the fear of COVID infection increased, self-care decreased which is the opposite of what would be expected and difficult to interpret (Sharifi et al, 2021). In a similar study, death anxiety and death–related depression were correlated with each other (N= 344) (Erbesler et al, 2022). This was not surprising given that depression and anxiety are typically comorbid.

Anxiety and Depression

The prevalence of anxiety and depression has varied across cultures. These mood states are often considered together given their comorbidity. In a theoretical review from Korea, 37% of the elderly experienced depression or anxiety (Lee et al, 2020). The authors suggested that fear and anger should also be considered as the two are often comorbid with anxiety and depression. These findings are tentative given that this was a theoretical not a systematic review based on data.

A slightly greater prevalence has been noted in a sample from Italy at 45% depression, anxiety or anger (Maggi et al, 2021). The authors noted that resilience mediated the relationship between these problems and the fear of COVID.

The sample (N=334) was, surprisingly, noted to have a similar prevalence of depression during the quarantine (time one of the study) and two months after the quarantine (time two). However, severe depression at time one was associated with post-traumatic stress symptoms at time two, although it was unclear how much of the variance in posttraumatic stress was explained by depression. The measurement of anger was unique to this COVID study which is surprising given that aggression was prevalent during COVID which often derives from anger (Field, 2021) and has also been comorbid with anxiety and depression (Field et al, 2003). The measurement of post-traumatic stress in the elderly was also unique to this study. Conceivably it was rarely addressed in this literature because post-traumatic symptoms often don't appear until after the stress situation subsides.

In a study involving telephone interviews by family medicine residents, 38% of participants reported depression (Levkovich et al, 2021). A significant amount of the variance in depression was explained by a lack of optimism and social support (29%). A significantly lower rate of depression (14%) was reported in another study based on the Geriatric Depression Scale (Kurniawidjaja et al, 2022). However, an additional 40% reported a "tendency for depression". The combined prevalence of depression and the "tendency for depression" in this survey study was linked to retirement and income as well as illness, family and social support.

The Geriatric Depression Scale has typically yielded a greater prevalence of depression which may relate to its inclusion of those with a "tendency for depression". Also it has typically been assessed via survey as opposed to telephone interviews that were used in the study just noted with lower prevalence (Levkovich et al, 2021). Folks may feel less stigmatized reporting depression via survey than via phone interviews given that surveys are typically anonymous.

In a study on anxiety in the elderly (>65-years-old) from Turkey (N=278), 32% scored above the cutpoint on the Geriatric Anxiety Inventory (Sirin et al, 2021). The risk factors were not only age but also female gender (38% in females versus 24% in males), economic loss, uncertainty and time watching news on COVID. The authors mistakenly referred to their sample as having generalized anxiety disorder based on the survey inventory rather than a diagnostic interview. Surprisingly, in a longitudinal study no change was reported for affective or anxiety disorders between time one at the beginning of the lockdown and time two which was four months later (Seethaler et al, 2021). In this telephone interview study, an increase was noted in psychosocial support and demand for sports, OT, PT and psychotherapy. It was surprising that no change occurred across these time periods even though less stress would be expected following the end of the lockdown and especially with the additional supports and therapies that were experienced. Perhaps even more surprisingly, only mild negative emotions were noted in most of a large sample study (N=1278) from 31 provinces in China (Zhou et al, 2021). In this study, chronic diseases and BMI index were noted to affect depression, neurasthenia, fear, anxiety and hypochondria. It would appear that the pre-existing conditions, i.e. the chronic diseases and BMI index outweighed the negative effects of the pandemic in this large sample from China which is not surprising especially if those with pre-existing conditions worried more about their pre-existing condition than about the risk for COVID infection.

And in other surprising findings, stress, anxiety and depression were the same for quarantine and non-quarantine age-matched controls (Ouanes et al, 2021). This sample from Qatar again considered the elderly anyone older than 60 years. Higher scores were noted in females but the scores were not linked to any other variables including age, psychiatric history, duration of the quarantine or religiosity. The lack of quarantine effects on these emotions and the

Table 1. COVID-19 infection symptoms in elderly versus young groups (and first authors)

Symptoms	First authors
More frequent asymptomatic and severe cases	Mori
Lower levels C-reactive protein	Liu
Greater prevalence dyspnea	Zang, Ping
Greater mortality	Seong, Pepe
Greater prevalence pneumonia	Hwang, Lee
Higher levels d-dimer	Zeng
Greater prevalence Long COVID	Aly, Krupp, Iodice

Table 2. Psychological problems in infected elderly during COVID-19 (and first authors)

Problems	First author
Anxiety	Rana, Morola, Mazza
Depression	Rana, Morola, Mazza
Insomnia	Rana, Mazza
Post-traumatic stress disorder	Mazza
Inflammatory markers	Mazza, Groli

Table 3. Psychological problems in non-infected elderly during COVID-19 (and first authors).

Problems	First authors
Loneliness	Dziedzic, Ju, Heidinger, Field, Guner, Parveen, Labadi, Kasar
Fear of COVID and death	Agrawal, Yadav, Mistry, Erbesler
Anxiety and depression	Lee, Maggi, Levkovich, Kurnidirdjaja, Garcia-Fernandez, Gangwar, Field
Suicide	Rana, Chou
Sleep disturbances	Parveen, Kasar, Amicucci, Yazici, Field
Lower levels melatonin	Ozturk

Table 4. Behavior problems in the elderly during COVID-19 (and first authors).

Problems	First authors
Inactivity	Hofmann, Oliveira, Champonniere, Takunbo
Lacking social media skills	Delgado, VanJaarsveld, Lorente-Barrero, Yildirin

Table 5. Buffers for elderly problems during COVID-19 (and first authors).

Buffers		First authors
	Personal Qualities	
Optimism		Levkovich, Sardella
Resilience		Lee
	Behaviors	
Exercise		Cruz, Kasar, Tokunbo, Colucci
	Therapies	
Cognitive behavior therapy		Kasar
Acupuncture		Zhao
Melatonin		Cardinali, Ozturk

lack of links to all variables except gender raises questions about limited variability on these factors and/or limited statistical power.

In a study that compared a greater than 60-year-old with a younger than 60-year-old group (N=639), the older group reported less stress and depression than the younger group (Garcia-Fernandez et al, 2020). These findings from a Spanish sample are consistent with those from a survey study in the U.S. (Field et al, 2020). In the U.S. study (N= 167), the young (20-40-years-old) and especially the young living alone experienced greater stress and depression than the older sample (60-80 years-old). And, in a study from India (N=119), the younger participants also reported more anxiety and depression than the elderly group (Gangwar et al, 2021). An interesting variable called "number days of lifestyle change" was also predictive of depression and anxiety.

Despite the significant variability across studies on the elderly being more or less depressed than young adults, depression can be a serious problem that has resulted in suicides in the elderly. In a study from India, suicide was significantly correlated with daily COVID deaths (a significant correlation of.20) (Rana, 2020). The only other paper that relates to suicide in this literature was a discussion of the different suicide theories including interpersonal, three-step and hopelessness theories (Chou et al, 2020). The authors concluded that interviews with the elderly should match the intrinsic belief of the suicide attempter, highlighting the significance of identifying depression in the elderly.

Sleep Disturbances

Sleep disturbances have also been a prevalent problem for the elderly during COVID-19 (Parveen et al, 2021). In this review of studies on sleep problems during COVID, 50% of the elderly reputedly suffered from sleep problems. Sleep disturbances were noted to relate to social isolation and loneliness, as might be expected. And, mental health issues and comorbidities were overlapping. Although the authors referred to them as overlapping, they are likely reciprocal as well as overlapping problems. In another review, sleep quality was notably inferior in the elderly, especially the older living alone (Kasar & Karaman, 2021).

In a very unusual comparison between adolescents and the elderly in Italy during COVID-19, the adolescents were noted to have more severe insomnia, worse sleep quality, longer sleep latency, daytime dysfunction, greater disruption of sleep habits including bedtime, risetime and naptime and greater depression and stress (Amicucci et al, 2021). The elderly, in contrast, were noted to have shorter sleep duration, lower sleep efficiency and greater use of sleep medications which might at least explain their lesser insomnia and latency to sleep. Despite the significant age difference between these two groups with the adolescents averaging 19 and the elderly averaging 68, the sample sizes are extremely unequal with the number of adolescents being twice the number of elderly, statistically limiting these results.

At least two research groups have reported significant relationships between poor sleep quality and loneliness. In one study from Turkey (N =412), loneliness and insomnia were correlated based on the UCLA Loneliness Scale and the Insomnia Severity Index (Yazici et al, 2022). This seemingly was a bidirectional relationship. And, in the study from China, sleep quality was considered a risk factor for loneliness (Ju et al, 2022). However, loneliness would be expected to affect sleep quality, again in a bidirectional relationship.

In a review paper on melatonin in the elderly, sleep problems were associated with decreasing melatonin (Ozturk et al, 2020). Notably, melatonin has significant effects on circadian rhythms including sleep which was highlighted in this review that unfortunately did not include illustrative data.

Behavior Problems in Non-Infected Elderly

89

Two of the most prevalent and frequently studied behavior problems for the elderly during COVID-19 are inactivity and lack of social media skills. Although inactivity has been widespread and a significant problem for all age groups during COVID-19, the lack of social media skills seems to be unique to the elderly.

Inactivity

In a study from the Netherlands (N = 5777), as many as 59% did not meet World Health Organization criteria for physical activity during COVID-19 (Hofman et al, 2021). In this study there was a steadily low trajectory based on latent class trajectory analysis of three different time points. Those who were less active were also older, less educated, had poorer health, were more depressed, had a less healthy diet, engaged in more smoking and less drinking and were less often retired. Unfortunately, the relative significance of these variables was not determined. The lesser activity in the non-retired individuals may have related to their doing desk work at home with less time for physical activity.

In a systematic review of 25 studies (14 cross–sectional and 11 cohort studies) on physical activity and physical fitness, decreases in physical activity and physical fitness were noted along with increased sedentary lifestyle during COVID-19 (Oliveira et al, 2022). It's not clear how directionality was determined based on so many cross-sectional studies and a meta-analysis apparently could not be conducted because of the three different types of measures that were used across studies.

Just as for adolescents during COVID-19 (Field, 2021), the decreased activity noted in the elderly was also related to increased screen time. In a study from France, for example, physical inactivity and sedentary behavior were noted to increase during lockdown in a sample of 1178 elderly participants (Chambonniere et al, 2021). Those who met physical activity recommendations before lockdown experienced a greater decrease in physical activity during lockdown, as might be expected.

In a paper with the interesting title "COVID-19 sitting is the new smoking", a review of studies revealed that more activity during COVID-19 was associated with fewer falls, less osteoarthritis and cancer, decreases in depression and anxiety, decreases in inflammatory markers including IL-6, TNF-alpha and C-reactive protein as well as an increase in IL-6, IL-15 and brain derived neurotrophic factor (Tokunbo et al, 2021). The authors interpret the paradoxical finding that IL-6 was both a pro-inflammatory and an anti-inflammatory by saying that IL-6 can be considered pro-inflammatory if expressed by macrophages and anti-inflammatory if expressed by muscle cells. The decrease in IL-15 is significant inasmuch as it can regulate metabolic diseases including obesity and diabetes, which have both been significant pre-existing conditions for COVID-19 infection.

Lacking social media skills

Some have called social media during COVID-19 an "infodemic". In a scoping review of 33 articles, younger adults and females were most affected by exposure time to COVID-19 social media (Delgado et al, 2021). More exposure time to COVID-19 information led to greater anxiety, depression and stress in the younger adults versus the elderly. This was not a systematic review but the conclusions are consistent with other literature on excessive exposure to social media by the youth (Field, 2021).

In contrast, social media for the elderly has been referred to as a "digital divide" or the "gray digital divide" and the importance of closing the digital divide was noted by this author (Van Jaarsveld, 2020). Data were also cited in this paper that 40% of the elderly are unprepared to use telehealth. In a study exploring risk factors in the elderly, a structural equations analysis revealed that insufficient knowledge about the pandemic led to being worried about the negative effects on family in turn leading to loneliness, boredom, distress and depression (Yildirim et al, 2021).

Others have highlighted the importance of information and communication technology for the elderly (Llorente-Barroso et al, 2021). These authors claim that both information and communication technology would "prevent infection, provide access to entertainment and hobbies and improve self-esteem", although the degree of the effectiveness of these technologies for the elderly has not been assessed.

Buffers for Elderly Problems During COVID-19

Several buffers for elderly problems have been reported in the COVID-19 literature. These include the personal qualities of optimism, self-worth, self-efficacy and resilience. Behaviors that have been studied as buffers for problems of the elderly during COVID-19 include emotion-focused coping, religiosity and exercise. Effective therapies have included cognitive behavior therapy, acupuncture and melatonin.

Personal Qualities as Buffers

Optimism has been noted as a buffer for elderly problems in at least two COVID-19 studies. In a longitudinal study on 141 outpatients both before and during a lockdown, optimism was noted to contribute to the mental component of The Quality of Life Scale (Sardella et al, 2021). In another study, optimism combined with social support led to less depression with a combination of these variables contributing to 29% of the variance in depression (Levkovich et al, 2021). In a theoretical review, several personal qualities were considered buffers including self-esteem, self-efficacy and resilience (Lee et al, 2020).

Behaviors as Buffers

Exercise has had buffering effects in a few studies for inactivity of the elderly during COVID-19. In one study it was viewed as a buffer against all mental health problems (Cruz et al, 2021). In a study on elderly living alone and experiencing loneliness, several behaviors/activities in addition to exercise were recommended as buffers (Kasar & Karaman, 2021). These

included laughter, meditation, gardening therapy, dance and yoga. Surprisingly, one of the most popular activities of the elderly, namely tai chi, was not mentioned. Importantly, in a review on inactivity in the elderly, activity was noted for its significant role in reducing inflammatory markers including IL-6, TNF-alpha and C-reactive protein, markers that have been associated with COVID-19 (Tokunbo et al, 2021).

Physical activity was also a significant predictor variable for changes that occurred pre-lockdown to lockdown periods (Colucci et al, 2022). In this study pre-lockdown was compared to 3 months after the start of a lockdown and during a second lockdown in healthy elderly individuals (N =72). Although there were differences between pre-lockdown and the first lockdown and between pre-lockdown and the second lockdown, there were no differences between the first and the second lockdown on quality of life. Physical activity buffered these changes along with levels of energy, happiness, and memory. Although these are interesting variables, It's not clear why these variables were selected except that they were of interest to the researchers just as many of the study variables are selected for that reason.

Therapies as Buffers

The intervention literature for elderly problems during COVID-19 has been very limited. Cognitive behavior therapy, acupuncture and melatonin have received some attention. In a review paper on seven studies on loneliness in the elderly during lockdowns, the authors suggested cognitive behavior therapy and technology opportunities as potential buffers (Kasar & Karaman, 2021). Seemingly, education on technology for the elderly would lead to more communication and less loneliness and would be less costly than cognitive therapy, but these interventions have not yet been tested.

Emotional therapy has also been suggested and assessed in a study that compared emotional therapy with a combination of emotional therapy plus acupuncture (Zhao et al, 2021). Not surprisingly, the combined therapy group versus emotional therapy alone showed a decrease in depression at three, six, nine and 12 weeks following the therapy. Surprisingly, the researchers didn't include an acupuncture only group.

Melatonin as therapy has been the focus of at least two studies probably following on the sleep disturbances that have been noted in the elderly during COVID-19. In one study, the elderly are considered a high risk COVID group for diminished melatonin that occurs with age (Cardinali et al, 2020). Melatonin counteracts infection as an antioxidant, anti-inflammatory and immunomodulatory antiviral. Chronotherapy by melatonin restores the optimal circadian pattern of the sleep-wake cycle. In that sense melatonin would be considered a mediating variable for the restorative sleep effects on immune function. In a review paper, melatonin effects have also been related to neuroendocrine and cardiovascular functions (Ozturk et al, 2020). The authors concluded that melatonin can prevent age-related oxidative stress that would have implications for COVID risk.

Methodological Limitations of this Literature

Starting with the type of studies that are frequently conducted, surveys are limited to computer-literate elderly samples which are not representative. Surveys might be compared to phone interviews to determine whether older and less computer-literate individuals might be more frequently recruited by phone interviews. Although, the elderly might be more self-revealing on surveys than phone interviews because surveys are typically anonymous and the elderly might not feel as much stigma reporting moods like depression on anonymous surveys.

The 60-year-old cut-off for the elderly for most studies may be on the young side given that many sixty and seventy-year-olds are still working and active as well as being computer-literate. The relatively young cut-off might be masking elderly/youth differences. Some have said, for example, that the elderly responses to the pandemic have been similar to that of folks in their 50s based on responses they received in 27 countries (Daoust et al, 2020).

Other types of variability in recruitment including infected versus non-infected individuals and lockdown versus non-lockdown periods are limiting in terms of conducting systematic reviews and meta-analyses. Surprisingly, these groups have rarely been compared even though differences would be expected with infected looking worse than non-infected groups and lockdown groups being more affected than non-lockdown groups.

A reporting bias might also exist for the elderly. For example, they might have a greater inclination to report loneliness if they are living alone when loneliness might be expected. Or, they they might be less inclined to report depression because depression was seemingly more stigmatic in their earlier years.

Regarding measures, a comparison between traditional and geriatric measures, for example, for depression and anxiety might reveal differences in the severity level being assessed. It's conceivable that because the geriatric measures of depression and anxiety are more specific to that age group, they may be more sensitive in detecting those problems than the traditional measures like the State Anxiety Inventory or the Beck Depression Inventory. In any case, the variability on the measures being used has contributed to the literature lacking systematic reviews and meta-analyses.

The pre-existing conditions or comorbidities that the elderly typically experience may contribute to their anxiety in addition to their worry about COVID infection. Knowing that their age and pre-existing condition compounds their risk for infection may contribute to additional stress. In that sense, these are more than confounding covariate variables which may be need to be considered as group comparison, mediating or moderating variables.

Mediators have rarely been assessed in the COVID-19 literature on elderly problems. Mediator/moderator analyses may be more appropriate than correlation analyses and even hierarchical regression analyses. The most frequent focus on prevalence has led to the primary use of hierarchical regression analyses. Using more complex data analyses such as structural equation modeling, although rarely used in this literature, may be desirable for determining complex relationships between multiple variables.

Etiology and mechanism research has less frequently appeared in this literature that has focused mainly on prevalence data. An example of the benefits of mechanism research comes from the sleep/melatonin data revealing that melatonin is needed to restore the natural sleep cycle which has been interrupted during the COVID-19 pandemic for many elderly people.

Despite these methodological limitations, this literature on COVID-related problems in the elderly has alerted providers of their risk not only for COVID infection but for psychological and behavior problems deriving from the pandemic lockdown and non-lockdown periods. Further, it will likely help inform prevention/intervention research and clinical programs that are needed to reduce the pandemic-related problems for the elderly.

References

[1]. Agrawal S, Dróżdż M, Makuch S, Pietraszek A, Sobieszczańska M, Mazur G. The Assessment of Fear of COVID-19 among the Elderly Population: A Cross-Sectional Study. J Clin Med. 2021 Nov 26;10(23):5537. doi: 10.3390/jcm10235537. PMID: 34884241; PMCID: PMC8658105.

[2]. Aly MAEG, Saber HG. Long COVID and chronic fatigue syndrome: A survey of elderly female survivors in Egypt. Int J Clin Pract. 2021 Dec;75(12):e14886. doi: 10.1111/ijcp.14886. Epub 2021 Sep 24. PMID: 34537995; PMCID: PMC8646426.

[3]. Amicucci G, Salfi F, D'Atri A, Viselli L, Ferrara M. The Differential Impact of COVID-19 Lockdown on Sleep Quality, Insomnia, Depression, Stress, and Anxiety among Late Adolescents and Elderly in Italy. Brain Sci. 2021 Oct 11;11(10):1336. doi: 10.3390/brainsci11101336. PMID: 34679402; PMCID: PMC8533758.

[4]. Cardinali DP, Brown GM, Reiter RJ, Pandi-Perumal SR. Elderly as a High-risk Group during COVID-19 Pandemic: Effect of Circadian Misalignment, Sleep Dysregulation and Melatonin Administration. Sleep Vigil. 2020;4(2):81-87. doi: 10.1007/s41782-020-00111-7. Epub 2020 Sep 26. PMID: 33015537; PMCID: PMC7519696.

[5]. Chambonniere C, Lambert C, Tardieu M, Fillon A, Genin P, Larras B, Melsens P, Baker JS, Pereira B, Tremblay A, Thivel D, Duclos M. Physical Activity and Sedentary Behavior of Elderly Populations during Confinement: Results from the FRENCH COVID-19 ONAPS Survey. Exp Aging Res. 2021 Oct-Dec;47(5):401-413. doi: 10.1080/0361073X.2021.1908750. Epub 2021 Apr 7. PMID: 33827390.

[6]. Chou HC, Tzeng DS, Lin SL. Suicide and the Elderly During the COVID-19 Pandemic: An Overview of Different Suicide Theories. Prim Care Companion CNS Disord. 2020 Oct 22;22(5):20nr02676. doi: 10.4088/PCC.20nr02676. PMID: 33095519.

[7]. Colucci E, Nadeau S, Higgins J, Kehayia E, Poldma T, Saj A, de Guise E. COVID-19 lockdowns' effects on the quality of life, perceived health and well-being of healthy elderly individuals: A longitudinal comparison of pre-lockdown and lockdown states of well-being. Arch Gerontol Geriatr. 2022 Mar-Apr;99:104606. doi: 10.1016/j.archger.2021.104606. Epub 2021 Dec 5. PMID: 34896795; PMCID: PMC8645291.

[8]. Cruz WM, D' Oliveira A, Dominski FH, Diotaiuti P, Andrade A. Mental health of older people in social isolation: the role of physical activity at home during the COVID-19 pandemic. Sport Sci Health. 2021 Aug 25:1-6. doi: 10.1007/s11332-021-00825-9. Epub ahead of print. PMID: 34457072; PMCID: PMC8386142.865.

[9]. Daoust JF. Elderly people and responses to COVID-19 in 27 Countries. PLoS One. 2020 Jul 2;15(7):e0235590. doi: 10.1371/journal.pone.0235590. PMID: 32614889; PMCID: PMC7332014.

[10]. Delgado CE, Silva EA, Castro EAB, Carbogim FDC, Püschel VAA, Cavalcante RB. COVID-19 infodemic and adult and elderly mental health: a scoping review. Rev Esc Enferm USP. 2021 Dec 1;55:e20210170. English, Portuguese. doi: 10.1590/1980-220X-REEUSP-2021-0170. PMID: 34855932.

[11]. Dziedzic B, Idzik A, Kobos E, Sienkiewicz Z, Kryczka T, Fidecki W, Wysokiński M. Loneliness and mental health among the elderly in Poland during the COVID-19 pandemic. BMC Public Health. 2021 Nov 2;21(1):1976. doi: 10.1186/s12889-021-12029-4. PMID: 34727897; PMCID: PMC8561080.

[12]. Erbesler ZA, Demir G. Determination of Death Anxiety and Death-Related Depression Levels in the Elderly During the COVID-19 Pandemic. Omega (Westport). 2022 Mar 26:302228221082429. doi: 10.1177/00302228221082429. Epub ahead of print. PMID: 35343311; PMCID: PMC8958305.

[13]. Field, T. (2021). Aggression and violence affecting youth during COVID-19: A narrative review. Journal of Psychiatry Research Reviews and Reports. 3, 1-7. doi.org/10.47363/JPSR/2021 (3)130.

[14]. Field, T. (2021). Social media use and mental health in youth during COVID-19: A narrative review. Journal of Psychological Research and Reviews,4:54. DOI: 10.28933/ijprr-2021-08-2905

[15]. Field, T. (2021). Inactivity in youth during COVID-19: A narrative review. International Journal of Integrative Pediatrics and Environmental Health.

[16]. Field, T., Diego, M., Hernandez-Reif, M., Schanberg, S., Kuhn, C., Yando, R. & Bendell, D. (2003). Pregnancy Anxiety and Comorbid Depression and Anger Effects on the Fetus and Neonate. Depression and Anxiety, 17, 140-151.

[17]. Field, T., Mines, S., Poling, S., Bendell, D. & Veazey, C. (2020). Young, alone, and young alone during a COVID-19 lockdown. Mental Health and Clinical Psychology, 4 (4), 31-38.

[18]. Field, T., Mines, S., Poling, S., Diego, M., Bendell, D. & Veazey, C. (2020). Anxiety and depression in a COVID-19 lockdown. Journal of Anxiety and Depression, 3 (2), 124-137.

[19]. Gangwar V, Singh A, Verma M, John NA, Gangwar RS, John J, Jasrotia RB. Mental health indicators in the later phase of lockdown due to COVID-19 pandemic in healthy youth combined elderly people: a web-based cross-sectional survey. Int J Physiol Pathophysiol Pharmacol. 2021 Aug 15;13(4):117-125. PMID: 34540132; PMCID: PMC8446773.

[20]. García-Fernández L, Romero-Ferreiro V, López-Roldán PD, Padilla S, Rodriguez-Jimenez R. Mental Health in Elderly Spanish People in Times of COVID-19 Outbreak. Am J Geriatr Psychiatry. 2020 Oct;28(10):1040-1045. doi: 10.1016/j.jagp.2020.06.027. Epub 2020 Jul 7. PMID: 32718855; PMCID: PMC7340042.

[21]. Grolli RE, Mingoti MED, Bertollo AG, Luzardo AR, Quevedo J, Réus GZ, Ignácio ZM. Impact of COVID-19 in the Mental Health in Elderly: Psychological and Biological Updates. Mol Neurobiol. 2021 May;58(5):1905-1916. doi: 10.1007/s12035-020-02249-x. Epub 2021 Jan 6. PMID: 33404981; PMCID: PMC7786da

[22]. Guner TA, Erdogan Z, Demir I. The Effect of Loneliness on Death Anxiety in the Elderly During the COVID-19 Pandemic. Omega (Westport). 2021 Apr 20:302228211010587. doi: 10.1177/00302228211010587. Epub ahead of print. PMID: 33878967; PMCID: PMC8060692.

[23]. Heidinger T, Richter L. The Effect of COVID-19 on Loneliness in the Elderly. An Empirical Comparison of Pre-and Peri-Pandemic Loneliness in Community-Dwelling Elderly. Front Psychol. 2020 Sep 30;11:585308. doi: 10.3389/fpsyg.2020.585308. PMID: 33101154; PMCID: PMC7554575.

[24]. Hofman A, Limpens MAM, de Crom TOE, Ikram MA, Luik AI, Voortman T. Trajectories and Determinants of Physical Activity during COVID-19 Pandemic: A Population-Based Study of Middle-Aged and Elderly Individuals in The Netherlands. Nutrients. 2021 Oct 27;13(11):3832. doi: 10.3390/nu13113832. PMID: 34836085; PMCID: PMC8618734.

[25]. Hwang J, Ryu HS, Kim HA, Hyun M, Lee JY, Yi HA. Prognostic Factors of COVID-19 Infection in Elderly Patients: A Multicenter Study. J Clin Med. 2020 Dec 4;9(12):3932. doi: 10.3390/jcm9123932. PMID: 33291617; PMCID: PMC7761972.

[26]. Iodice F, Cassano V, Rossini PM. Direct and indirect neurological, cognitive, and behavioral effects of COVID-19 on the healthy elderly, mild-cognitive-impairment, and Alzheimer's disease populations. Neurol Sci. 2021 Feb;42(2):455-465. doi: 10.1007/s10072-020-04902-8. Epub 2021 Jan 7. PMID: 33409824; PMCID: PMC7787936.

[27]. Ju J, Qi WB, Zhang J, Cao ZJ, Tsai CL, Liu P. A Cross-Sectional Study on the Cross-Talk of the COVID-19-Related Degree of Loneliness and the Etiological Factors Among the Elderly in Central China. Front Psychiatry. 2022 Feb 11;13:805664. doi: 10.3389/fpsyt.2022.805664. PMID: 35237190; PMCID: PMC8883135.

[28]. Kasar K, Karaman E. Life in lockdown: Social isolation, loneliness and quality of life in the elderly during the COVID-19 pandemic: A scoping review. Geriatr Nurs. 2021 Sep-

Oct;42(5):1222-1229. doi: 10.1016/j.gerinurse.2021.03.010. Epub 2021 Mar 12. PMID: 33824008; PMCID: PMC8566023.

[29]. Krupp K, Madhivanan P, Killgore WDS, Ruiz JM, Carvajal S, Coull BM, Grandner MA. Neurological Manifestations in COVID-19: An Unrecognized Crisis in Our Elderly? Adv Geriatr Med Res. 2021;3(3):e210013. doi: 10.20900/agmr20210013. Epub 2021 Jun 16. PMID: 34268500; PMCID: PMC8279204.

[30]. Kurniawidjaja M, Susilowati IH, Erwandi D, Kadir A, Hasiholan BP, Al Ghiffari R. Identification of Depression Among Elderly During COVID-19. J Prim Care Community Health. 2022 Jan-Dec;13:21501319221085380. doi: 10.1177/21501319221085380. PMID: 35333667; PMCID: PMC8958696.

[31]. Lábadi B, Arató N, Budai T, Inhóf O, Stecina DT, Sík A, Zsidó AN. Psychological well-being and coping strategies of elderly people during the COVID-19 pandemic in Hungary. Aging Ment Health. 2022 Mar;26(3):570-577. doi: 10.1080/13607863.2021.1902469. Epub 2021 Mar 29. PMID: 33779424.

[32]. Lee K, Jeong GC, Yim J. Consideration of the Psychological and Mental Health of the Elderly during COVID-19: A Theoretical Review. Int J Environ Res Public Health. 2020 Nov 3;17(21):8098. doi: 10.3390/ijerph17218098. PMID: 33153074; PMCID: PMC7663449.

[33]. Levkovich I, Shinan-Altman S, Essar Schvartz N, Alperin M. Depression and Health-Related Quality of Life Among Elderly Patients during the COVID-19 Pandemic in Israel: A Cross-sectional Study. J Prim Care Community Health. 2021 Jan-Dec;12:2150132721995448. doi: 10.1177/2150132721995448. PMID: 33576290; PMCID: PMC7883147.

[34]. Liu K, Chen Y, Lin R, Han K. Clinical features of COVID-19 in elderly patients: A comparison with young and middle-aged patients. J Infect. 2020 Jun;80(6):e14-e18. doi: 10.1016/j.jinf.2020.03.005. Epub 2020 Mar 27. PMID: 32171866; PMCID: PMC7102640.

[35]. Llorente-Barroso C, Kolotouchkina O, Mañas-Viniegra L. The Enabling Role of ICT to Mitigate the Negative Effects of Emotional and Social Loneliness of the Elderly during COVID-19 Pandemic. Int J Environ Res Public Health. 2021 Apr 8;18(8):3923. doi: 10.3390/ijerph18083923. PMID: 33917966; PMCID: PMC8068368.

[36]. Maggi G, Baldassarre I, Barbaro A, Cavallo ND, Cropano M, Nappo R, Santangelo G. Mental health status of Italian elderly subjects during and after quarantine for the COVID-19 pandemic: a cross-sectional and longitudinal study. Psychogeriatrics. 2021 Jul;21(4):540-551. doi: 10.1111/psyg.12703. Epub 2021 May 6. PMID: 33955115; PMCID: PMC8242477.

[37]. Mazza MG, De Lorenzo R, Conte C, Poletti S, Vai B, Bollettini I, Melloni EMT, Furlan R, Ciceri F, Rovere-Querini P; COVID-19 BioB Outpatient Clinic Study group, Benedetti F. Anxiety and depression in COVID-19 survivors: Role of inflammatory and clinical predictors. Brain Behav Immun. 2020 Oct;89:594-600. doi: 10.1016/j.bbi.2020.07.037. Epub 2020 Jul 30. PMID: 32738287; PMCID: PMC7390748.

[38]. Mistry SK, Ali ARMM, Akther F, Yadav UN, Harris MF. Exploring fear of COVID-19 and its correlates among older adults in Bangladesh. Global Health. 2021 Apr 14;17(1):47. doi: 10.1186/s12992-021-00698-0. PMID: 33853616; PMCID: PMC8045579.

[39]. Mori H, Obinata H, Murakami W, Tatsuya K, Sasaki H, Miyake Y, Taniguchi Y, Ota S, Yamaga M, Suyama Y, Tamura K. Comparison of COVID-19 disease between young and elderly patients: Hidden viral shedding of COVID-19. J Infect Chemother. 2021 Jan;27(1):70-75. doi: 10.1016/j.jiac.2020.09.003. Epub 2020 Sep 6. PMID: 32950393; PMCID: PMC7474868.

[40]. Mowla A, Ghaedsharaf M, Pani A. Psychopathology in Elderly COVID-19 Survivors and Controls. J Geriatr Psychiatry Neurol. 2022 May;35(3):467-471. doi: 10.1177/08919887211002664. Epub 2021 Mar 22. PMID: 33745373.

[41]. Oliveira MR, Sudati IP, Konzen VM, de Campos AC, Wibelinger LM, Correa C, Miguel FM, Silva RN, Borghi-Silva A. Covid-19 and the impact on the physical activity level of elderly people: A systematic review. Exp Gerontol. 2022 Mar;159:111675. doi: 10.1016/j.exger.2021.111675. Epub 2021 Dec 23. PMID: 34954282; PMCID: PMC8695515.

[42]. Ouanes S, Kumar R, Doleh ESI, Smida M, Al-Kaabi A, Al-Shahrani AM, Mohamedsalih GA, Ahmed NE, Assar A, Khoodoruth MAS, AbuKhattab M, Maslamani MA, AlAbdulla MA. Mental Health, resilience, and religiosity in the elderly under COVID-19 quarantine in Qatar. Arch Gerontol Geriatr. 2021 Sep-Oct;96:104457. doi: 10.1016/j.archger.2021.104457. Epub 2021 Jun 6. PMID: 34146999.

[43]. Öztürk G, Akbulut KG, Güney Ş. Melatonin, aging, and COVID-19: Could melatonin be beneficial for COVID-19 treatment in the elderly? Turk J Med Sci. 2020 Oct

22;50(6):1504-1512. doi: 10.3906/sag-2005-356. PMID: 32777902; PMCID: PMC7605095.

[44]. Parveen S, George SM, Chand S. Was Sleep a Problem for the Elderly During COVID-19? Sleep Vigil. 2021;5(2):197-203. doi: 10.1007/s41782-021-00164-2. Epub 2021 Sep 6. PMID: 34514292; PMCID: PMC8420144.

[45]. Pepe M, Maroun-Eid C, Romero R, Arroyo-Espliguero R, Fernàndez-Rozas I, Aparisi A, Becerra-Muñoz VM, Garcia Aguado M, Brindicci G, Huang J, Alfonso-Rodríguez E, Castro-Mejía AF, Favretto S, Cerrato E, Albiol P, Raposeiras-Roubin S, Vedia O, Feltes Guzmän G, Carrero-Fernández A, Perez Cimarra C, Buzón L, Jativa Mendez JL, Abumayyaleh M, Corbi-Pascual M, Macaya C, Estrada V, Nestola PL, Biondi-Zoccai G, Núñez-Gil IJ. Clinical presentation, therapeutic approach, and outcome of young patients admitted for COVID-19, with respect to the elderly counterpart. Clin Exp Med. 2021 May;21(2):249-268. doi: 10.1007/s10238-021-00684-1. Epub 2021 Feb 8. PMID: 33555436; PMCID: PMC7868661.

[46]. Rana U. Elderly suicides in India: an emerging concern during COVID-19 pandemic. Int Psychogeriatr. 2020 Oct;32(10):1251-1252. doi: 10.1017/S1041610220001052. Epub 2020 Jun 3. PMID: 32487275; PMCID: PMC7322164.

[47]. Sardella A, Lenzo V, Bonanno GA, Basile G, Quattropani MC. Expressive Flexibility and Dispositional Optimism Contribute to the Elderly's Resilience and Health-Related Quality of Life during the COVID-19 Pandemic. Int J Environ Res Public Health. 2021 Feb 10;18(4):1698. doi: 10.3390/ijerph18041698. PMID: 33578873; PMCID: PMC7916547.

[48]. Seethaler M, Just S, Stötzner P, Bermpohl F, Brandl EJ. Psychosocial Impact of COVID-19 Pandemic in Elderly Psychiatric Patients: a Longitudinal Study. Psychiatr Q. 2021 Dec;92(4):1439-1457. doi: 10.1007/s11126-021-09917-8. Epub 2021 Apr 26. PMID: 33904123; PMCID: PMC8075010.

[49]. Seong GM, Baek AR, Baek MS, Kim WY, Kim JH, Lee BY, Na YS, Lee SI. Comparison of Clinical Characteristics and Outcomes of Younger and Elderly Patients with Severe COVID-19 in Korea: A Retrospective Multicenter Study. J Pers Med. 2021 Nov 29;11(12):1258. doi: 10.3390/jpm11121258. PMID: 34945730; PMCID: PMC8708855.

[50]. Sharifi N, Rezaei N, Fathnezhad-Kazemi A, Ghiasi F. Association between Fear of COVID-19 with Self-care Behaviors in Elderly: A Cross-Sectional Study. Soc Work Public Health. 2021 Jul 4;36(5):606-614. doi:

10.1080/19371918.2021.1937435. Epub 2021 Jul 6. PMID: 34225566.

[51]. Sirin H, Ahmadi AA, Ketrez G, Ozbeyaz C, Dikmen AU, Ozkan S. Assessment of anxiety in elderly population during the COVID-19 pandemic and the impact of compulsory home-stay in the central districts of Ankara, Turkey: A quantitative, qualitative mixed method study. Int J Geriatr Psychiatry. 2021 Nov;36(11):1785-1794. doi: 10.1002/gps.5600. Epub 2021 Jul 19. PMID: 34231924; PMCID: PMC8420385.

[52]. Song J, Hu W, Yu Y, Shen X, Wang Y, Yan J, Yang X, Gong S, Wang M. A Comparison of Clinical Characteristics and Outcomes in Elderly and Younger Patients with COVID-19. Med Sci Monit. 2020 Jul 28;26:e925047. doi: 10.12659/MSM.925047. PMID: 32720649; PMCID: PMC7412913.

[53]. Tokunbo O, Abayomi T, Adekomi D, Oyeyipo I. COVID-19: sitting is the new smoking; the role of exercise in augmenting the immune system among the elderly. Afr Health Sci. 2021 Mar;21(1):189-193. doi: 10.4314/ahs.v21i1.25. PMID: 34394297; PMCID: PMC8356589.

[54]. Van Jaarsveld G. The Effects of COVID-19 Among the Elderly Population: A Case for Closing the Digital Divide. Front Psychiatry. 2020 Nov 12;11:577427. doi: 10.3389/fpsyt.2020.577427. PMID: 33304283; PMCID: PMC7693633.

[55]. Yadav UN, Yadav OP, Singh DR, Ghimire S, Rayamajhee B, Kanti Mistry S, Rawal LB, Ali AM, Kumar Tamang M, Mehta S. Perceived fear of COVID-19 and its associated factors among Nepalese older adults in eastern Nepal: A cross-sectional study. PLoS One. 2021 Jul 26;16(7):e0254825. doi: 10.1371/journal.pone.0254825. PMID: 34310639; PMCID: PMC8312955.

[56]. Yazici H, Ökten Ç. The Insomnia and Loneliness of Elderly Individuals and Affecting Factors During the COVID-19 Pandemic in Turkey. Soc Work Public Health. 2022 Mar 14:1-8. doi: 10.1080/19371918.2022.2053630. Epub ahead of print. PMID: 35287564.

[57]. Yildirim H, Işik K, Aylaz R. The effect of anxiety levels of elderly people in quarantine on depression during covid-19 pandemic. Soc Work Public Health. 2021 Feb 17;36(2):194-204. doi: 10.1080/19371918.2020.1868372. Epub 2021 Jan 7. PMID: 33413035.

[58]. Zeng F, Deng G, Cui Y, Zhang Y, Dai M, Chen L, Han D, Li W, Guo K, Chen X, Shen M, Pan P. A predictive model for the severity of COVID-19 in elderly patients. Aging (Albany NY). 2020 Nov 10;12(21):20982-20996. doi:

10.18632/aging.103980. Epub 2020 Nov 10. PMID: 33170150; PMCID: PMC7695402.

[59]. Zhang L, Fan T, Yang S, Feng H, Hao B, Lu Z, Xiong R, Shen X, Jiang W, Wang W, Geng Q. Comparison of clinical characteristics of COVID-19 between elderly patients and young patients: a study based on a 28-day follow-up. Aging (Albany NY). 2020 Oct 26;12(20):19898-19910. doi: 10.18632/aging.104077. Epub 2020 Oct 26. PMID: 33106442; PMCID: PMC7655161.

[60]. Zhao F, Tong X, Wang C. Acupuncture Combined With Emotional Therapy of Chinese Medicine Treatment for Improving Depressive Symptoms in Elderly Patients With Alcohol Dependence During the COVID-19 Epidemic. Front Psychol. 2021 May 26;12:635099. doi: 10.3389/fpsyg.2021.635099. PMID: 34122226; PMCID: PMC8187785.

[61]. Zhou R, Chen H, Zhu L, Chen Y, Chen B, Li Y, Chen Z, Zhu H, Wang H. Mental Health Status of the Elderly Chinese Population During COVID-19: An Online Cross-Sectional Study. Front Psychiatry. 2021 May 12;12:645938. doi: 10.3389/fpsyt.2021.645938. PMID: 34054603; PMCID: PMC8149938.

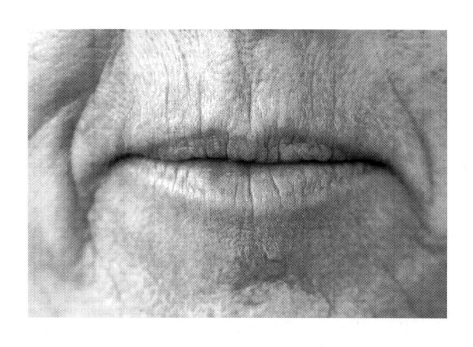

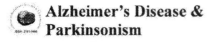

Field, J Alzheimers Dis Parkinsonism 2015, 5:1
http://dx.doi.org/10.4172/2161-0460.1000186

Alzheimer's Disease & Parkinsonism

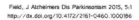

Review Article   **Open Access**

Smell and Taste Dysfunction as Early Markers for Neurodegenerative and Neuropsychiatric Diseases

Tiffany Field[1,2]

[1]University of Miami School of Medicine, USA
[2]Fielding Graduate University, USA

Abstract

During the last few decades a significant literature has evolved, suggesting that sensory dysfunction, particularly smell and taste dysfunction, can be early markers for neurodegenerative diseases such as Parkinson's and Alzheimer's and neuropsychiatric diseases including ADHD and Schizophrenia, all diseases that involve dopaminergic pathology. Smell loss and taste dysfunction appear in clinical versus non-clinical groups, and in longitudinal studies these symptoms have been noted years earlier than motor signs in the first degree relatives of individuals who already have the diseases. This paper is a review of the recent literature on empirical studies and reviews that have documented the results of sensory screenings of several groups with neurodegenerative and neuropsychiatric diseases and those first-degree relatives at risk for those diseases. Although early biomarkers could be useful in identifying those needing preventive intervention, the treatment literature is very limited.

Keywords: Smell and taste dysfunction; Neurodegenerative and neuropsychiatric diseases

Introduction

Smell is one of the oldest senses in evolution, plays a key role in development, relationships, pleasure, health, safety and survival [1]. Smell is associated with memories, moods and emotions, food preferences, pheromones, mating and parent-infant bonding. Although humans are less dependent on smell for survival than other mammals, smell is critical for detecting polluted air and water, smoke and leaking gas, and spoiled foods [2]. Despite these important functions, smell has been one of the neglected senses.

Although the sense of smell functions as early as the fetal stage,decreased olfactory function occurs with aging, with over half of those between the ages of 65 and 80 and over three quarters of those over the age of 80 experiencing this problem [3]. In a sample with olfactory disorder, 68% of the patients presented with hyposmia and 32% with anosmia [4]. Olfaction has been notably worse in men in most studies [2,5] ,although there are some exceptions[6]. In the latter study, lower olfaction scores were also related to lower educational status.

An inability to identify smells or tastes predates the clinical symptoms of several neurodegenerative and neuropsychiatric diseases, highlighting their importance as markers for early interventions. Neurodegenerative diseases that have been associated with inferior smell identification include Parkinson's [7-12], Alzheimer's [9, 13,14] and a myotrophic lateral sclerosis [8] and the neuropsychiatric/smell disorder conditions include ADHD [15,16], anxiety disorders [17], Autism Spectrum Disorder [18-20], depression [21], eating disorders [22] and schizophrenia [23-26].

Most of the empirical studies have compared clinical and non-clinical groups on smell tests, although more recently, some longitudinal studies have documented sensory dysfunction in at-risk, first degree relatives who later show the cardinal motor signs [8,27]. The University of Pennsylvania Smell Identification Test (UPSIT) is the most frequently used test [8], although several other shorter and less expensive versions have been developed including the Sniffin Sticker Test (SST) [9], the Brief Smell Identification Test (B-SIT) [28], the Odor Stick Identification Test (OSIT) [8] and the San Diego Odor Identification Test (SDOIT) [28] and most recently the peanut butter smell test [14]. These tests, for example the Sniffin' Sticks test has been significantly correlated with a visual analogue scale in at least one study [29].

Because of cross-cultural differences in smell identification, researchers from other countries have developed alternative versions that feature smells that are prevalent in their cultures including Brazil [30], Japan [31] and South Korea (who call theirs the cross-cultural smell test) [32]. Although most of the smell tests were designed for adults, a child's version exists called the Sensory Identification Score [15], and infants with developmental delays are also being tested for sensory integration problems [33]. Others have evaluated the relationships between smell identification, taste threshold, dopamine transporter scan (DaTSCAN) and motor function and their diagnostic accuracy in early Parkinson's disease and have suggested that a basic smell test is as sensitive as the DaTSCAN in the diagnosis of Parkinson's [34],and, still others claim that they have not been as sensitive as the self-report measures [8].

Tests for taste have also been developed including sweetness, creaminess and pleasantness [35]. In that study, pleasantness identification was the most reliable of the three tests for taste. Liquid taste solutions for sweet, sour, salty and bitter have also been developed and have acceptable reliability [36]. Less conclusive data have been documented for taste dysfunction, although smell and taste disorders might be expected to be comorbid as those senses are often interactive, and many patients who have lost their sense of smell complain that their sense of taste is also blunted [9]. Some have noted that a damaged olfactory system reduces taste perception including sweet, sour, bitter and salty via the facial, glossopharyngeal and vagus nerves [37]. Comorbid smell and taste dysfunction has been reported for eating disorders, both bulimia nervosa and anorexia nervosa [22]. These were determined using the "Sniffin Sticks" method and the "Taste Strip" kit. Taste has been tested less often, probably because its assessment has been more difficult and aversive for research participants [35].

*Corresponding author: Tiffany Fie, University of Miami School of Medicine. Tel: 305 975 5029; E-mail: tfield@med.miami.edu

Received February 12, 2015; Accepted March 18, 2015; Published April 25, 2015

Citation: Field T (2015) Smell and Taste Dysfunction as Early Markers for Neurodegenerative and Neuropsychiatric Diseases. J Alzheimers Dis Parkinsonism 5: 186. doi: 10.4172/2161-0460.1000186

Citation: Field T (2015) Smell and Taste Dysfunction as Early Markers for Neurodegenerative and Neuropsychiatric Diseases. J Alzheimers Dis Parkinsonism 5: 186. doi: 10.4172/2161-0460.1000186

The etiology and development of these sensory dysfunctions are not known, but the dopamine, norepinephrine, serotonin, acetylcholine and orbitofrontal cortex systems have been implicated in several of the neurodegenerative and neuropsychiatric conditions associated with smell dysfunction [8,38]. These include, for examples, Parkinson's and ADHD. Although sensory tests have been developed for infants and young children who are noted to have hypo or hypersensitivity as well as sensory integration problems [33], longitudinal studies have not been conducted to determine whether the negative effects that these problems have on child development persist into adulthood

Olfactory dysfunction appears to precede the motor and cognitive symptoms of several conditions, making it an earlier marker forpreventive interventions, althoughvery few effective interventions have been identified. Reportedly the medications that are effective for motor symptoms are not effective for sensory dysfunction [8]. Some corticosteroid and anti-inflammatory medications have been effective. For example, estradiolhas been effective but has only been tested in the rat [39]. And, methylprednisolone has been an effective medication in at least two studies [9]. Reputedly, olfactory training has also been effective [9].

Olfactory functions and development

The sense of smell is the oldest in evolution and functions as early as the fetal stage [1]. Some have noted fetal perception of aromas based on increased fetal activity and neonatal perception by changes in respiration, heart rate and facial expressions [40-42]. The newborn has shown positive reactions to amniotic fluid and breast milk odors [43,44] and negative responses to acetic acid odors [45]. In a study we conducted, 2-month-old infants cried less, had lower cortisol levels and spent more time in deep sleep after a bath in lavender oil than one without lavender [46]. In another study from our lab EEG recordings of 3-week-old infants showed a shift to greater left frontal EEG activation (which is a positive shift) following exposure to lavender aroma [47].

Adults show a similar relaxation response to lavender (as compared to rosemary) as measured by their EEG patterns and decreased heart rate and they also performed math computations in less time and with greater accuracy [48]. In still another study in our laboratory, adults who were exposed to lavender fragrance showed decreased heart rate, increased theta power and greater left frontal EEG activation, variables that are typically associated with relaxation [49]. Thus smell perception happens very early in life and smell preferences of young infants mimic those of older adults. These studies have been limited to lavender and rosemary aromas, and while lavender seems to have calming effects and rosemary arousing effects, the underlying mechanisms for these differential responses are not clear, and other odorants need to be tested for their effects on heart rate and EEG patterns.

Olfactory functions, anatomy and demographic factors

The sense of smell plays a critical role in the quality of life from infancy to old age [1], serving many functions in safety, e.g. detecting hazardous smells, in health, e.g. in food preferences and getting adequate nutrition, in emotions, e.g. memories of pleasurable experiences, feelings of pleasure, in behavior, e.g. sensing pheromones, in mother-infant attachment, and in longevity.Odorants that enter the nose are absorbed by the nasal mucosa and once absorbed stimulate olfactory receptors in the epithelium located over the cribriform plate [50]. Smell is then transmited via the olfactory bulb to the olfactory cerebral cortex and the orbitofrontal cortex. The orbitofrontal cortex receives both olfactory and taste stimuli.

Olfactory functions and dysfunctions are affected by several demographic factors.Demographic factors that affect the sense of smell include at leastgender, education and aging. Women have been noted to have a better sense of smell [8], although studies in other cultures have yielded mixed results. In a study on healthy Turkish adults the Sniffin Sticks scores were lower than in other countries and they decreased with age, and adults with less education had lower scores, but the scores were not related to gender or smoking [6]. In contrast, in a cross-sectional population-based survey in Spain in which four microencapsulated odorants (rose, banana, musk and gas) were distributed, the olfaction scores for men werelower, smell recognition declined after the sixth decade and scores were also lower for less educated adults [5]. The data on declining function with age appear to be consistent. In a recent review by [3],decreased olfactory function appeared in over half the population ages 65 to 80 years and in 75% of those over the age of 80. They further suggested that a disproportionate number of the elderly have died in accidental gas poisonings.

Incidence of olfactory dysfunction

In the cross-sectional population-based survey already mentioned, olfaction was normal for detection in 81% of the sample, for recognition/memory in 56% of the individuals and for identification in 51% of the sample [5]. Dysfunction was defined as hyposmia or anosmia if the adults recognized or identified one to three odors in the case of hyposmia or none of the odors as in anosmia. Most of the dysfunction was hyposmia (19%). This happened for recognition (44%) and identification (48%). Surprisingly,smoking and exposure to noxious substances were positively related to smell recognition in that study.

The incidences of hyposmia and anosmia were notably higher in a sample of patients seeking treatment for smell disorders in a study conducted in Portugal [4]. In this study, 68% of the patients had hyposmia and 32% had anosmia. The primary diagnoses were idiopathic (32%).

Psychophysical tests for olfactory dysfunction

Smell functions are most frequently assessed by psychophysical, self-report measures including odor identification and discrimination tests (central) and odor threshold tests (peripheral) [51]. Most of the studies to date have assessed odor identification using the UPSIT (the University of Pennsylvania Smell Identification Test) or some variation of that test. Most of the results from the different tests are highly correlated, although they feature different odorants and vary in their reliability and sensitivity [8].

The UPSIT is comprised of 4 booklets (10 pages each) with 40 microencapsulated "scratch and sniff" odorant strips that are scratched with a pencil tip and an odor selected from 4 odor descriptors. The UPSIT is strongly correlated with odor threshold tests and is reported to have a sensitivity of 91% and a specificity of 88% which are higher than the sensitivity/specificity measures of other biomarkers including PET and SPECT [8].

The Brief Smell Identification Test (B-SIT) which includes 12 odorants has been compared to the San Diego Odor Identification Test (SDOIT) comprised of 8 odors. In this comparison, both tests were in agreement on identifying impairment in 96% of the participants [28]. The "Sniffin Sticks" (SST) system features pen-like odor dispensers that are held under the nose and each odor is identified from a list of four choices [52]. The dispensers have the advantage of being reusable, and in one study the Sniffin Sticks scores were correlated with the participants' ratings of their sense of smell on a visual analogue scale [29].

Citation: Field T (2015) Smell and Taste Dysfunction as Early Markers for Neurodegenerative and Neuropsychiatric Diseases. J Alzheimers Dis Parkinsonism 5: 186. doi: 10.4172/2161-0460.1000186

Perhaps the simplest and shortest of the odor tests is a container of 14 g of peanut butter [14] that is held at the bottom of a 30 cm ruler and is moved gradually (1 cm at a time) up the ruler while the participant is exhaling and with eyes closed. The score is the distance the jar was from the nose when the peanut butter was detected. This inexpensive test also had good sensitivity and specificity, and the authors reported dysfunction for the left but not the right nostril. However, others have failed to replicate at least their left/right nostril asymmetry findings [53].

A self-report measure is the Screening Questionnaire for Parosmia (inability of the brain to identify an odor's natural smell) [54]. This is a four-item questionnaire with the first and fourth questions having the highest sensitivity and specificity (#1 Food tastes different than it should because of a problem with odors and #4 The biggest problem is not that I do not or only weakly perceive odors, but that they smell different than they should).

The UPSIT has been translated into a dozen languages and modified by replacing unfamiliar with familiar odors, for example, in Portugal [30], Taiwan and Australia. In the Portuguese version, the popcorn odor was replaced by rubber because more participants thought the popcorn odor smelled more like rubber. And, in Japan, the Japanese Odor Stick Identification Test includes odors like the bromine of China ink, curry, rose, cypress, menthol, sweaty socks and condensed milk [31], and a Cross-Cultural Smell Identification Test has been used in Korea [32].

A cross-cultural difference is one of the problems with cross-study comparisons. Others are that the tests assess different types of odorants and different odorant intensities. These problems are further compounded by the different alternative responses, both number and types of alternative responses. Nonetheless, the sensitivity, specificity and test-retest reliabilities are relatively high for most studies.

Olfactory tests have also been developed for children and infants. In one study children were presented with the essences of apple, banana, lemon and orange and asked to smell the essence from a bottle for 3 seconds and choose the smell from a list of 4 descriptors [15]. No age or gender differences were noted. Sensory Rating Scales have also been developed for parents' ratings on the senses of their infants and toddlers that include the degree of responsively to all the senses, i.e. to taste, smell and touch stimuli along with hearing and vision [33]. A laboratory paradigm called The Sensory Challenge Protocol has also been developed for use with children with Autism Spectrum Disorder [55]. In that protocol all senses except taste are assessed by presenting timed stimuli like a fire engine siren and wintergreen oil.

Psychophysiological and electrophysiological measures have also been used such as changes in heart rate, blood pressure and respiration, odor event-related potentials (OERP) and the electro-olfactogram (EGM)[56]. These have not been widely used because of their variability and the invasiveness of the measures (e.g. electrodes in the nose for the electro-olfactogram). In one study, several of these measures were used in addition to a dopamine transporter scan (DaTSCAN) [34]. In this study the sensitivity of the UPSIT (86%) was not significantly different from the DaTSCAN (92%) and these measures were moderately correlated. However, The OERP was not correlated with the DaTSCAN and the EGM was not correlated with any of the other measures, highlighting again the clinical utility of the UPSIT for assessing odor identification.

Taste testing

The sense of taste is less often tested even though it is closely interconnected with the sense of smell. The less frequent assessment of taste function may relate to the lesser frequency of taste dysfunction. Some 95% of perceived taste disorders are reputedly caused by olfactory rather than gustatory loss [57]. The gustatory system (facial,glossopharyngeal and vagus nerves) is closely related to the olfactory system [9]. Often the same individuals who lose their sense of smell also complain that they have lost their sense of taste. One set of contradictory findings including data from both regional and whole mouth tests of 581 patients at a smell and taste center suggests that olfactory dysfunction did not affect taste perception when the effects of sex, age and etiology were controlled [37].

The taste buds (approximately 10,000 of them) are located in the mucosa of the epiglottis, the palate, the pharynx and the tongue with each taste bud having a receptor [58]. The sensory nerve fibers from the taste receptors are transmitted to the gustatory nucleus of the medulla oblongata by the facial, glossopharyngeal and vagal cranial nerves and from there to the thalamus and to the gustatory cortex [50]. Some have speculated that the involvement of multiple nerves in taste may explain the lower incidence of taste versus olfactory dysfunction [50]. Taste has typically been categorized as sweet, sour, bitter, salty and umami (savory) and the disorders ageusia (complete loss), dysgeusia (distorted perception) and hypogeusia (reduced ability to taste) can involve one or more of these 5 basic tastes [50].

A common test for taste perception includes ratings of 20 mixtures of 5 dairy drinks on sweetness, creaminess and pleasantness [59]. The participants are asked to take a sip of the mixture and swirl it around in their mouth and then make the ratings and spit out the mixture. In a recent study these ratings were tested for their test-retest reliability, and only the pleasantness ratings were reliable [35]. The authors suggested that simply rating pleasantness would make the test 83% shorter and result in less burden and unpleasantness for the participants as well as unconfined the test that was affected by negative states experienced by the participants.

Liquid taste solutions for sweet, sour, salty and bitter tastes have also been developed [36]. In this study, taste discrimination was superior in women but declined with age. Whole mouth and Taste Strip Tests have also been used [60].

Questionnaires are perhaps the simplest. In one study a 4 item questionnaire was used including ratings on 1)saltiness in chips, pretzels or salted nuts; 2)sourness in vinegar, pickles or lemons; 3) sweetness in soda, cookies or ice cream and 4)bitterness in coffee, beer or tonic water [57]. These authors claimed that patients who had no difficulty detecting these tastes rarely had taste dysfunction based on other tests. Perhaps with these less aversive taste tests more research will be conducted on taste dysfunction and its relationship to smell dysfunction.

Drug-induced taste disorder was the most common diagnosis among patients attending a taste clinic in Japan. Other disorders that have been associated with taste dysfunction include Parkinson's disease, multiple sclerosis, chronic kidney disease and cancer, studies that are reviewed in a later section on dysfunction.

Sensory Dysfunction in Neurodegenerative Diseases

Sensory dysfunction has been noted in neurodegenerative diseases including Parkinson's, Alzheimer's, and amyotrophic lateral sclerosis (Table 1). The commonality across these diseases is dopaminergic pathology and possibly damage to cholinergic, serotonergic and noradrenergic systems [8]. As some have noted,olfactory

Citation: Field T (2015) Smell and Taste Dysfunction as Early Markers for Neurodegenerative and Neuropsychiatric Diseases. J Alzheimers Dis Parkinsonism 5: 186. doi: 10.4172/2161-0460.1000186

Neurodegenerative diseases	Parkinson's –odor detection threshold, recognition and identification, taste, comorbid smell and color, smell and pain
	Alzheimer's-odor detection threshold, recognition and identification
	Amyotrophic lateral sclerosis-smell
	Autism spectrum disorder-odor identification
	Attention deficit/hyperactivity disorder-odor detection and identification
Neuropsychiatric diseases	Obsessive compulsive disorder-odor identification
	Posttraumatic stress disorder-odor identification
	Depression-odor detection threshold
	Schizophrenia-odor detection threshold, recognition and identification
	Irritable bowel syndrome- smell and taste
	Diabetes type 2-smell
Other diseases	Kidney disease-taste
	Multiple sclerosis-smell and taste
	Child survivors of cancer-taste

Table 1: Summary of smell and taste dysfunctions in different diseases.

dysfunction and less frequently gustatory dysfunction are early markers of neurodegenerative disease that precede the motor and cognitive disturbances by several years. Early diagnoses could lead to interventions including, for example, anti-inflammatory medications and olfactory training.

Parkinson's: Reputedly 95% of those with Parkinson's (PD) show dysfunctional smell (75% having hyposmia or anosmia) which apparently precedes the motor symptoms by approximately 4-6 years [9]. The smell dysfunction is more prevalent than tremors (approximately 75% more prevalent) and other signs [61]. Surprisingly, most of the individuals with PD are unaware of their smell dysfunction until they are tested [8]. Longitudinal studies have documented smell dysfunction in a significant number of asymptomatic first degree relatives of those with PD [62].

In a review of the literature on smell dysfunction in several diseases [8] made several "generalizations" about smell dysfunction in PD including: 1)the dysfunction is bilateral and is a better diagnostic marker than motor tests [63]; 2) as already mentioned, women with PD perform better on the tests than men [64]; 3)usually there is not a total loss of smell, i.e. the loss is usually hyposmia; 4)the poor performance on smell tests is not related to specific odorants; 5)the average score across many diseases including PD and early stage Alzheimer's is 20 on the UPSIT; 6)medications that are effective for the motoric dysfunction in PD are not effective for the olfactory dysfunction(e. g. dopamine agonists); 7)the olfactory dysfunction in PD is stable and is not stage-dependent or related to severity of the disease;8) the olfactory deficit precedes the motor signs often by several years, serving as a pre-motor marker [65]; and 9) some asymptomatic relatives have olfactory dysfunction that predicts later PD.

Some exceptions to the generalizations made by Dotty [8] have appeared in the literature. For example, in a recent study using the 16 Sniffin' sticks with 148 PD patients and 148 healthy controls, disease severity was associated with low odor identification scores [7]. In addition, although [8] suggested that poor performance on smell tests is not related to specific odorants, [7] reported that their Parkinson's patients had the most difficulty identifying the coffee, peppermint and anise odorants.

In a study on taste in Parkinson's, 61 patients were compared to controls on Whole Mouth and Taste Strip Tests [60]. Although the Parkinson's patients' Taste Strip Test scores were lower, their Whole Mouth Test scores did not differ from those of the control group. The authors suggested that these contradictory results may relate to taste dysfunction not being detectable at supra-threshold concentrations of daily life foods. In contrast, in another study on Parkinson's patients only the women patients' Taste Strip Test scores were inferior to controls [66]. The authors attributed this finding to the women's Mini-Mental State Examination score being lower. This potentially confounding variable may explain some of the mixed findings in the literature, although this exam on mental function typically has not been included in research protocols on taste and smell.

Comorbid sensory dysfunction has also been noted in PD patients including color and smells discrimination and pain and smell disturbances. In a study on color and smell discrimination in PD patients the UPSIT and the Farnsworth-Munsell Color Discrimination Tests were given [67]. Both color and smell discrimination were impaired in the PD patients, and color and smell scores were significantly correlated in the PD group.To assess pain and olfactory disturbance in PD patients, somatosensory evoked potentials (SEPs) were recorded and the Odor Stick Identification Test for Japanese (OSIT-J) was used [68]. Pain processing was impaired in the PD group and their OSIT-J scores were correlated with their SEP amplitude.

Several other non-motor symptoms have been reportedly associated with smell dysfunction in PD including sleep disturbances, gastric and bowel dysfunction, cardiovascular conditions, mood and cognition problems, depression and anxiety [34]. These authors reported that 26% of theparticipants in their Parkinson At-Risk Syndrome study who had four or more nonmotor complaints were hyposmic compared to only 12% who had three or fewer symptoms [34]. However, as [10] has suggested, these non-motor symptoms are common in the general population, except idiopathic REM sleep behavior disorder which is predictive of PD. These researchers suggest the use of more specific markers, i.e. serial dopamine transporter imaging even though the sensitivity of the scan is reportedly similar to the sensitivity of the UPSIT which is much cheaper [34]. Nonetheless, identification deficits have effectively differentiated idiopathic from non-idiopathic Parkinsonism in at least one study [69].

Alzheimer's: Olfactory dysfunction is reputedly as serious in patients with Alzheimer's (AD) as it is in those with PD [9]. A meta-analysis studyrevealed that early AD could not be distinguished from early PD by odor tests [70]. However, unlike the mixed literature on the relationship between olfactory dysfunction and severity of PD, olfactory dysfunction and severity of AD were correlated. A more recent meta-analysis suggested that while both AD and PD patients were more impaired on odor identification and recognition tasks than odor detection thresholds, the PD patients did not perform as well as AD patients on detection thresholds [11]. A study on first-degree relatives at risk for Alzheimer's disease also reported olfactory dysfunction as an early biomarker [27].

The recent study using peanut butter odor detection suggested that AD patients had left nostril detection problems but not right nostril problems which is consistent with their having more degeneration of their left than right hemisphere (olfactory detection being ipsilateral) [14]. However, as already mentioned, another group failed to replicate this asymmetry using the same test [3].

In AD patients the olfactory dysfunction symptoms apparently emerge before cognitive deficits [71]. In a study using the Sniffin'Sticks odor identification test, AD patients also had significantly higher levels

Citation: Field T (2015) Smell and Taste Dysfunction as Early Markers for Neurodegenerative and Neuropsychiatric Diseases. J Alzheimers Dis Parkinsonism 5: 186. doi: 10.4172/2161-0460.1000186

of apathy relative to non-AD participants, but odor identification deficits were correlated with apathy levels, not depression, across the AD and non-AD samples [13].

Amyotrophic lateral sclerosis

In a study on amyotrophic lateral sclerosis (ALS) also known as Lou Gehrig's disease ALS patients' UPSIT scores were significantly lower than they were for a control group [72].

Sensory dysfunction in neuropsychiatric diseases

Sensory dysfunction is also an early marker for neuropsychiatric diseases including autism spectrum disorder, attention deficit/hyperactivity disorder, eating disorders, depression, obsessive compulsive disorder, posttraumatic stress disorder and schizophrenia, with the lion's share of the published research being on attention deficit/hyperactivity disorder and schizophrenia. And, as in neurodegenerative diseases, smell testing has been the most prevalent assessment of early biomarkers.

Autism spectrum disorder (ASD): Children and adolescents with autism spectrum disorder have shown poor performance on smell tests [73]. Although they are noted to have hypersensitive responses to visual and auditory stimuli, they have diminished olfactory function. In a study comparing individuals with ASD and Asperger syndrome, olfactory identification (higher-order olfactory processing) was impaired in the individuals with ASD relative to the participants with Asperger's [19]. However, their odor detection thresholds and discrimination abilities (lower-order processing) were not affected. In a recent review, two unpublished data sets on olfactory dysfunction in children with autism were consistent with the published data [16]. Potential confounding effects are related to the cognitive dysfunction, attention problems and sleep disorders of these children [74]. These data on children with ASD are, nonetheless,similar to findings on detection thresholds in adults with ASD [20].

Attention deficit/hyperactivity disorder (ADHD): In a review of olfactory function in children and adolescents with psychiatric disorders, the authors noted that those disorders that involved smell dysfunction also had pathology related to dopamine metabolism and orbito frontal cortex functioning including ASD, ADHD, obsessive compulsive disorder (OCD) and schizophrenia [16]. They also suggested that the child and adolescent smell dysfunction literature is much more limited than the adult literature and mentioned the heterogeneity of findings that they ascribed to methodological limitations including confounding variables like intelligence and infections and the use of different tests and odors. Their attention deficits alone could contribute to their smell dysfunction along with their sleep disorders.

Studies on children and adolescents with ADHD suggest alterations in olfactory processing (identification and detection threshold) [75,76] that are consistent with findings on ADHD adults [77,78]. In a more recent study odor detection was assessed with phenyl ethyl alcohol and odor identification with the essences of apple, banana, lemon and orange [15]. Both the Sensory Threshold Score and the Sensory Identification Score were lower for the group of children with ADHD than a group of non-ADHD children who were matched on age, gender and Mean School Scores. Further, the dysfunctions in detection and identification wereunrelated to age, gender and School Scores.

In contrast, thereare studies showing increased olfactory sensitivity in ADHD. For example, in one study odor sensitivity (lower thresholds) was noted in those ADHD individuals who were not on medications [76].This enhanced function was normalized under stimulant

medication. Just as individuals with ADHD may be hyperactive without stimulant medication, they may be hypersensitive without medication. Other sensory modalities might be examined in this population to determine whether this hypersensitivity crosses senses.

Anxiety disorders: A recent review suggests that anxiety disorders have rarely been assessed for olfactory dysfunction.However, those with obsessive compulsive disorder (OCD) and posttraumatic stress disorder (PTSD) appear to have identification deficits [17].

Depression: Depressed individuals have been characterized as having normal olfactory function except for detection threshold [79,17]. In a study on depressed individuals, smell threshold, discrimination and identification as well as chemosensory event related potentialsand functional magnetic resonance imagingwas assessed[21]. At the beginning of psychotherapy the female inpatients with depression had reduced smell discrimination, prolonged latencies on the event related potentials and reduced activation in olfactory structures including the thalamus, insula and left middle orbitofrontal cortex. By the end of the psychotherapy period the depressed women did not differ from the healthy age-matched women.It is not clear how psychotherapy could alter smell discrimination and the associated event related potentials and activation of olfactory structures. The preserved performance on identification tasks by individuals with depression has made it a suitable tool for differential diagnosis of other pathologies like Alzheimer's disease [80]. As in Parkinson's and Alzheimer's, depressed individuals have sleep disorders and are often on medications that can confound the assessments of sensory function[81].

Schizophrenia: Deficits in the odor identification domain have been reported consistently across many studies on individuals with schizophrenia [79,82]. In the [82] meta-analytic study, substantial olfactory deficits were noted across all domains (identification, detection threshold sensitivity, discrimination and memory) in patients with schizophrenia.And no differential deficits were noted across those domains. Further, they noted no significant gender, medication or smoking effects. These authors suggested that their meta-analytic review "supports the hypothesis of primary dysfunction in the olfactory system that is regulated by brain regions where structural and functional abnormalities have also been reported in neuroimaging studies" [82].

In contrast, in a recent study, patients with schizophrenia did not differ from psychiatric outpatients on olfactory function, although those with schizotypy rated smells as less pleasant than healthy control participants [23]. The authors concluded that olfactory identification problems may be characteristic of several severe mental illnesses. On the other hand, at least two research groups have identified relationships between olfactory dysfunction and negative symptoms of schizophrenia (blunted affect, apathy and anhedonia). One group used the UPSIT and assessed positive and negative symptoms using the Scales for the Assessment of Positive and Negative Symptoms (SAPS and SANS) [24]. They reported a correlation of SANS with UPSIT performance, but particularly with blunted affect, apathy and anhedonia. The positive symptom scores (hallucinations, delusions) were not correlated with smell identification. In a more complex study, similar findings were noted [25]. In this paradigm, the severity of negative symptoms in individuals with schizophrenia was associated with reduced olfactory event-related potentials and poorer odor detection, identification and thresholds. Sex differences were noted in a third study that explored the relationship between olfaction and cognition in patients with schizophrenia [26]. In this study better smell identification was associated with better cognition on several measures, but especially in female patients.

Citation: Field T (2015) Smell and Taste Dysfunction as Early Markers for Neurodegenerative and Neuropsychiatric Diseases. J Alzheimers Dis Parkinsonism 5: 186. doi: 10.4172/2161-0460.1000186

Other diseases: Smell and/or taste dysfunctions have also been noted in other diseases including irritable bowel disease, diabetes type 2, kidney disease, multiple sclerosis and child survivors of cancer. Diabetes type 2 patients as compared with a group with Diabetes type 1 showed impaired smell function but no taste dysfunction in at least one study [83]. Patients with irritable bowel disease (Crohn's disease and ulcerative colitis), on the other hand, have been noted to have both smell and taste dysfunction [84]. In that study 58% of the patients were hyposmic (less olfactory function) and 31% were hypogeusic (less gustatory function).

Gustatory function and olfactory function have also been assessed in patients with multiple sclerosis by the Taste-Powder Test and the Threshold, Discrimination and Identification Sniffin' Sticks [85]. There was a significant loss in gustatory function in 22% of the patients and a significant loss in olfactory function in 40% of the patients. The complex cognitive tasks on the olfactory test may confound these results as might the disability status of the patients as well as the depression and fatigue that they often experience.

Children with various medical conditions have also been given taste and smell tests. For example, children with advanced chronic kidney disease have scored lower on taste tests than clinical and healthy control children [86]. Their smell test scores did not differ from the control children, although their smell scores were correlated with their BMIs which were an expressed concern of the authors inasmuch as these children often have loss of appetite and delayed growth.

Child survivors of cancer who were assessed more than five years after the end of chemotherapy scored lower on a taste identification test (25 sample taste test) but not on a smell test (16 common odorants) [87]. Taste dysfunction was noted in 28% of the children while smell dysfunction was only noted in 4% of the children. Food preferences were also assessed on a 94-item list. Although the children preferred less healthy foods such as flavored drinks, takeaway and snack foods, taste dysfunction and food preferences were not related. It is not clear whether these apparent side effects of cancer therapy on taste dysfunction also affect the actual diet of these children.

Potential Underlying Mechanisms

Underlying mechanism studies havebeen conducted, most frequently in animal models, although with the increasing use of fMRI and neuro transmitter metabolite testing, central nervous systems have been implicated including the orbito frontal cortex and several neurotransmitter systems, mainly the nor adrenergic, serotonergic and dopaminergic systems [8]. Although several of the neurodegenerative diseases, e.g. Parkinson's and Alzheimer's and the neuropsychiatric conditions, e.g. ADHD and schizophrenia, involved opaminergic pathology, the research on that pathology is lacking, probably because of the complex interactions between the dopaminergic and other neurotransmitter systems(i.e.serotonergic and noradrenergic systems) and the greater expense of the research (urine metabolites still being the only non-invasive assays of these).

Other mechanisms have been explored including damaged olfactory epithelium, aberrant proteins in the olfactory bulb and altered transmission through the primary and secondary olfactory centers and intersensory region of the brain [3]. Examples of these are neuropathology studies on the olfactory bulb [88], including studies on Lewy bodies in the olfactory bulb [89,90] and studies showing limited gray matter volume in the right piriform cortex and the right amygdala [91].

Environmental agents such as herbicides, pesticides, solvents and viruses have also been implicated. Data on the effects of these agents come from large sample studies. For example, in a study on 5000 patients at The Taste and Smell Clinic in Washington, D.C. 27% of the patients had influenza-related smell loss and 15% of smell loss patients had allergic rhinitis [92]. And, in a study on 132 patients from the first Smell and Taste Clinic in Thailand, as many as 67% of the smell disorder patients had sinonasal disease followed by head injury (12%), idiopathic cause (11%), and upper respiratory tract infection (7%) [93]. Sinonasal disease has been implicated in 52-72% of olfactory disorders [54] and head trauma is a frequent cause of olfactory loss [50].

Medications can also affect the dopamine system, interfering with the ability to detect olfactory dysfunction. For example, a rat study showed that antipsychotics (haloperidol) increased dopamine (D2) receptors in schizophrenia which were most noticeable in the olfactory tubercle [94]. Methylphenidate (an amphetamine-like drug commonly used by those with ADHD) has been noted to increase dopamine transporter inhibition in mice [95]. This effect could explain the mixed findings on olfactory dysfunction in children with ADHD. A further example is the use ofL-dopa therapy which increases dopamine metabolism in the mouse model of Parkinson's disease [96].

Potential Interventions

As already noted in[8] list of generalizations regarding the sensory dysfunction in individuals with Parkinson's, the medications that have been effective with the motor dysfunction of PD have no effect on the loss of sense of smell, specifically L-DOPA, the dopamine agonists and the anticholinergic drugs [8,97]. Odor discrimination deficits have been noted in mice who are lacking the dopamine transporter [98]. However, giving a dopamine agonist to rats has enhanced their odor detection performance [99], although these effects were weak,and there is no evidence that these findings would generalize to humans. Some have noted positive effects of estradiol on induced smell dysfunction in rats [39]. Others have reported that anti-inflammatory medicationssuch as methylprednisolone are effective [9].

The psychosocial stress that reduces serotonin also influences odor detection [100]. Massage therapy (and similar treatments like acupuncture and progressive muscle relaxation) have been noted to increase serotonin and dopamine, two systems that have been implicated in olfactory impairment [101]. Massage therapy has also been effective in reducing sleep disturbances in Parkinson's along with enhancing their activities of daily living as well as increasing the production of serotonin and dopamine [102], although we did not assess the patients' motor or olfactory function. The positive effects of massage therapy have been especially noted following moderate pressure massage and attributed to the stimulation of pressure receptors and enhanced vagal activity [103].

Repetitive trans cranial magnetic stimulation has also been assessed for its effects on smell and taste dysfunction [104]. In this study both taste and smell acuity were improved in 88 percent of the patients, although repeated sessions were necessary to achieve these effects. Acupuncture has been assessed for its effects on olfactory function [105]. In this placebo-controlled, randomized trial, acupuncture (laser needle) enhanced olfactory sensitivity (lowered olfactory detection thresholds) in healthy subjects even though half the subjects were skeptical about the treatment. Although the authors called this a double-blinded study, it's not clear how an acupuncture study could be single-blinded let alone double-blinded. Nonetheless, the stimulation of pressure receptors by acupuncture, as in massage therapy, might be expected to have positive effects on sensory functioning.

Citation: Field T (2015) Smell and Taste Dysfunction as Early Markers for Neurodegenerative and Neuropsychiatric Diseases. J Alzheimers Dis Parkinsonism 5: 186. doi: 10.4172/2161-0460.1000186

Limitations of The Literature and Future Directions

Odor identification deficits have been documented in many studies on neurodegenerative (mostly Parkinson's and Alzheimer's) and neuropsychiatric diseases (mostly ADHD and schizophrenia) since the development of the UPSIT. The UPSIT as well as several other abbreviated, less expensive and more culturally appropriate forms of the olfactory test have had high sensitivity and specificity ratings and they have been highly correlated. They are easy to administer and inexpensive (especially the latest peanut butter identification test) even though they are difficult to compare and to meta-analyze because of the different odorants used, the different cognitive demands made by the tests and the cross-cultural differences noted.

Comorbid sensory dysfunction is also probable given the interacting nervous systems.Research that assessesmultiple senses may further enhance the identification of early markers of these diseases, e.g. smell and taste, smell and pain.Studies on comorbid sensory dysfunction have been limited. For example, taste research, as already mentioned, has been limited possibly because it is more expensive to assess and, except for ratings of pleasantness, can be more aversive for participants. And, the assessment of pain is more difficult for human subjects forethical reasons, except for some limited assessments, for example, thresholds of different pressure points with a dolorimeter. Nonetheless, the study of other dysfunctional senses may more accurately identify and differentiate the risk, for example, for Parkinson's versus Alzheimer's. Making differential diagnoses is increasingly a problem as these sensory dysfunctions are associated with increasing numbers of neurodegenerative and neuropsychiatric conditions.

The treatment literature has been primarily limited to animal models, and the human treatment research has not been blinded, let alone double-blinded. Treatments have not been compared and effective treatment studies have not been replicated. The treatment literature is far less developed than the literature on the use of olfactory identification tests as early biomarkers of neurodegenerative and neuropsychiatric diseases. The purpose of identifying early biomarkers is to be able to identify those at risk for the development of the diseases and to then provide preventive interventions. Having documented olfactory dysfunction might naturally lead to olfactory training [106], but these training needs to be replicated and compared with other treatments using randomized trials and at least blind assignment to groups.

Anti-inflammatory medications may be promising inasmuch as they have been effective in the animal model. Having shown that dopamine and serotonin deficits are associated with olfactory dysfunction may lead to the use of agonists, although at least in two studies [8,97],agonists have not been effective for the olfactory dysfunction as they had been for motor impairment.

A further consideration is the target intervention groups and whether they should have multiple risk factors including being the first-degree relatives of those who have the disease and having tested positive for anosmia or at least hyposmia. Identifying early biomarkers for neurodegenerative and neuropsychiatric diseases may be a moot process ifthere are no effective preventive interventions. Although olfactory testing has identified several neurodegenerative and neuropsychiatric diseases, the intervention literature is lacking, and it is not clear whether different preventive interventions may need to be tailored to different diseases.

Potential future directions are suggested by the current limitations of the literature. More replications are needed, using the same olfactory assessments and including the same odorants. More research is needed on central olfactory problems like discrimination and memory and peripheral problems like sensory threshold.Research on multiple senses is needed to more accurately differentiate the at-risk disease that close relatives may ultimately experience. Cost-effective tests like the UPSIT need to be developed for the other senses so that comorbidities can be identified. Having multiple reliable early sense biomarkers may help with differential diagnoses and with designing protocols for preventive interventions. Studies are needed on the relationships between the senses biomarkers like olfactory dysfunction and the motor signs of the different diseases, e.g. the bradykinesia, tremors, rigidity and postural instability of Parkinson's. Little is known about the relationships between the early sensory and motor biomarkers. Additional research is needed on the interactions between the neurotransmitter systems. In the interim, at least those who are at risk by virtue of being first- degree relatives can be tested with these cost-effective reliablesensory tests.

Acknowledgements

I would like to thank all the adults and mothers and infants who participated in our studies and most especially my colleagues who collaborated on them. Our studies were supported by an NIMH Merit Award (#MH46586)and NIH Senior Scientist Awards (#MH00331 and #AT01585) to Tiffany Field and funding from Johnson and Johnson and Colgate-Palmolive to the Touch Research Institute. Correspondence can be addressed to tfield@med.miami.edu or Tiffany Field, 2889 McFarlane Rd, Miami, Fl 33133. Phone 305-975-5029.

References

1. Hoskison EE (2013) Olfaction, pheromones and life. J Laryngol Otol 127: 1156-1159.

2. Doty RL (2009) The olfactory system and its disorders. Semin Neurol 29: 74-81.

3. Doty RL, Kamath V (2014) The influences of age on olfaction: a review. Front Psychol 5: 20.

4. Gregorio LL, Caparroz F, Nunes LM, Neves LR, Macoto EK (2014) Olfaction disorders: retrospective study. Braz J Otorhinolaryngol 80: 11-17.

5. Mullol J, Alobid I, Marino-Sanchez F, Quinto L, de Haro J, et al. (2012). Furthering the understanding of olfaction, prevalence of loss of smell and risk factors: a population-based survey (OLFACAT study). BMJ Open 2: 1-13.

6. Orhan KS, Karabulut B, KeleÂŸ N, DeÂŸer K (2012) Evaluation of factors concerning the olfaction using the Sniffin' Sticks test. Otolaryngol Head Neck Surg 146: 240-246.

7. Casjens S, Eckert A, Woitalla D, Ellrichmann G, Turewicz M, et al. (2013) Diagnostic value of the impairment of olfaction in Parkinson's disease. PLoS One 8: e64735.

8. Doty RL (2012) Olfaction in Parkinson's disease and related disorders. Neurobiol Dis 46: 527-552.

9. Huttenbrink, KB, Hummel, T, Berg, D, Gasser, T, Hahner, A (2013) Olfactory Dysfunction: Common in Later Life and Early Warning of Neurodegenerative Disease. Deutsches Arzteblatt International, 110: 1-7.

10. Iranzo, A (2013) Parkinson Disease and Sleep: Sleep-Wake changes in the Premotor Stage of Parkinson Disease; Impaired Olfaction and Other Prodromal Features. Current Neurology and Neuroscience Reports 13:373

11. Rahayel S, Frasnelli J, Joubert S (2012) The effect of Alzheimer's disease and Parkinson's disease on olfaction: a meta-analysis. Behav Brain Res 231: 60-74.

12. Siderowf A, Jennings D, Eberly S, Oakes D, Hawkins KA, et al. (2012) Impaired olfaction and other prodromal features in the Parkinson At-Risk Syndrome Study. MovDisord 27: 406-412.

13. Seligman SC, Kamath V, Giovannetti T, Arnold SE, Moberg PJ (2013) Olfaction and apathy in Alzheimer's disease, mild cognitive impairment, and healthy older adults. Aging Ment Health 17: 564-570.

14. Stamps JJ, Bartoshuk LM, Heilman KM (2013) A brief olfactory test for Alzheimer's disease. J NeurolSci 333: 19-24.

Citation: Field T (2015) Smell and Taste Dysfunction as Early Markers for Neurodegenerative and Neuropsychiatric Diseases. J Alzheimers Dis Parkinsonism 5: 186. doi: 10.4172/2161-0460.1000186

15. Ghanizadeh A, Bahrani M, Miri R, Sahraian A (2012) Smell identification function in children with attention deficit hyperactivity disorder. Psychiatry Investig 9: 150-153.

16. Schecklmann M, Schwenck C, Taurines R, Freitag C, Warnke A, et al. (2013) A systematic review on olfaction in child and adolescent psychiatric disorders. J Neural Transm 120: 121-130.

17. Burón E, Bulbena A (2013) Olfaction in affective and anxiety disorders: a review of the literature. Psychopathology 46: 63-74.

18. Ben-Sasson A, Hen L, Fluss R, Cermak SA, Engel-Yeger B, et al. (2009) A meta-analysis of sensory modulation symptoms in individuals with autism spectrum disorders. J Autism DevDisord 39: 1-11.

19. Galle SA, Courchesne V, Mottron L, Frasnelli J (2013) Olfaction in the autism spectrum. Perception 42: 341-355.

20. Tavassoli T, Baron-Cohen S (2012) Olfactory detection thresholds and adaptation in adults with autism spectrum condition. J Autism DevDisord 42: 905-909.

21. Croy I, Symmank A2, Schellong J2, Hummel C3, Gerber J4, et al. (2014) Olfaction as a marker for depression in humans. J Affect Disord 160: 80-86.

22. Dazzi F, Nitto SD, Zambetti G, Loriedo C, Ciofalo A (2013) Alterations of the olfactory-gustatory functions in patients with eating disorders. Eur Eat Disord Rev 21: 382-385.

23. Auster TL, Cohen AS, Callaway DA, Brown LA (2014) Objective and subjective olfaction across the schizophrenia spectrum. Psychiatry 77: 57-66.

24. Ishizuka K, Tajinda K, Colantuoni C, Morita M, Winicki J, et al. (2010) Negative symptoms of schizophrenia correlate with impairment on the University of Pennsylvania smell identification test. Neurosci Res 66: 106-110.

25. Kayser J, Tenke CE, Kroppmann CJ, Alschuler DM, Ben-David S, et al. (2013) Olfaction in the psychosis prodrome: electrophysiological and behavioral measures of odor detection. Int J Psychophysiol 90: 190-206.

26. Malaspina D, Keller A, Antonius D, Messinger JW, Goetz DM, et al. (2012) Olfaction and cognition in schizophrenia: sex matters. J Neuropsychiatry Clin Neurosci 24: 165-175.

27. Serby M, Mohan C, Aryan M, Williams L, Mohs RC, et al. (1996) Olfactory identification deficits in relatives of Alzheimer's disease patients. Biol Psychiatry 39: 375-377.

28. Krantz EM, Schubert CR, Dalton DS, Zhong W, Huang GH, et al. (2009) Test-retest reliability of the San Diego Odor Identification Test and comparison with the brief smell identification test. Chem Senses 34: 435-440.

29. Haxel BR, Bertz-Duffy S, Fruth K, Letzel S, Mann WJ, et al. (2012) Comparison of subjective olfaction ratings in patients with and without olfactory disorders. J LaryngolOtol 126: 692-697.

30. Fornazieri MA, Doty RL, Santos CA, Pinna Fde R, Bezerra TF, et al. (2013) A new cultural adaptation of the University of Pennsylvania Smell Identification Test. Clinics (Sao Paulo) 68: 65-68.

31. Seki K, Tsuruta K, Inatsu A, Fukumoto Y, Shigeta M (2013) [Classification of reduced sense of smell in women with Parkinson's disease]. Nihon Ronen Igakkai Zasshi 50: 243-248.

32. Hong JY, Chung SJ, Lee JE, Sunwoo MK, Lee PH et al. (2013) Predictive Value of the Smell Identification Test for Nigrostriatal Dopaminergic Depletion in Korean Tremor Patients. Parkinsonism and Related Disorders 19: 1018-1021.

33. Eeles AL, Spittle AJ, Anderson PJ, Brown N, Lee KJ, et al. (2013) Assessments of sensory processing in infants: a systematic review. Dev Med Child Neurol 55: 314-326.

34. Deeb J, Shah M, Muhammed N, Gunasekera R, Gannon K, et al. (2010) A basic smell test is as sensitive as a dopamine transporter scan: comparison of olfaction, taste and DaTSCAN in the diagnosis of Parkinson's disease. QJM 103: 941-952.

35. Coulon SM, Miller AC, Reed JM, Martin CK (2012) Reliability of a common solution-based taste perception test: implications for validity and a briefer test. Eat Behav 13: 42-45.

36. Pingel J, Ostwald J, Pau HW, Hummel T, Just T (2010) Normative data for a solution-based taste test. Eur Arch Otorhinolaryngol 267: 1911-1917.

37. Stinton N, Atif MA, Barkat N, Doty RL (2010) Influence of smell loss on taste function. Behav Neurosci 124: 256-264.

38. Sara SJ (2009) The locus coeruleus and noradrenergic modulation of cognition. Nat Rev Neurosci 10: 211-223.

39. Bernal-Mondragón C, Rivas-Arancibia S, Kendrick KM, Guevara-Guzmán R (2013) Estradiol prevents olfactory dysfunction induced by A-I² 25-35 injection in hippocampus. BMC Neurosci 14: 104.

40. Cowart B, Beauchamp G (1998) Development of taste and smell in the neonate. In Poln R.A. & Fox, W.W. (eds). Fetal Neonatal Physiology, W.B. Saunders. Co., Philadelphia.

41. Menella JA, Beauchamp GK (1991)Olfactory preferences in children and adults. In Laing, D.G., Doty, R.L. &Breipohl (eds) The Human Sense of Smell, Springer-Verlag, New York.

42. Schaal B (1998) Olfaction in infants and children: Developmental and functional perspectives. Chemical Senses, 13:145-190.

43. Marlier L, Schaal B, Soussignan R (1998) Neonatal responsiveness to the odor of amniotic and lacteal fluids: a test of perinatal chemosensory continuity. Child Dev 69: 611-623.

44. Varendi H, Christensson K, Porter RH, Winberg J (1998) Soothing effect of amniotic fluid smell in newborn infants. Early Hum Dev 51: 47-55.

45. Rieser J, Yonas A, Wikner K (1976) Radial localization of odors by human newborns. Child Dev 47: 856-859.

46. Field T, Field T, Cullen C, Largie S, Diego M, et al. (2008) Lavender bath oil reduces stress and crying and enhances sleep in very young infants. Early Hum Dev 84: 399-401.

47. Fernandez M, Hernandez-Reif M, Field T, Diego M, Sanders Cet al. (2004) EEG during lavender and rosemary exposure in infants of depressed and non-depressed mothers. Infant Behavior and Development, 27:91-100.

48. Diego MA, Jones NA, Field T, Hernandez-Reif M, Schanberg S, et al. (1998) Aromatherapy positively affects mood, EEG patterns of alertness and math computations. Int J Neurosci 96: 217-224.

49. Field T, Diego M, Hernandez-Reif M, Cisneros W, Feijo L, et al. (2005) Lavender fragrance cleansing gel effects on relaxation. Int J Neurosci 115: 207-222.

50. Malaty J, Malaty IA (2013) Smell and taste disorders in primary care. Am Fam Physician 88: 852-859.

51. Naudin M, Mondon K, Atanasova B (2013) [Alzheimer's disease and olfaction]. GeriatrPsycholNeuropsychiatrVieil 11: 287-293.

52. Hummel T, Landis BN, Hüttenbrink KB (2011) [Dysfunction of the chemical senses smell and taste]. Laryngorhinootologie 90 Suppl 1: S44-55.

53. Doty RL, Bayona EA, Leon-Ariza DS, Cuadros J, Chung I, et al. (2014) The lateralized smell test for detecting Alzheimer's disease: failure to replicate. J NeurolSci 340: 170-173.

54. Landis BN, Stow NW, Lacroix JS, Hugentobler M, Hummel T (2009) Olfactory disorders: the patients' view. Rhinology 47: 454-459.

55. Mcintosh DN, Miller LJ, Shyu V, Hagerman RJ (1999) Sensory-Modulation Disruption, Electrodermal Responses and functional Behaviours. Developmetal Medicine & Child Neurology 41: 608-615.

56. Doty RL, Cometto-Muñiz JE, Jalowayski AA, Dalton P, Kendal-Reed M, et al. (2004) Assessment of upper respiratory tract and ocular irritative effects of volatile chemicals in humans. Crit Rev Toxicol 34: 85-142.

57. Soter A, Kim J, Jackman A, Tourbier I, Kaul A, et al. (2008) Accuracy of self-report in detecting taste dysfunction. Laryngoscope 118: 611-617.

58. Deems DA, Doty RL, Settle RG, Moore-Gillon V, Shaman P, et al. (1991) Smell and taste disorders, a study of 750 patients from the University of Pennsylvania Smell and Taste Center. Arch Otolaryngol Head Neck Surg 117: 519-528.

59. Drewnowski A, Greenwood MR (1983) Cream and sugar: human preferences for high-fat foods. PhysiolBehav 30: 629-633.

60. Cecchini MP, Osculati F, Ottaviani S, Boschi F, Fasano A, et al. (2014) Taste performance in Parkinsonâ€™s disease. J Neural Transm 121: 119-122.

61. Alves G, Forsaa EB, Pedersen KF, Dreetz Gjerstad M, Larsen JP (2008) Epidemiology of Parkinson's disease. J Neurol 255 Suppl 5: 18-32.

62. Ponsen MM, Stoffers D, Wolters EC, Booij J, Berendse HW (2010) Olfactory Testing Combined with Dopamine Transporter Imaging as a Method to Detect Prodromal Parkinson´s Disease. Journal of Neurology. Neurosurgery & Psychiatry 81: 396-399.

Citation: Field T (2015) Smell and Taste Dysfunction as Early Markers for Neurodegenerative and Neuropsychiatric Diseases. J Alzheimers Dis Parkinsonism 5: 186. doi: 10.4172/2161-0460.1000186

63. Bohnen NI, Studenski SA, Constantine GM, Moore RY (2008) Diagnostic performance of clinical motor and non-motor tests of Parkinson disease: a matched case-control study. Eur J Neurol 15: 685-691.

64. Stern MB, Doty RL, Dotti M, Corcoran P, Crawford D, et al. (1994) Olfactory function in Parkinson's disease subtypes. Neurology 44: 266-268.

65. Haehner A, Hummel T, Hummel C, Sommer U, Junghanns S, et al. (2007) Olfactory loss may be a first sign of idiopathic Parkinson's disease. Mov Disord 22: 839-842.

66. Kim HJ, Jeon BS, Lee JY, Cho YJ, Hong KS, et al. (2011) Taste function in patients with Parkinson disease. J Neurol 258: 1076-1079.

67. Kertelge L, Bruggemann N, Schmidt A, Tadic V, Wisse C, et al. (2010) Impaired Sense of Smell and Color Discrimination in Monogenic and Idiopathic Parkinson's Disease. Movement Disorders 25: 2665-2669.

68. Hara T, Hirayama M, Mizutani Y, Hama T, Hori N, et al. (2013) Impaired pain processing in Parkinson's disease and its relative association with the sense of smell. Parkinsonism RelatDisord 19: 43-46.

69. Müller A, Müngersdorf M, Reichmann H, Strehle G, Hummel T (2002) Olfactory function in Parkinsonian syndromes. J ClinNeurosci 9: 521-524.

70. Mesholam RI, Moberg PJ, Mahr RN, Doty RL (1998) Olfaction in neurodegenerative disease: a meta-analysis of olfactory functioning in Alzheimer's and Parkinson's diseases. Arch Neurol 55: 84-90.

71. Wilson RS, Arnold SE, Schneider JA, Boyle PA, Buchman AS, et al. (2009) Olfactory impairment in presymptomatic Alzheimer's disease. Ann N Y Acad Sci 1170: 730-735.

72. Hawkes CH, Shephard BC, Geddes JF, Body GD, Martin JE (1998) Olfactory disorder in motor neuron disease. Exp Neurol 150: 248-253.

73. Bennetto L, Kuschner ES, Hyman SL (2007) Olfaction and taste processing in autism. Biol Psychiatry 62: 1015-1021.

74. Escalona A, Field T, Singer-Strunck R, Cullen C, Hartshorn K (2001) Brief report: improvements in the behavior of children with autism following massage therapy. J Autism Dev Disord 31: 513-516.

75. Karsz FR, Vance A, Anderson VA, Brann PG, Wood SJ, et al. (2008) Olfactory impairments in child attention-deficit/hyperactivity disorder. J Clin Psychiatry 69: 1462-1468.

76. Romanos M, Renner TJ, SchecklmannM, Hummel B, RoosM,et al. (2008) Improved odor Sensitivity in Attention-Deficit/Hyperactivity Disorder. Biological Psychiatry 64: 938-940.

77. Gansler DA, Fucetola R, Krengel M, Stetson S, Zimering R, et al. (1998) Are there cognitive subtypes in adult attention deficit/hyperactivity disorder? J Nerv Ment Dis 186: 776-781.

78. Murphy KR, Barkley RA, Bush T (2001) Executive functioning and olfactory identification in young adults with attention deficit-hyperactivity disorder. Neuropsychology 15: 211-220.

79. Atanasova B, GrauxJ, EHage W, Hommet C, Camus V, et al. (2008) Olfaction: a potential cognitive marker of psychiatric disorders. Neurosci Biobehav Rev 32: 1315-1325.

80. McCaffrey RJ, Duff K, Solomon GS (2000) Olfactory dysfunction discriminates probable Alzheimer's dementia from major depression: a cross-validation and extension. J Neuropsychiatry ClinNeurosci 12: 29-33.

81. Field T, Diego M, Hernandez-Reif M, Figueiredo B, Schanberg S, et al. (2007) Sleep disturbances in depressed pregnant women and their newborns. Infant Behav Dev 30: 127-133.

82. Moberg PJ, Agrin R, Gur RE, Gur RC, Turetsky BI, et al. (1999) Olfactory dysfunction in schizophrenia: a qualitative and quantitative review. Neuropsychopharmacology 21: 325-340.

83. Naka A, Riedl M, Luger A, Hummel T, Mueller CA (2010) Clinical significance of smell and taste disorders in patients with diabetes mellitus. Eur Arch Otorhinolaryngol 267: 547-550.

84. Steinbach S, Reindl W, Dempfle A, Schuster A, Wolf P, et al. (2013) Smell and taste in inflammatory bowel disease. PLoS One 8: e73454.

85. Dahlslett SB, Goektas O, Schmidt F, Harms L, Olze H, et al. (2012) Psychophysiological and electrophysiological testing of olfactory and gustatory function in patients with multiple sclerosis. Eur Arch Otorhinolaryngol 269: 1163-1169.

86. Armstrong JE, Laing DG, Wilkes FJ, Kainer G (2010) Smell and taste function in children with chronic kidney disease. Pediatr Nephrol 25: 1497-1504.

87. Cohen J, Laing DG2, Wilkes FJ3, Chan A4, Gabriel M5, et al. (2014) Taste and smell dysfunction in childhood cancer survivors. Appetite 75: 135-140.

88. Braak H, Ghebremedhin E, Rüb U, Bratzke H, Del Tredici K (2004) Stages in the development of Parkinson's disease-related pathology. Cell Tissue Res 318: 121-134.

89. Hubbard PS, Esiri MM, Reading M, Mc Shane R, Nagy Z (2007) Alpha-synuclein pathology in the olfactory pathways of dementia patients. J Anat 211: 117-124.

90. Wilson RS, Yu L, Schneider JA, Arnold SE, Buchman AS, et al. (2011) Lewy bodies and olfactory dysfunction in old age. Chem Senses 36: 367-373.

91. Wattendorf E, Welge-Lüssen A, Fiedler K, Bilecen D, Wolfensberger M, et al. (2009) Olfactory impairment predicts brain atrophy in Parkinson's disease. J Neurosci 29: 15410-15413.

92. Henkin RI, Levy LM, Fordyce A (2013) Taste and smell function in chronic disease: a review of clinical and biochemical evaluations of taste and smell dysfunction in over 5000 patients at The Taste and Smell Clinic in Washington, DC. Am J Otolaryngol 34: 477-489.

93. Kaolawanich A, Assanasen P, Tunsuriyawong P, Bunnag C, Tantilipikorn P (2009) Smell disorders: a study of 132 patients from the first Smell and Taste Clinic of Thailand. J Med Assoc Thai 92: 1057-1062.

94. Joyce J (2001) D2 but not D3 receptors are elevated after 9 or 11 months chronic haloperidol treatment: Influence of withdrawal period. Synapse 40: 137-44.

95. Calipari E, Ferris M, Salahpour A, Caron M, Jones S (2013) Methylphenidate amplifies the potency and reinforcing effects of amphetamines by increasing dopamine transporter expression. Nat Commun 4: 272-3.

96. Smith ML, King J, Dent L, Mackey V, Muthian G, et al. (2014) Effects of acute and sub-chronic L-dopa therapy on striatal L-dopa methylation and dopamine oxidation in an MPTP mouse model of Parkinsons disease. Life Sci 110: 1-7.

97. Roth J, Radil T, RÄ¯zicka E, Jech R, TichÂ J (1998) Apomorphine does not influence olfactory thresholds in Parkinson's disease. Funct Neurol 13: 99-103.

98. Tillerson JL, Caudle WM, Parent JM, Gong C, Schallert T, et al. (2006) Olfactory discrimination deficits in mice lacking the dopamine transporter or the D2 dopamine receptor. Behav Brain Res 172: 97-105.

99. Doty RL, Li C, Bagla R, Huang W, Pfeiffer C, et al. (1998) SKF 38393 enhances odor detection performance. Psychopharmacology (Berl) 136: 75-82.

100. Jovanovic H, Perski A, Berglund H, Savic I (2011) Chronic stress is linked to 5-HT(1A) receptor changes and functional disintegration of the limbic networks. Neuroimage 55: 1178-1188.

101. Field T, Hernandez-Reif M, Diego M, Schanberg S, Kuhn C (2005) Cortisol decreases and serotonin and dopamine increase following massage therapy. Int J Neurosci 115: 1397-1413.

102. Hernandez-Reif M, Field T, Largie S, Cullen C, Beutler J, et al. (2002) Parkinson's Disease Symptoms are Differentially Affected by Massage Therapy vs. Progressive Muscle Relaxation: a Pilot Study. Journal of Bodywork and Movement Therapies, 6. 177-182.

103. Diego MA, Field T (2009) Moderate pressure massage elicits a parasympathetic nervous system response. Int J Neurosci 119: 630-638.

104. Henkin RI, Potolicchio SJ Jr, Levy LM (2011) Improvement in smell and taste dysfunction after repetitive transcranial magnetic stimulation. Am J Otolaryngol 32: 38-46.

105. Anzinger A, Albrecht J, Kopietz R, Kleeman AM, Schopf V, et al. (2009) Effects of laserneedle acupuncture on olfactory sensitivity of healthy human subjects: a placebo-controlled, double-blinded, randomized trial. Rhinology 47: 153-9.

106. Hummel T, Rissom K, Reden J, Hähner A, Weidenbecher M, et al. (2009) Effects of olfactory training in patients with olfactory loss. Laryngoscope 119: 496-499.

Citation: Field T (2015) Smell and Taste Dysfunction as Early Markers for Neurodegenerative and Neuropsychiatric Diseases. J Alzheimers Dis Parkinsonism 5: 186. doi: 10.4172/2161-0460.1000186

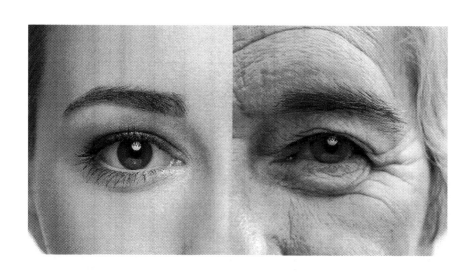

OBM Geriatrics

LIDSEN Publishing Inc.

Review

Online Dating Profiles and Problems in Older Adults: A Review

Tiffany Field*

Department of Pediatrics, School of Medicine, University of Miami, USA; E-Mail: tfield@med.miami.edu

* **Correspondence:** Tiffany Field; E-Mail: tfield@med.miami.edu

Academic Editor: Lisa Hollis-Sawyer

Special Issue: Got Aging? Examining Later-life Development from a Positive Aging Perspective

OBM Geriatrics	**Received:** April 28, 2018
2018, volume 2, issue 3	**Accepted:** August 10, 2018
doi:10.21926/obm.geriatr.1803012	**Published:** September 25, 2018

Abstract

This narrative review is based on literature searches of PubMed and PsycINFO using the terms online dating in older adults. The papers that met inclusion criteria include content analyses of online dating profiles and interviews with online dating individuals. The issues that emerged from this literature included online versus off-line advantages and disadvantages, online profile characteristics that differ by age and gender and online use problems. Online versus off-line dating older adults have reputedly experienced greater disclosure and expression of what they referred to as the "true-self" online. In their profiles, online older adults have also expressed greater interest in relationships and more selective relationships as well as health-related issues and have been willing to travel further for dates, whereas online younger adults have been more focused on work and achievement. Gender differences include males at all ages being more interested in physically attractive, younger dates. In contrast, online females have expressed more interest in communication and in older men, until they are 75- years-old when they have expressed more interest in younger men. These differences are discussed in the context of socioemotional selectivity theory and investment theory. Limitations of the literature include non-representative samples of individuals who are more educated and higher income than off-line individuals. The

OBM Geriatrics 2018; 2(3), doi:10.21926/obm.geriatr.1803012

interviews may also reflect socially desirable responses and the content analyses may be biased by deception.

Keywords
Online dating profiles; online dating problems; older adults

1. Introduction

Increasingly, older adults are using technology and turning to online dating sites to expand their social networks, to alleviate their loneliness, and to find friends and romantic partners [1, 2]. These sites have provided a rich database for several studies on internet use by older adults. Surprisingly, the literature on online dating in older populations is rather sparse, and there is considerable need for more investigation on romantic relationships among persons in this age group. The recent published research has included questionnaire, interview, content analysis and experimental studies. Comparisons have been made across ages, across gender and different types of single status, for example, widows versus divorcees. Coding of online profiles has yielded data on these differences and other factors including matching qualities. Online dating problems have also emerged including deception, excessive searching for potential friends/romantic partners, rejection, sexting and scamming.

Older adults may differ from younger age groups on their patterns of online dating. They may, for example, view online dating as one of their only alternatives for finding relationships as they have less access to those via school or work. They may invest more time on their online profiles and contacts for that reason. On the other hand, they may be disadvantaged for having less internet experience and expertise. They may also experience more online dating problems such as self-deception in order to look younger and more attractive as well as spend more time excessively searching as they feel more time-limited given their older age and lonely given their greater isolation. For those reasons, they may feel more desperate to find a relationship. They may also be more vulnerable to online dating problems like rejection, sexting and scamming due to their lesser experience with online dating. Given the apparent unique characteristics and problems among older online dating adults, it is unusual that the literature is limited and has rarely been reviewed. These questions highlighted the importance of conducting this review.

For this literature search on PubMed and PsycINFO, the terms online dating in older adults were used, and only studies in English were selected. Older adults are variously defined by the different researchers and the literature comes from primarily English-speaking countries and has the additional limitation of having sampled heterosexual individuals and not including LGBTQ individuals. Literature prior to the last twelve years was excluded because it had already been reviewed. In that review respondents between 30 and 50 were the most active online daters. Thus, older online adult issues were not included [3]. Online dating has become increasingly popular among older adults so that cohort differences might be expected between the earlier and more recent research. Surprisingly, despite increased online dating by older adults, only 22 studies met inclusion criteria for the current review. The fast growing popularity of online dating among older adults in contrast to the slow growing research literature highlighted the need for a recent review to hopefully inspire new research.

This brief narrative review of those studies on online dating in older adults is organized by the issues covered by the research. The first section of the paper is focused on online dating profiles and profile characteristics that differ by age and gender [2, 4] and includes studies on online versus off-line dating advantages and disadvantages [5]. The second section of the paper includes online use problems that have been cited by older adults in interviews on online dating but have primarily been researched in younger adults [6]. The problems section is followed by a discussion on socioemotional selectivity theory [7] and investment theory [8] as potential theoretical interpretations for the differences between the younger and the older adult online dating profiles .This is followed by a discussion on the limitations of the literature on online dating profiles and problems in older adults. Age and gender distribution data for these studies are included in Table 1. Types of data collection and primary results of the studies are also included in Table 1 and are grouped by each type of comparison that was made. The clinical relevance of online dating profiles and problems research includes issues of loneliness, forming new relationships and finding social support in later life.

Table 1 First author, country of study, N (sample size), gender, age, methods and results from studies grouped by comparisons made in this review on online dating profiles and problems in older adults ([1]=gender and age not given in the review or meta-analysis, [2]=gender and age given earlier in this table).

First Author	Country	N/gender/Age	Methods	Results
Advantages and disadvantages online versus off-linedating in older adult				
Vanderweerd	U.S.	N=45 women 50-80 years	interviews	> pacing relationship but >deceptive messages
Whitty	Australia	N=60 50% males, 23-60 years, M=44 years	Telephone interviews	>selective relationships and relationships moved faster
Age effects (older versus younger)				
Davis	England	N=4000 profiles 18-95 years	analysis profiles	>focus on relationships & health
Wada2016[1]	Canada	N=320 profiles	coding profiles	>focus on active life
Wada2015[1]	Canada	N=144 articles	coding profiles	continuing sexual interest
McIntosh	U.S.	N=200 profiles 50% males, Younger age group M=29 years, Older age group M=68 years	coding profiles	>income & willing to drive >distance,
Toma[1]	U.S.	N=80 online daters	self-ratings	deception about age
Alterovitz	U.S.	N=450 profiles 50% males, 40-54, 60-74, 75+ years	content anal	>loneliness, <adventure <seeking soulmate, <sexual interest

Gender effects (females versus males)				
Alterovitz[2]	U.S.	N=450 profiles	content anal	No gender effects
McIntosh[2]	U.S.	N=200 profiles	coding	taller dates, older men, >independence >income, <interracial tolerance
Whitty	Australia	N=60 50% males, 23-60 years, M=44 years	telephone	<deception age, height, looks and relationship status
Menkin	U.S.	N=5434 quest. 50% males, 20-95 years	coding	<sexual attraction,> communication
Relationship status (widowed versus divorced)				
Young		N=240 widowed, 280 divorced Males N=274, Females N=246 18-40 years, M=35 years	Coding	>discussion about loss
Profile qualities (popular)				
Khan[1]	U.S.	N=86 studies	Meta-synthesis	>realistic, simple language, humor, mention trait of recipient, disclosure, complimentary
Taylor[1]			Review	> matching, attractiveness, popularity, self-worth
Online problems, Self-deception (females versus males)				
Toma[1]		N=80 online daters	self-ratings	>lying re wt, < re ht
Whitty[2]	Australia	N=60	Interviews	<deception relationships
Excessive searching bias				
Wu	Taiwan	N=128 50% males, 18-36 years, M=26 years	Laboratory	>search options lead to worse choices
Chiou	Taiwan	N=120 50% males, M=24 years	Laboratory	>need for cognition leads to >searching& bad choices
Rejection				
Ford	U.S.	N=78 50% males, M=22 years	Online rejection	>cortisol, >self-blame

OBM Geriatrics 2018; 2(3), doi:10.21926/obm.geriatr.1803012

Sexting				
Klettke[1]	U.S.	N=31 studies	Syst. Lit. Rev.	>prevalent in older adults
Scamming				
Whitty 2012	Great Britain	N= 2028 50%males, 18-75 years	online dating site	230,000 British citizens are victims of this crime
Self-protection				
Cali	U.S.	N=82 18-36 years, M=25 years	online vs. offline	>self-protective scenarios

2. Online Versus Offline Dating Advantages and Disadvantages

Both advantages and disadvantages have been noted for online versus off-line dating. In one study on 45 women ages 50+ who dated online, interviews were recorded, transcribed and coded for themes [5]. The positive aspects of online dating noted by these women included expanding their social networks, pacing their relationships and having greater knowledge about potential friends/partners before meeting them. The negative aspects reported by these women were the risks of receiving deceptive messages, unwanted sexual advances and scams. Surprisingly, very few studies have addressed these problems in older online dating adults. While the negative aspects mentioned by these women are suggestive of future research, these data are tenuous as they are based on a small sample of solely heterosexual women who were exclusively dating online. A more heterogeneous sample of both online and off-line, younger and older men and women would yield more generalizable data.

In a more heterogeneous sample of 60 Australian men and women, one third of the sample reported via telephone interviews that online dating was the only method of finding potential dates [9]. Although this study was more heterogeneous than the previous study in that it included both men and women who were online as well as off-line dating, the sample was skewed towards a better educated group, and as many as 11% had a partner or were married. Based on the already existing literature, the authors suggested that online versus off-line dating would be advantaged by allowing for greater impression management, more controllable interactions, and greater self-disclosure, intimacy and expression of what they referred to as "true selves" as opposed to "actual selves". This was especially true for socially anxious individuals who typically had difficulty self-disclosing in face-to-face social situations. The participants in this study were recruited from the largest Australian online dating site. Transcripts were made from the telephone interviews and submitted to grounded theory analysis to identify categories/themes from the participants' comments [10]. After the themes were identified, the transcripts were coded for the presence of the themes. Surprisingly, many of the gender differences that had been identified in the off-line dating literature did not appear in this study [9]. For example, there were no gender differences on looking for partners based on their physical attractiveness, on their similar interests or on their socioeconomic status. According to Whitty (2008) [9], in the off-line dating literature, men typically looked for physical appearance more than women and women were notably more interested in partners with high socioeconomic status. Online daters in the Whitty (2008) [9] study were seemingly more selective and had greater expectations for their potential dates, likely

OBM Geriatrics 2018; 2(3), doi:10.21926/obm.geriatr.1803012

because they had a greater number of potential dates online than they would find off-line. The relationships that were formed online versus off-line also seemed to move faster from being solely online communications to dating, possibly related to the greater self-disclosure that was evident on the online interactions.

3. Profiles Differ by Age, Gender and Relationship Status

Online profiles have differed not only by age, but also by gender and by relationship status. Typically, these differences have been identified on profiles from popular online dating sites by the use of word count software. The focus on profiles may relate to their being readily accessible on online dating sites as opposed to deriving data from more costly interviews and self-report methods.

3.1 Older Age Effects

Age differences are the most frequently studied effects in the recent literature on online dating in older adults. In an age comparison study on 4000 dating profiles from two popular websites, the authors hypothesized that younger adults would likely focus on themselves and their achievements, attractiveness and sexuality, while older adults would present themselves positively but focus on their relationships and physical health probably to clarify that older adults were not too old for relationships and physical health [2]. The younger adults more often used first–person singular pronouns (i.e. I and my) and comments that were related to work and achievement. In contrast, older adults more often used first person plural nouns (i.e. we and our) that were related to health and positive emotions. While the younger adults focused more on self, the older adults commented more on their relationships and connectedness. References to attractiveness and sexuality as they relate to health did not differ between the age groups.

Profiles of older adults have also been coded for three criteria for successful aging including low incidence of disease, high functioning and active life engagement. In a cross-sectional study, for example, 320 profiles of older adults were coded for these criteria [11]. Logistic regression analysis suggested that low disease was characteristic of the younger profiles, while the older profiles were characterized by active life engagement, especially among older women. In another study, the same research group reviewed 144 newspaper and magazine articles about older people and their online dating profiles that were published between 2009 and 2011 [12]. Sexuality was idealized in 13% of the articles on "older adults and online dating" including sexual attractiveness and optimal sexual engagement. In 19% of the articles, sexual interest and functioning were shown as declining in older people while 15% of the articles showed sexuality as sustained in older people. Another 15% of the articles on older adults and online dating implied that older adults might explore new techniques to boost their sexual pleasure. The authors suggested that these articles challenge the stereotype of older adults being non-sexual. That might be even more characteristic of a future review, as the average lifespan has increased since then. A review of more contemporary news articles would be more informative inasmuch as the zeitgeist of dating online has changed within recent times including that more older adults are using online dating sites and more sites are available.

While the review on news articles focused on sexuality, online profiles typically elaborate demographic variables. For example, in a study on Match profiles, 200 of those were randomly

OBM Geriatrics 2018; 2(3), doi:10.21926/obm.geriatr.1803012

selected to assess the demographic characteristics that older online versus younger online daters preferred [13]. The older adults were defined as 65 and older and the younger adults as 25 to 35 years, suggesting a wide age gap in their sample. The variables included age, gender, youngest acceptable age, oldest acceptable age, height, income requirement, distance willing to travel, willingness to date interracially and to date other religions. Older as compared to younger individuals were willing to date younger individuals, but preferred taller individuals with a greater income. The older adults were less willing to date adults of different races and religions. Surprisingly, the older as opposed to the younger adults indicated that they were willing to travel greater distances for their dates. Gender differences also emerged suggesting that males were more interested in younger dates with less income and more tolerant of interracial and cross-religion dating. Females, on the other hand, preferred taller dates and older men until age 75 at which time they began to prefer younger men. As the authors noted, this is a problem inasmuch as there are three single women for every single man over the age of 65. They contrasted the interests of older men and women as being men looking for stability and domestic help from a marriage, while older women are reluctant to lose their independence and afraid that they will find a companion who needs caregiving. Thus, the authors suggested that women may have to relax their standards to perhaps date other races and religions as well as men who are not as tall or as well-off financially [13]. On the other hand, women may be advantaged by their being more selective regarding age, race, religion, income and height of a prospective partner as they have a profile of preference which might help them identify someone sooner without extensive searching. And, as others have noted, women have expressed the advantages of online dating expanding their social networks, pacing their relationships and having greater knowledge about potential friends/partners before meeting them [5].

The data from these four studies are seemingly consistent including that older people are less willing to date people of other races and they are not wanting to have a financial burden [2, 11-13]. Further, women have consistently held a stronger preference for men who are taller than them. And, economic status has been more important for women than men, who seem to have a greater desire for a confidante who provides emotional support. Of note here was the frequent finding that men who are married tend to live longer, while this health benefit is less obvious for women, which may lead the women to being more selective.

The data from these four studies also have the limitations that the older adults from some online data sites may not be representative of other dating sites or of older singles in general, inasmuch as older people use the Internet less often [2, 11-13]. Once again, the samples were more educated and higher socioeconomic status and perhaps even healthier than older singles who are not online daters. Further, there may have been socially desirable responses in these interviews as, for example, approximately 13% of women and 24% of men have been noted to lie about their age [14]. However, there were no age differences in deception in the Toma et al (2008) [14] study. Further, these data reflect peoples' stated criteria, not their actual dating behavior which would be more difficult to tap given the methodological difficulty of monitoring internet behavior. The participants may have been "faking good" or stating more socially desirable preferences Finally, the age differences may be simple cohort effects. For example, the younger adults were reaching dating age at a time when dating others from different races and religions was more socially accepted.

OBM Geriatrics 2018; 2(3), doi:10.21926/obm.geriatr.1803012

These studies also featured wide age gaps between young and old samples. But even when the age gap is reduced, age differences have emerged. For example, important age distinctions were noted between middle-age, younger-old, and older-old groups when online daters were divided that way in another study [4]. In this case, 3 groups were compared including the younger-old, (60-74 years) the older-old (75+) and the middle-aged (40-54 years). According to the authors, these three age groups were based on previous research on physical and cognitive aging [15](Abrams, Trunk & Merrill, 2017). The 3 groups were compared on their dating motivations based on salient themes that were identified by a qualitative content analysis of personal profiles including: 1) expressing loneliness, 2) seeking adventure or exploration,3) searching for a "soulmate",4) desiring romantic activities,5) expressing sexual interests, and 6) mentioning health. Personal ads (N=450) were downloaded from "Yahoo! Personals" by random quota sampling without replacement to have 75 "men seeking women" and 75 "women seeking men". The online daters were a representative sample from three geographic areas across the US. These areas included a 200 mile radius around Austin, Texas, Seattle, Washington and Pittsburgh, Pennsylvania. Although online personal ads are more common among middle-aged adults, a sufficient sample was selected for all three groups. The mean age of each group was the same for men and women, although the groups differed on other dimensions. For example, 70% of the older–old adults were widowed and 66% of the middle-aged adults were divorced, a difference that could confound the group comparisons. Employment status also differed by age group, and the sample was not representative given that 36% had a college degree and 88% were white, raising the question of the generalizability of these data. Nonetheless, the qualitative approach of these authors revealed interesting data.

The qualitative content analysis was conducted on the written portions of the profiles (the section entitled"in my words") to determine the motivations/themes of the online daters [4]. The profiles were then coded for these motivations/themes. No gender differences were noted on these motivations/themes. Loneliness was the only theme that the two old adult groups expressed more than the middle-age adult group (15% vs. 5%). The adventure/exploration theme was expressed significantly less often by the older–old adult group than the other two groups (14% versus 27% for the younger-old and 32% for the middle-aged adult group). Looking for a soulmate was expressed significantly less often by the older-old adult group than the other two groups (4% versus 13% and 19%). Less interest for romantic activities was mentioned by the older–old adult group (13%) than the younger-old (30%) or the middle-age (32%) adult groups. Similarly, the older–old adult group expressed less sexual interest (2%) than the younger–old (10%) and the middle-aged (13%) adult groups. Health was the only interest that the older-old adult group expressed more often than the other two adult groups (39% versus 19% and 18%).

These results were unique in that there is very little related research on the romantic lives of these different age adult groups and virtually none on the older–old age adult group. The results suggest that at least on this online dating site, the younger–old adult group was closer to the middle-age adult group than the older–old age adult group, suggesting that old age begins later than the typical 65-year marker, at least for online dating motivations. The fact that both "old" adult groups expressed loneliness motivations suggests the value of online dating at least to 75+ years. As the authors pointed out, these data highlight the importance of improving computer literacy for older adults and for facilitating online dating. The authors also discussed limitations of their study including lack of generalizability given that the sample was better educated and less

OBM Geriatrics 2018; 2(3), doi:10.21926/obm.geriatr.1803012

ethnically diverse than the general population and the fact that a greater percentage of the older-old adult group was widowed. Finally, they suggested that their results likely reflect both age and cohort effects. Without having longitudinal data, there is no way to estimate the relative contributions of these two effects. The absence of expected gender effects and gender by age interaction effects may relate to the even distribution of gender across the age groups or an insufficient sample size or simply that these motivations/themes are shared by both genders.

3.2 Gender Differences

Gender differences would be expected in this literature just as they have been noted in many other studies on behaviors/activities/attitudes of older people. However, they were not reported in the study just described [4]. No gender differences emerged on the motivations of the middle-age, younger-old and older-old online dating adults including the loneliness, adventure-seeking, looking for a soulmate, romantic activities, sexual interests or health themes. Gender differences did emerge, however, in the Match study [13]. The males were more interested in younger dates with less income and expressed more tolerance of interracial and cross-religion dating. Females, on the other hand, preferred taller dates and older men until age 75 at which time they preferred younger men. As the authors noted, this is a problem inasmuch as there are three single women for every single man among people over age 65. They contrasted the interests of older men and women. That is, men were looking for stability and domestic help from a marriage, while older women were reluctant to lose their independence and afraid that they would find a companion who needed caregiving. Unfortunately, the disadvantages cited for women's online dating were not counterbalanced by any noted advantages in this study, although the women in the Vanderweed et al (2016) study cited the advantages of expanding social networks, pacing relationships and having greater knowledge about partners before meeting.

Gender differences also appeared in the Australian study including that women more often included a photo, most especially a glamour photo [9]. Men more often misrepresented their looks and included a photo that was over a year out of date or even a photo of a different person, as in "stealing another's identity" [9]. The men also described themselves as being better looking than they actually were and more often misrepresented their height and their relationship status (did not report that they were married).No gender differences, however, emerged with regard to what the daters were looking for in a partner

More typically, age by gender interactions have been noted. For example, in a study on 5,434 relationship questionnaires that were completed by new users of eHarmony, older age users rated sexual attraction as less important than younger age users [16]. Although the users generally valued interpersonal communication more than sexual attraction, the men valued sexual attraction more than women at all ages and the women expressed a greater interest in communication as opposed to sexual attraction.

3.3 Relationship Status

As suggested by the men misrepresenting their relationship status in the Whitty (2008) study, relationship status may be a meaningful variable in online profiling. However, only one study could be found on a comparison between divorced and widowed individuals, and no research appeared on single but never married versus other status individuals. In the study on divorced versus

OBM Geriatrics 2018; 2(3), doi:10.21926/obm.geriatr.1803012

widowed individuals entitled "Online dating and conjugal bereavement", online dating profiles of 241 widowed and 280 divorced individuals were content analyzed for the backstory of their relationship and any meaning--making about the lost relationship [17]. The results suggested that about one-third of those who were widowed discussed their loss and about 16% reappraised their bereavement. In contrast, the divorcees made very little mention of their loss and made less meaning-making about future partners. This finding was not surprising inasmuch as widowed individuals often idealize their lost spouses while divorced individuals often denigrate their former partners. And, profiles are most frequently positive, as already mentioned, so negative referents would be unusual.

4. Profile Qualities and Motivations

Most online dating site profiles begin with a photo, an online name along with location of residence and an opening line. They then give basic demographics including age, height, body type, relationship status, drinking, smoking, profession, income, education, astrological sign, number of children and interests along with an adjacent column that specifies the characteristics wanted in the potential significant other. In at least the Australian study, no gender differences were noted on any of these factors in terms of characteristics/interests they were looking for in a partner [9]. However, as noted, men more often misrepresented their looks including an outdated photo or a photo of another person, their height and their relationship status. In the Whitty (2008) study, the participants talked about keeping their profiles "real" (actual self) as well as selling themselves or describing who they would like to be. Many reported that they showed their profiles to their friends and family to ensure that their profile was a true reflection of themselves. Over half the participants stated that they met their date within a week or two after being contacted on the site. As many as 68% of the participants suggested that the first meeting determined if the relationship would progress. Phone calls made prior to the first date were meant to organize the date and verify information about the person.

Surprisingly, no data could be found in this literature on the proportion of phone calls that successfully led to face-to-face meetings. Further, age differences have not been reported for phone calls or face-to-face meetings, although online dating has been said to result in faster-moving relationships in general [9]. The types of phone conversations would be an important variable for future research including, for example, superficial versus intimate and long versus short conversations. Some have at least explored the profile characteristics that lead to face-to-face meetings. One study, for example, used electronic searches to perform a meta-narrative synthesis of the profiles that resulted in a face-t-o-face meeting [18]. This synthesis included 86 studies. Results suggested that capturing initial interest required an attractive photo, a screen name, and a headline message. The profiles, according to this study, increased likability when they featured a 70:30 ratio of who the dater was to qualities of the desirable person [18]. Popular profiles also stayed close to reality and used simple language with humor. The invitations that were most successful gave a short personalized message that addressed a trait in the profile of the recipient and, they were generally complimentary. Typically, an in-person meeting was scheduled if the sender expressed genuine interest in a short turnaround time. This also happened when the individuals had a similar level of self–disclosure, humor, lack of criticism and an early move from being online chatting to a date. These data would support the "matching hypothesis" that

OBM Geriatrics 2018; 2(3), doi:10.21926/obm.geriatr.1803012

individuals would select partners who were similar on these qualities. Another research group assessed the matching hypothesis but on different qualities [19]. In this review on data collected in laboratories and popular online dating sites, the reviewers reported that matching was based on the individual's selection of someone who was similar on physical attractiveness, popularity and self-worth. However, the matching on these qualities varied by degree of matching and by different stages of the dating process.

5. Online Dating Problems

Despite attempts to optimize online profiles, phone calls and ultimate face-to-face meetings, potential online dating problems are a downside of this practice. Several problems have been cited by older adults in the literature on online dating profiles in older adults. Those have included deceptive self–presentation, excessive searching bias, rejection, sexting and scamming. Although these problems have been raised by older adults in the online dating interview research, they are not unique to older adults and have rarely been studied in older adults.

5.1 Deceptive Self-presentation

Deceptive self-presentation has been self-reported in several of the studies already reviewed but has been measured more objectively by using a novel cross–validation technique [14]. In this study, 80 online daters rated the accuracy of their self–presentation. The researchers then gathered information on the physical characteristics of the participants including their age, weight and height and compared those data with their online profile data. Women lied about their weight and men lied about their height. In general, the photographs were the least accurate (typically outdated photographs) and the relationship information was the most accurate, although the latter is inconsistent with the Australian study reporting deception about relationships by men [9]. In addition, the observed accuracy was correlated with the participants' self–ratings of accuracy, suggesting that the individuals were deliberately deceptive. Intentional deception would not be surprising given the attempt to be socially desirable online and especially among older adults who have a more limited "playing field". It is also possible that online daters have simply neglected to update their profiles including their photographs, despite the importance of not deceiving their viewers.

5.2 Excessive Searching Bias

Older online dating adults may need to "excessively search" including across several dating sites, although this has not been studied in older adults. Again, this may be related to the limited number of online participants in the older age category and/or the large number of individuals (especially men) who have a stated preference for younger individuals [13]. Excessive searching was explored in two studies demonstrating that excessive searching has led to poor decision-making and reduced selectivity among online dating people [20, 21]. In the first study, the research participants were asked to enter characteristics they find desirable in a partner and then they were randomly assigned to three levels of available profiles [21]. The results supported their thesis that more search options triggered excessive searching leading to worse choices/poorer selectivity. In their second study, they investigated this "more–means-worse-effects"

OBM Geriatrics 2018; 2(3), doi:10.21926/obm.geriatr.1803012

phenomenon which they described as searching leads to poorer choices because the online users get distracted by irrelevant information which reduces their ability to screen out inferior choices [20]. They tested the research participants on their "need-for-cognition" (engaging in and enjoying intellectual activity) and then asked the participants to review either a small or large number of their most desirable romantic partners on an online dating site. The high need-for-cognition participants did more excessive searching and the effects of their searching were worse than for the low-need-for-cognition participants. Although education is often given on online dating sites, intellectual activity would not necessarily relate to education level. The "need for cognition" individuals may need to search more to find matches on intellectual activity. Other variables that may lead to excessive searching include being perfectionistic as in looking for "a match made in heaven". This may happen more frequently in older online dating adults, especially if they have been widowed and have idealized their deceased partner or if they have been divorced and are looking for a very different person than their ex-spouse. Excessive searching would also provide alternative choices in anticipation of being rejected.

5.3 Rejection

Rejection by online users is a common experience given the significant number of contacts typically made online. In a simulated rejection study, 78 online dating individuals experienced an ambiguous interpersonal rejection or no rejection from a partner in the context of an online dating interaction [22]. In that situation, individuals who had low self-esteem blamed themselves, had greater cortisol reactivity and criticized the rejecter. These results might be expected in a real-life online situation. However, it is difficult to believe that the participants were not aware that this study was a contrived deception, especially if they were given informed consent that had been approved by an institutional review board. On the other hand, the participants may have vividly imagined this happening in real life and accordingly had negative reactions and elevated cortisol.

5.4 Sexting

Sexting, or sending unwanted sexual material, has become so common that it is the topic for one of the only systematic literature reviews that is relevant to online dating [23]. In this separate literature, thirty-one studies met criteria for the review that covered behavioral, psychological and social factors influencing sexting. The results revealed no gender differences but suggested that sexting was more prevalent among older age individuals. This age difference is difficult to interpret, especially since others have reported the lesser focus on sexuality in older adults [4]. Further research is needed to confirm this unexpected finding.

5.5 Scamming

Scamming is a major risk factor for online dating. Typically, someone with a stolen identity initiates an online relationship and after sometimes months of positive interaction dupes the online partner into sending large sums of money via reputable wiring and banking companies [6](Whitty & Buchanan, 2012). Despite being a relatively new form of fraud, an estimated 230,000 British citizens have been victims of this crime. An entire blog devoted to this problem features the stolen identity photos along with templates of the poetry and material shared by these

OBM Geriatrics 2018; 2(3), doi:10.21926/obm.geriatr.1803012

Internet café scammers. Although online dating sites have warned their members about potential scamming, they do not provide information about the institutions that are enabling the crime. And, because there are no gatekeepers to monitor and prevent this scamming, the crime continues. It has likely dissuaded many potential online daters, especially older adults who have hard-earned monies and may be targeted more often for that reason. Online dating sites might alert members to specific scamming episodes, to blogs that describe the details and to self-protective behaviors. Research on this topic is rare, likely because it is is difficult to identify potential scammers online.

5.6 Self-protection

The felt need for self-protection may derive from knowledge about the preceding online dating problems, especially sexting and scamming. Self-protection is the topic of a paper called "Stranger danger? Women's self-protection intent and the continuing stigma of online dating". In this study, 82 women were asked to read scenarios on a prospective date who was only known through an online dating site or a date who was known through a face-to-face interaction [24]. After the participants read the scenario they rated the importance of self–protection behaviors that they would use if they were in that scenario. As might be expected, those who were in an online scenario rated self-protection behaviors as more important than those who experienced the face-to-face scenario. The authors reported that those participants who had not been on a date with someone online had particularly high self–protection ratings. The same study might be conducted with sexting and non-sexting and scamming and non-scamming online dating scenarios to highlight the importance of self-protection behaviors during those situations. Although different age groups have not been compared on self-protection behavior, it is conceivable that older adults might feel more vulnerable to online dating problems like these and show more self-protection behavior.

6. Discussion

This recent literature on online dating profiles and problems in older adults generally suggests that going online for potential dating is a positive experience that is focused on finding relationships, although online dating has potential problems. In the studies comparing the online dating profiles of older and younger adults, the older adults commented more often about connectedness and relationships while the younger adults more often focused on work and achievement [2]. And, notably, the older adults talked about selective relationships [9] and they more often used plural nouns (we, our), unlike the younger adults who more often used singular nouns (I, my). In addition, they often commented on an active life [11] and expressed positive emotions [2], suggesting that going online for dating is generally a positive experience despite the frequently mentioned potential problems.

Given that these studies have been conducted in English-speaking countries (U.S., Canada, Australia)and exclusively on heterosexual adults, these data might not be generalizable and could be considered ethnocentric as opposed to universal by cross-cultural psychologists [25]. In addition, the data are subjective versus objective and descriptive versus theoretical. Most of the research reviewed here was based on self-reports and interviews rather than observations and was not based on theoretical models.

OBM Geriatrics 2018; 2(3), doi:10.21926/obm.geriatr.1803012

The positive-emotion and relationship-oriented profiles of the older online dating adults could be considered in the context of socioemotional selectivity theory [7].In that theory, age is associated with increasing motivation to derive emotional meaning from life. For example, in a study by Carstensen and her colleagues on age-related patterns in social networks of European Americans and African Americans, older people "became more selective in their choice of social partners, favoring emotionally meaningful relationships over peripheral ones" [26]. This occurred across a wide age range (18-90 year-olds) and among both ethnic groups. Online dating may provide a broader array of potential partners and a greater opportunity to be selective in choosing social partners and to find more emotionally meaningful relationships. The greater focus on relationships and emotional well-being in the profiles of the older online dating adults versus the focus on work and economic well-being of the younger adults may derive from the socioemotional selectivity concept that "When time is perceived as limited, emotional goals assume primacy" [7].

Further, Carstensen and her colleagues in a growth curve analysis of longitudinal data noted that the "peak of emotional life may not occur until well into the 7th decade" [27]. This sample ranged from 18 to 94 years of age (ethnicity, gender and socioeconomic status stratified across age). The participants were interviewed three times at five year intervals on physical and mental health problems, happiness and personality variables and daily emotion sampling was done 5 times per day for 7 days following the interviews. The authors noted better physical health for those who pursued emotionally meaningful goals and suggested that they also "invested more psychological and social resources to optimize emotional well-being" [27]. The Carstensen et al (2011) sample may have been self-selected for old people who "feel younger". In a recent study on visual representations of people on 39 dating sites intended for older adults, for example, the sample was comprised of older adults who "felt younger" [28]. These authors did a visual thematic analysis of the older adults on these sites. They reported that the majority of the older men and women were smiling, fair complexion, light eye color and looked younger than 60. The "looking younger" was consistent with the older adults "feeling younger" [28].

Another possible interpretation for the older adults focusing on emotional connection is that older adults have been accustomed to emotional well-being from longer-term relationships they have experienced as compared to younger adults. This raises another potential theoretical framework for these data, namely investment theory, which posits that relationships are based on the investment of time, emotional energy and commitment [8]. The primacy of emotional goals in the profiles of older online dating adults may reflect their greater previous experience investing in long-term relationships that have been based on emotional connections. And looking for emotional connections may be more salient and more pressing given their lesser longevity and greater loneliness that has resulted in part from spending more time alone.

A more mundane explanation for the focus on emotional connection is that emotional goals and emotionally meaningful relationships may also be more affordable when one is retired and no longer occupied with working, mating and parenting responsibilities. And, time for preparing profiles and for finding relationships may also be more available. Further research as in that modeled by Carstensen and her colleagues [26] and Rusbult (1980) would inform potential theoretical models for these age differences. More theoretically derived and empirically robust research is needed on this topic.

The studies reviewed here have several limitations including that they may not be representative of other dating sites or of older singles given that older people use the Internet less often. Most of the samples were also more educated and higher socioeconomic status and perhaps even healthier than older adults who do not engage in online dating. They were also not representative of different gender individuals in that LGBTQ adults were not included in the samples. And, they were limited to English-speaking countries, suggesting that they were not cross-culturally representative.

Several of the studies were based on self-reports or interviews that may have been biased by "socially desirable" responses. Other studies were based on content analyses of profiles which have been subject to deception. Further, most of these studies were based on stated criteria for online dating preferences rather than actual dating behavior. And, the age differences may be simple cohort effects. The older adults reached a dating age at a time when dating across race and religion was less socially acceptable. Nonetheless, the data are suggestive of older versus younger and female versus male online dating preferences which, in turn, suggest ways that online dating older adults can improve their profiles and perhaps move faster from online to face-to-face relationships.

Multivariate research is needed to explore multiple variables within studies rather than single variable studies. And, more experimental and observational research is needed on the online dating behaviors as most of the research has been on profile-stated preferences. Longitudinal research is also needed on several features of online dating including the pacing of the relationships and the transitions from online to offline and how the "stories ended". Future research might assess whether online dating actually alleviates loneliness, expands social networks and helps the consumer find a partner. Comparisons might be made between private dating agencies that perform the matching of potential partners versus traditional online dating. Finally, this research literature has not been driven by theoretical perspectives. Several aspects of online dating including motivations, attitudes and personality characteristics have not been addressed either empirically or theoretically in the current literature. Theories like socioemotional selectivity theory and investment theory might generate further hypotheses as, for example, older people being more selective in their choice of social partners and online dating affording that selectivity more than offline dating. This would especially pertain to older adults since they have less opportunity for face-to-face encounters. As in many other behavioral phenomena, the popularity of the practice has outpaced the scientific study of the behavior, and the data reviewed here highlight the need for further research.

Author Contributions

The author did all works.

Competing Interests

The author has declared that no competing interests exist.

References

1. Alterovitz SS, Mendelsohn GA. Partner preferences across the life span: online dating by older adults. Psychol Aging. 2009; 24: 513-517.

OBM Geriatrics 2018; 2(3), doi:10.21926/obm.geriatr.1803012

2. Davis EM, Fingerman KL. Digital dating: online profile content of older and younger adults. J Gerontol B Psychol Sci Soc Sci 2016; 71: 959-967.
3. Valkenburg PM, Peter J. Who visits online dating sites? Exploring some characteristics of online daters. Cyberpsychol Behav. 2007; 10: 849-852.
4. Alterovitz SS, Mendelsohn GA. Relationship goals of middle-aged, young-old, and old-old internet daters: an analysis of online personal ads. J Aging Stud. 2013; 27: 159-165.
5. Vandeweerd C, Myers J, Coulter M, Yalcin A, Corvin J. Positives and negatives of online dating according to women 50+. J Women Aging. 2016; 28: 259-270.
6. Whitty MT, Buchanan T. The online romance scam: a serious cybercrime. Cyberpsychol Behav Soc Netw. 2012; 15: 181-183.
7. Carstensen LL, Isaacowitz DM, Charles ST. Taking time seriously: a theory of socioemotional selectivity. Am Psychol. 1999; 54: 165.
8. Rusbult CE. Commitment and satisfaction in romantic associations: a test of the investment model. J Exp Soc Psychol. 1980; 16: 172-186.
9. Whitty MT. Revealing the 'real'me, searching for the 'actual'you: presentations of self on an internet dating site. Comput Human Behav. 2008; 24: 1707-1723.
10. Glaser BG, Strauss AL. The discovery of grounded theory: strategies for qualitative theory. New Brunswick: Aldine Transaction. 1967.
11. Wada M, Mortenson WB, Clarke LH. Older adults' online dating profiles and successful aging. Can J Aging. 2016; 35: 479-490.
12. Wada M, Clarke LH, Rozanova J. Constructions of sexuality in later life: analyses of Canadian magazine and newspaper portrayals of online dating. J Aging Stud. 2015; 32: 40-49.
13. McIntosh WD, Locker Jr L, Briley K, Ryan R, Scott AJ. What do older adults seek in their potential romantic partners? Evidence from online personal ads. Int J Aging Hum Dev. 2011; 72: 67-82.
14. Toma CL, Hancock JT, Ellison NB. Separating fact from fiction: an examination of deceptive self-presentation in online dating profiles. Pers Soc Psychol Bull. 2008; 34: 1023-1036.
15. Abrams L, Trunk DL, Merrill LA. Why a superman cannot help a tsunami: activation of grammatical class influences resolution of young and older adults' tip-of-the-tongue states. Psychol Aging. 2007; 22: 835.
16. Menkin JA, Robles TF, Wiley JF, Gonzaga GC. Online dating across the life span: Users' relationship goals. Psychol Aging. 2015; 30: 987.
17. Young DG, Caplan SE. Online dating and conjugal bereavement. Death stud. 2010; 34: 575-605.
18. Khan KS, Chaudhry S. An evidence-based approach to an ancient pursuit: systematic review on converting online contact into a first date. BMJ Evid Based Med. 2015: ebmed-2014-110101.
19. Shaw Taylor L, Fiore AT, Mendelsohn G, Cheshire C. "Out of my league": a real-world test of the matching hypothesis. Pers Soc Psychol Bull. 2011; 37: 942-954.
20. Chiou W, Yang M. The moderating role of need for cognition on excessive searching bias: a case of finding romantic partners online. ARCTT. 2010: 120-122.
21. Wu P-L, Chiou W-B. More options lead to more searching and worse choices in finding partners for romantic relationships online: An experimental study. Cyberpsychol Behav. 2009; 12: 315-318.
22. Ford MB, Collins NL. Self-esteem moderates neuroendocrine and psychological responses to interpersonal rejection. J Pers Soc Psychol. 2010; 98: 405.

OBM Geriatrics 2018; 2(3), doi:10.21926/obm.geriatr.1803012

23. Klettke B, Hallford DJ, Mellor DJ. Sexting prevalence and correlates: a systematic literature review. Clin Psychol Rev. 2014; 34: 44-53.
24. Cali BE, Coleman JM, Campbell C. Stranger danger? Women's self-protection intent and the continuing stigma of online dating. Cyberpsychol Behav Soc Netw. 2013; 16: 853-857.
25. Headland T. A dialogue between kenneth pike and marvin harrison emics and etics. Emics and Etics: The Insider/Outsider Debate London: SAGE. 1990.
26. Fung HH, Carstensen LL, Lang FR. Age-related patterns in social networks among European Americans and African Americans: Implications for socioemotional selectivity across the life span. Int J Aging Hum Dev. 2001; 52: 185-206.
27. Carstensen LL, Turan B, Scheibe S, Ram N, Ersner-Hershfield H, Samanez-Larkin GR, et al. Emotional experience improves with age: evidence based on over 10 years of experience sampling. Psychol Aging. 2011; 26: 21.
28. Gewirtz-Meydan A, Ayalon L. Forever young: visual representations of gender and age in online dating sites for older adults. J Women Aging. 2017: 1-19.
29. Fletcher, G. & Kerr, P. Through the eyes of love: reality and illusion in intimate relationships. Psychol Bull. 2010; 136; 627-658.

Senior citizens benefit from movement therapy

Kristen Hartshorn, Jesse Delage, Tffany Field, Loren Olds

Sixteen senior citizens participated in four, 50-min movement therapy sessions over a 2-week period and were compared to 16 senior citizens who belonged to a wait list control group who received the movement sessions only after the end of the study. The movement therapy participants improved in their functional motion on the Tinetti scale, and specifically on the gait scale, their leg strength increased, and their leg pain significantly decreased. # 2002 Harcourt Publishers Ltd

Kristen Hartshorn, Jesse Delage, Ti ɪ any Field, Loren Olds
University of Miami School of Medicine, P.O. Box 016820, (D-820), Miami, FL 33101, USA

Correspondence to: Tiffany Field, PhD
E-mail: tfield@med.miami.edu

Received February 2001
Revised and accepted March 2001

Journal of Bodywork and Movement Therapies (2002)
6(1), 55^58
2002 Harcourt Publishers Ltd doi:
10.1054/jbmt.2001.0229, available online at
http://www.idealibrary.com on I D E ▶ L®

Significant numbers of senior citizens are noted to experience chronic pain (Klinger & Spaulding 1998) with an incidence of 23% in nursing care experiencing daily pain (Finne-Soveri & Tilvis 1998), 55% of nursing home patients being diagnosed with at least one painful condition (Horgas & Tsai 1998) and up to three-quarters of seniors who require home nursing services reporting pain (Ross & Crook 1998). Chronic pain in senior citizens has been associated with impaired functioning (Gagliese & Melzack 1997; Weiner et al. 1996), anxiety (Parmelee et al. 1998), sleep disturbance and depression (Cook 1998; Ross & Crook 1998) and reduced quality of life (Hopman et al. 1997). Back pain ranked as the second leading chronic pain condition for physician visits among this age group (Berman & Swyers 1997).

Pain management for senior citizens is difficult because of side effects from medication, slower drug metabolism, decreased organ function and changes in their cardiovascular and respiratory reserves (Gloth 1996; Richardson & Bresland 1998). Because of finding little pain relief and many side effects from conventional Western treatments, an increasing number of senior citizens are turning to alternative treatments for their pain conditions (Berman & Swyers 1997).

Other problems for this age group include loss of lower-extremity strength, unstable gait and frequent occurrence of falls (Judge et al. 1993; Tse & Bailey 1998). A number of Tai Chi movement studies have been conducted to improve balance and muscle strength in older people. Loss of lower-extremity strength typically increases the risk of their falls. Balance has been improved in several studies (Judge et al. 1993; Schaller 1996; Tse & Bailey 1998; Wolf et al. 1997; Wolfson et al. 1996). These improvements in balance may have derived from improved muscle strength which has also been frequently reported including an 18% increase in muscle strength of knee extensors and a 15% increase of knee flexors following Tai Chi (Lan et al. 1998). The increase in muscle strength and balance may have in turn led to the fewer falls reported following Tai Chi training (Province et al. 1995; Wolf et al.).

The purpose of the current study was to try a different type of movement therapy, namely a more creative, larger movement-in-space therapy with senior citizens. The effects of this therapy were assessed by the Tinetti balance and gait evaluation (Tinetti 1986) and by the participants' self-reports on their mood states (depression, anger and vigor) and their pain and strength ratings including overall body pain, back pain and leg pain.

Method

Participants

The sample was comprised of 32 senior citizens (26 females; mean age=86 years, SD=3.3 years). All but one of these participants finished high school, and half had some college education. They were recruited from two retirement communities by the activity directors and randomly assigned to a movement therapy or a wait list control group who were given the movement therapy only after the end of the study. None of the participants had ever participated in movement therapy. A trained movement therapist led the four 50-min sessions over a 2 week period.

Assessments

The participants were informed that assessments would be made on the effects of movement therapy including physical (range of motion) and self-reports (of pain, anxiety, mood, depression, self-esteem, and daily activities). These assessments were collected before the movement therapy or control sessions on the first and last days of the study.

The Profile of Mood States (POMS). The abbreviated version of the POMS (McNair et al. 1971) consists of 35 items on three subscales of depression, anger, and vigor that are rated on a 5-point scale. The participants were asked to indicate how well an adjective (e.g. unhappy, hopeless, guilty) described their current mood state. This scale has high internal consistency (r=0.95; McNair & Lorr 1964) and is an adequate measure of intervention effectiveness (Pugatch et al. 1969).

Pain and strength ratings. Overall body pain, back pain, and leg pain were rated on visual analogue scales (VITAS) ranging from 0 (no pain) to 10 (worst possible pain), anchored with five faces at two-point intervals, including very happy (0), happy (2), contented (4), somewhat distressed (6), distressed (8), and very distressed (10). Criterion-related validity was established by correlating the VITAS with sleep disturbance (r=0.63, $P50.01$) since body pain has been associated with difficulty sleeping (Sunshine et al. 1996). Leg strength was rated on a 10-point scale ranging from very week (0) to moderate (5) to very strong (10).

Tinetti balance and gait evaluation. The Tinetti balance and gait evaluation was used to assess range of motion in the participants. This scale was completed for each participant by a physical therapy student or one of the researchers. Each functional item was rated from 0 to 2, and a higher total score was considered optimal. The balance scale includes items like sitting balance, arising, standing balance, turning 360 degrees, and sitting down. The gait scale includes items like step length and height (clearing the floor), step continuity, step symmetry, and walking stance.

Movement therapy sessions. The movement therapy sessions lasted 50 min each and for four sessions over the 2 week period. Music was played in the background for some of the session. Props were used for the subjects to rub themselves on different body parts, for example, rolling a 1-inch diameter yard-long wooden dowel under the feet, down the back or across the thighs for 1-min periods each. The dowels were also held at each end by two individuals as a way of moving in space together. The purpose of this was to stimulate deep pressure receptors which has been notably effective in massage therapy.

Stages of sessions

Warm-up
This is usually done while seated in chairs in a circle. Introductions may be done verbally and through movement (such as passing a movement for everyone to mimic or an object around the circle). Focusing on breathing (breathing deeply together) and doing gentle movements with all the body parts such as raising the arms and legs and rotating the head, to articulate and sense kinesthetically all the body parts. Self-massage can also be used as part of this process.

Thematic preparation
Larger, whole body movements are encouraged such as swaying, pushing, stamping, twisting, turning, stepping, swinging etc, so that people expand and stretch themselves and use the space more fully. All participants are encouraged to contribute a movement, that is, to initiate a movement which can be followed and shared by everyone in the group.

Resting and sharing
This is an opportunity for the participants to rest physically and

notice any changes in themselves, such as increased heart rate, expanded respiration, and how their bodies have responded to moving. Although many shared their feelings of well-being during this segment, we did not record these comments because of their subjective nature.

Developing the theme

This is the time when the group works more specifically with movements that emerged during the second section. People are encouraged to let go more fully into the dynamics of a movement, for example, to intensify the movement and feeling of swaying or rocking. Sometimes this process is enhanced by working in pairs and mirroring or providing mutual support. A prop such as a ball or rope helps enlarge or focus a movement. There may be work with breathing, progressive relaxation of all body parts, and the use of imagery and visualization.

Results

Group by repeated measures ANOVAs were performed to compare the groups with the first session and last session as the repeated measures. As can be seen in Table 1, the participants improved in their functional motion on the Tinetti scale score, F $(1,31)=8.13$, $P50.01$, and specifically on the Gait scale, F $(1,31)=4.91$, $P50.05$. Leg strength increased, F $(1,31)=5.03$, $P50.05$, and leg pain was significantly decreased, F $(1,31)=6.18$, $P50.05$. Even though the change in the means for the overall pain and back pain were in a positive direction, these changes were not significant.

Discussion

The significantly greater improvement in leg strength noted in the movement group probably directly derived from the leg

Table 1 Means (SD) for measures taken before the first class and after the last class (wait list control group means are second line of each measure)

Measures	First day	Last day	P value
POMS-total[b]	20.80 (9.30)	20.39 (10.57)	ns
	19.72 (12.13)	20.45 (11.01)	ns
Overall pain[b]	3.69 (3.55)	3.19 (3.23)	ns
	3.51 (3.12)	3.29 (3.76)	ns
Back pain[b]	3.38 (4.01)	2.20 (2.97)	ns
	3.95 (3.87)	3.16 (2.59)	ns
Leg pain[b]	3.19 (3.31)	1.40 (1.99)	0.005
	3.16 (3.42)	2.93 (2.35)	ns
Leg strength[a]	5.50 (2.56)	6.38 (2.73)	0.05
	4.92 (2.19)	5.19 (2.45)	ns
Total Tinetti score[a]	17.19 (4.23)	19.38 (5.51)	0.01
	18.01 (5.16)	18.24 (5.02)	ns
-Balance[a]	9.19 (2.37)	9.94 (2.98)	ns
	9.07 (3.16)	9.49 (3.29)	ns
-Gait	8.00 (2.42)	9.56 (2.56)	0.001
	8.41 (2.17)	9.19 (2.45)	ns

[a]Higher is optimal.
[b]Lower is optimal.

movements during the movement therapy sessions. Strength may have contributed to the significant improvement in gait including step lengths and height (clearing the floor), step continuity, step symmetry and walking stance. These are consistent with many studies in the literature supporting improvements in muscle strength (Lan et al. 1998) and in balance (Schaller 1996; Wolf et al. 1997; Wolfson et al. 1996), although none of these investigators used the Tinetti scale and specifically assessed balance and gait.

Although, there were trends in the reduction of back pain, only the leg pain significantly decreased over the course of the study. This, again, may have directly derived from the active leg movements involved in the creative movement therapy sessions.

The combined effects of the movement therapy on leg strength, gait, and reduction of leg pain suggest that this may be an effective therapy for these problems in the elderly. The freer movements and the lesser degree of structure and concentration required of the elderly may make this a more

enjoyable kind of movement therapy than the more frequently studied Tai Chi.

Acknowledgements

The authors would like to thank the senior citizens who participated in this study and the researchers who assisted with data collection. This research was supported by an NIMH Senior Research Scientist Award to Tiffany Field (#MH00331), and funds from Johnson & Johnson to the Touch Research Institutes.

REFERENCES

Berman B, Swyers J 1997 Establishing a research agenda for investigating alternative medical interventions for chronic pain. Primary Care 24: 743–758

Cook A 1998 Elderly recipients of home nursing services: Pain, disability and functional competence. Journal of Advanced Nursing 53: 1117–1126

Finne-Soveri H, Tilvis R 1998 Daily pain, its associates and impact on work load in institutional long-term care. Archives of Gerontology and Geriatrics 27: 105–114

Gaglliese L, Melzack R 1997 Chronic pain in elderly people. Pain 70: 3–14

Gloth F 1996 Concerns with chronic analgesic therapy in elderly patients. American Journal of Medicine 101: 19–24

Hopman R, Kraaimaat F, Bijlsma J 1997 Quality of Life Research 6: 67–76

Horgas A, Tsai P 1998 Analgesic drug prescription and use in cognitively impaired nursing home residents. Nursing Research 47: 235–242

Judge JO, Lindsey C, Underwood M, Winsemius D 1993 Balance improvements in older women: Effects of exercise training. Physical Therapy 73: 254–262

Klinger L, Spaulding S 1998 Chronic pain in the elderly: Is silence really golden? Physical and Occupational Therapy in Geriatrics 15: 1–17

Lan C, Lai JS, Chen SY, Wong MK 1998 12-month Tai Chi training in the elderly: Its effect on health fitness. Med Science Sports Exercise 30: 345–351

McNair DM, Lorr M 1964 An analysis of mood in neurotics. Journal of Abnormal Social Psychology 69: 620–627

McNair DM, Lorr M, Droppleman LF 1971 Profile of Mood States. San Diego: Educational and industrial testing services.

Parmelee P, Lawton MP, Katz I 1998 The structure of depression among elderly institution residents: Affective and somatic correlates of physical frailty. Journal of Gerontology 53: 155–162

Province MA, Hadley EC, Hornbrook MC 1995 The effects of exercise on falls in elderly patiens. A preplanned meta-analysis of the FICSIT trials. Frailty and Injuries: Cooperative studies on intervention techniques. Journal of American Medical Association 273: 1341–1347

Pugatch D, Haskell, McNair DM 1969 Predictors and patterns of change associated with the course of time limited psychotherapy. Mimeo Report

Richardson J, Bresland K 1998 The management of postsurgical pain in the elderly population. Drugs Aging 13: 17–31

Ross M, Crook J 1998 Elderly recipients of home nursing services: pain, disability and functional competence. Journal of Advance Nursing 18: 1117–1126

Schaller KJ 1996 Tai Chi Chih: an exercise option for older adults. Journal of Gerontological Nursing 22: 12–17

Sunshine W, Field TM, Quintino O, Fierro K, Kuhn C, Burman I, Schanberg S 1996 Fibromyalgia benefits from massage therapy and tanscutaneous electrical stimulation. Journal of Clinical Rheumatology 2: 18–22

Tse SK, Bailey DM 1998 Tai chi and postural control in the well elderly. American Journal of Occupational Therapy 46: 295–300

Weiner D, Pieper C, McConnell E, Martinez S et al. 1996 Pain measurement in elders with chronic low back pain: Traditional and alternative approaches. Pain 67: 461–467

Wolf SL, Barnhart HX, Kutner NG, McNeely E, Coogler C, Xu T 1996 Reducing frailty and falls in older persons: an investigation of Tai Chi and computerized balance training. Atlanta FICSIT Group. Frailty and injuries: Cooperative studies of intervention techniques. Journal of the American Geriatrics Society 44: 489–497

Wolf SL, Barnhart HX, Ellison GL, Coogler CE 1997 The effect of Tai Chi Quan and computerized balance training on postural stability in older subjects. Atlanta FICSIT Group. Frailty and injuries: Cooperative studies on intervention techniques. Physical Therapy 77: 371–381

Wolfson L, Whipple R, Derby C, Judge J, King M, Amerman P, Schmidt J, Smyers D 1996 Balance and strength training in older adults: Intervention gains and Tai chi maintenance. Journal of the American Geriatrics Society 44: 498–506

Massage Therapy

Elder Retired Volunteers Benefit From Giving Massage Therapy to Infants

Tiffany M. Field
Maria Hernandez-Reif
Olga Quintino
University of Miami School of Medicine

Saul Schanberg
Cynthia Kuhn
Duke University Medical School

This exploratory within-subjects study compared the effects of elder retired volunteers giving massage to infants with receiving massage themselves. Three times a week for 3 weeks, 10 elder volunteers (8 females, mean age = 70 years) received Swedish massage sessions. For another 3 weeks, three times per week, the same elderly volunteers massaged infants at a nursery school. Receiving massage first versus giving massage first was counterbalanced across subjects. Immediately after the first- and last-day sessions of giving massages, the elder retired volunteers had less anxiety and depression and lower stress hormones (salivary cortisol) levels. Over the 3-week period, depression and catecholamines (norepinephrine and epinephrine) decreased and lifestyle and health improved. These effects were not as strong for the 3-week period when they received massage, possibly because the elder retired volunteers initially felt awkward about being massaged and because they derived more satisfaction massaging the infants.

Massage facilitates growth and development of healthy, preterm neonates (Field et al., 1986; Kuhn et al., 1991; Scafidi et al., 1990; Scafidi et al., 1986). Ottenbacher et al. (1987) conducted a meta-analysis of 19 stimulation studies and estimated that 72% of the preterm infants receiving massage were

AUTHORS' NOTE: This research was supported by a National Institute of Mental Health (NIMH) Research Scientist Award (#MH00331) and an NIMH Research Grant (#MH46586) to Tiffany Field and a grant from Johnson and Johnson to the Touch Research Institute. Correspondence and requests for reprints should be sent to Tiffany Field, Ph.D., Touch Research Institute, University of Miami School of Medicine, P. O. Box 016820, Miami, FL 33101.

The Journal of Applied Gerontology, Vol. 17 No. 2, June 1998 229-239 positively affected. Massage also decreases anxiety, depression and stress hormones (cortisol and norepinephrine levels) and increases sleep in child and adolescent psychiatric patients (Field et al., 1992). Further, massage reduces depression and enhances immune function in HIV patients (Ironson et al., 1996). Massage therapy appears to reduce the number of physical and psychiatric conditions observed in a variety of populations. Given the success of this therapeutic technique, it is possible that it will be used more frequently in the future for maintaining health and promoting well-being. However, it will first be necessary to find a cost-effective way to administer massage therapy.

Licensed massage therapists or student trainees typically provide massages. One additional potentially inexpensive source of therapists for infants is elder retired volunteers who provide various kinds of caregiving. It is also conceivable that they may benefit from the additional touch they receive as they massage infants. Research to date has only focused on the effects of receiving massage. Nothing is known about the effects on the person giving the massage.

Elder volunteers at hospitals and health care facilities are a good resource for providing infant massage for several reasons: (a) They volunteer their time and their services at no cost; (b) they are generally retired individuals who have the extra time needed to devote special attention to the care of others; and (c) research shows that some elderly people are prone to feelings of loneliness, depression, and decreased immune function. Because massage is noted to decrease depression and enhance immune function, the elder retired volunteers may benefit themselves from the extra touch they receive from providing massage (Hendrie & Crosset, 1990; McCullough, 1991; Ruegg, Zisook, & Swerdlow, 1988). For these reasons, elders are considered ideal for examining the effects of giving massages.

The aim of this exploratory study was to examine the therapeutic effects of elder retired volunteers giving massages. We expected that giving massages to infants would have positive effects on both the volunteers and the infants. Specifically, we predicted that the volunteers would have increased social contacts, fewer depressive symptoms, improved sleep and eating patterns, and improved self-esteem.

Method

Participants

The sample was composed of 10 elder volunteers (8 females; mean age = 70, range 63 to 84 years). A power estimate based on a moderate size effect at power = .80 and $p < .05$ indicated that a sample size of 10 was adequate. The elder volunteers were recruited from advertisements in a community newspaper and from flyers circulated at a social organization for retirees. Interested participants were screened for chronic medical conditions and scheduled for their first appointment. Two volunteers declined to participate due to scheduling conflicts. Informed consent was obtained and the participants were briefed that they would receive massage and also give massages to infants. After 2 weeks, 1 volunteer dropped out of the study due to the illness of a family member out of state. The final sample of elder volunteers were Caucasian ($n = 6$) or Hispanic ($n = 4$), middle socioeconomic status (SES) (3.1 on the Hollingshead Index) and averaged 15 years education. Half were married, and half saw other family members only infrequently (monthly or holidays only). None of the volunteers reported experiencing any chronic medical conditions. Only 4 of the volunteers had previously received a massage. This information suggested that receiving massage was a novel experience for this sample.

The 10 elder volunteers massaged 10 healthy, full-term infants between the ages of 1 to 3 months at their nursery school three times a week for 3 weeks. The elders also received massage themselves at a nearby clinic three times a week for 3 weeks. The frequency and duration of the massage period was based on previous studies showing that this was an adequate treatment time to demonstrate effects in this size sample (Field et al., 1992). The order of giving and receiving massages was counterbalanced for order effects. That is, half of the volunteers gave massage for the first 3 weeks and then received it for 3 weeks, and the other half received massage for the first 3 weeks and then gave massage for the second 3 weeks.

Giving massage. A trained research assistant taught Swedish massage techniques to the elder volunteers. The volunteers massaged their assigned infant three times a week for 3 weeks for a total of nine massages. Each massage lasted 15 minutes and consisted of two phases. For the first phase, the infant was placed in a face-up position, and oil was applied to ensure smooth, continuous stroking movements. The volunteer stroked five regions of the infant's body in the following sequence: (a) face—strokes along both sides of the face, flats of fingers across the forehead, circular strokes over the temples and hinge of the jaw, and flat finger strokes over the nose, cheeks, jaw, and chin; (b) chest—strokes on both sides of the chest with the flats of the fingers, going from midline outward, cross strokes from center of chest and going over the shoulders, and strokes on sides of the chest toward the shoulders; (c) stomach—hand-over-hand strokes in a paddlewheel fashion, avoiding the ribs and the tip of the rib cage, and circular motion with fingers in a clockwise direction starting at the appendix; (d) legs—strokes from hip to foot, squeezing and twisting in a wringing motion from hip to foot, massaging foot and toes, stretching the Achilles tendon, and stroking the legs upward toward the heart; and (e) arms—strokes from the shoulders to the hands, and then the same procedure as for the legs.

For the second phase, the infant was placed in a face-down position, and the infant's back was massaged in the following sequence: (a) downward strokes along the back; (b) hand-over-hand movements from the upper back to the buttocks; (c) hands from side to side across the back, including the sides; (d) circular motion from head to buttocks along, but not touching, the spine; (e) simultaneous strokes over the sides of the back from the middle to the sides; (f) rubbing and kneading shoulder muscles; (g) rubbing the neck; (h) stroking along the length of the back; and (i) gentle strokes from crown to feet.

Receiving Massage

The elder volunteers received a 30-minute massage by a trained therapist three times a week for 3 weeks, for a total of nine massages. Their massage also consisted of Swedish massage techniques and focused on the face, neck, shoulders, arms, legs, back, and feet, but was twice as long as the infants' massage because at least twice the body surface needed to be massaged in the elder volunteers versus the infants. For the first 15 minutes, the massage was performed in the face-up position and for the last 15 minutes, it was administered face down. The massage began with lengthening and stretching of the neck and spine, then stroking of the forehead and face. Depressing the shoulders and applying pressure to the tender points followed, and then the arms and legs were stretched and the arms were lifted and moved in a slow circular motion. Short, smooth strokes were used to massage the palms of the hands and the soles of the feet, with extra pressure applied to the tender points. While face down, medium pressure was applied to the upper shoulder and neck area, and brisk rubbing movements were performed along the spine.

Assessments ·

Subjects were informed that assessments were being made on massage effects on the elder volunteers including self-reports (of anxiety, mood, depression, self-esteem, and daily activities), behavior observations, and stress hormones from urine and saliva samples. On the first (Day 1) and last (Day 21) days of the treatment periods (both the giving-massage and receiving-massage periods), assessment measures were collected according to the following schedule: (a) 45 minutes prior to the massage, saliva and urine were collected from the elder volunteers; (b) 40 minutes prior to the massage, the self-report measures (Feeling Good Thermometer, Multiple Affect Adjective Check-List, Center for Epidemiologic Studies-Depression Scale, Duke-UNC Health Profile, and a Lifestyle Diary) were administered to the elder volunteers; (c) immediately after the massage, the volunteers received two of the self-report measures again (Feeling Good Thermometer and the Multiple Affect Adjective Check-List); and (d) 30 minutes following the massage, saliva samples were taken from the volunteers.

Short-Term Measures (immediate effects)

The following three measures were administered before and after the massage to obtain immediate effects of the therapy.

The Feeling Good Thermometer is a visual analog scale for measuring affect. The scale ranges from 0 to 10 with a higher temperature reflecting more positive feelings. This scale was selected because it offered a simple measure for the elderly to gauge their present mood state.

The Multiple Affect Adjective Check-List (MAACL) (Zuckerman & Lubin, 1965) provided a measure of anxiety and depressed mood. The total score is the number of positive items checked plus the number of zero items not checked. Subjects were given the Today form (as opposed to the General form) of the test. The MAACL is a brief checklist (taking less than 5 minutes to complete) designed to provide valid measures of clinically relevant negative affects including anxiety and depression (and hostility, which was not measured). It has been correlated with physiological and biochemical measures. No significant correlation has been found between the MAACL and age across a number of normal and clinical populations. The Today form of the MAACL has been reported as ideally suited for studies requiring repeated measures of affect over time and for measures of natural stress. Internal reliability ranges are reported between .79 and .90 (Zuckerman & Lubin, 1965).

Saliva samples were collected to assay stress hormone (cortisol) levels. Saliva cortisol is an index of short-term stress hormone change. It has consistently decreased following massage therapy (Field et al., 1992; Ironson et al., 1996). The saliva samples were obtained by placing a cotton dental swab dipped in sugar-free lemonade crystals along the subject's gumline for 30 seconds. The swab is then placed in a syringe, and the saliva is removed and inserted into a microcentrifuge tube for freezing and subsequent assaying. Saliva samples were collected before and 20 minutes after the first and last massage sessions. Due to the 20-minute lag in cortisol change, saliva samples reflect responses occurring 20 minutes prior to sampling.

Longer-Term Measures (first day-last day)

Four measures were obtained on the first and last days of each massage phase (giving and receiving) to determine longer term massage effects on stress hormones, depression, and health.

The Center for Epidemiologic Studies-Depression Scale (CES-D) (Radloff, 1977) was used to measure depressive symptoms of the elder volunteers. The 20-item scale contains items relating to depressed mood and psychophysiologic indicators of depression. Respondents rated how frequently each symptom was experienced during the past week on a 4-point scale. The ratings form a summed score ranging from 0 to 60. A score of 15 is the cut-point typically used in research samples to indicate depressive symptoms. This cut-point corresponds to the 80th percentile of scores in community samples. Both the reliability and validity of the CES-D have been supported across a variety of demographic characteristics, including age, education, and ethnic groups (Radloff, 1977; Radloff & Locke, 1986).

The Duke-UNC Health Profile (DUHP) (Parkerson, Gehlbach, & Wagner, 1981) was used to assess four dimensions of health: symptom status and physical, emotional, and social functioning. This 63-item questionnaire has been used to measure adult health status in primary care settings. Previous research supported the reliability and validity of the DUHP (Parkerson, Gehlbach, & Wagner, 1981).

The Lifestyle Diary was designed specifically for this study from interviews conducted with elderly individuals about their lifestyles. The diary assessed changes in (a) physical activity and health (number of hours of sleep, naps taken, headaches, medications or prescriptions taken, trips to the doctor's office), (b) entertainment-leisure (number of hours of television watching, phone calls made or received, visitors, sexual activities), and (c) eating and drinking (number of cups of coffee, alcoholic drinks, cigarettes smoked, meals eaten in or out). The volunteers completed this checklist about their previous weekend activities at the beginning and end of the study. According to the volunteers' ranking of stress indicators in their daily lives, at least three relevant stress variables were expected to change across the course of the study. The number of cups of coffee was expected to decrease, the number of social phone calls was expected to increase, and the number of doctors' office visits was expected to decrease.

Urine samples were collected from the elder volunteers 45 minutes prior to massage. Urine samples were assayed for longer-term changes in stress hormones (cortisol, norepinephrine, epinephrine, and dopamine). Decreased cortisol and catecholamine levels were expected after receiving massages, based on earlier massage therapy studies (Field et al., 1992; Ironson et al., 1996).

Results

Repeated measures MANOVAs were performed on the self-report data and the biochemical data. MANOVAs were used to correct for the probability of chance findings. Based on a large number of outcome measures, cause and effect could not be assessed reliably, but the relationship between variables could be determined. These were followed by repeated measures univariate ANOVAs on each of the variables with pre-post massage, first day-last day, and giving versus receiving as the repeated measures.

As can be seen in Table 1, the data analyses suggested the following for giving massage. For the pre-post massage comparisons: (a) Affect improved after the massage on the first and the last day; (b) anxiety was lower after the massage on the first and last day; (c) mood was less depressed after the massage on the first and last days; and (d) cortisol levels were lower after the massage on the first and last days.

For the first day-last day comparisons: (a) Depression decreased from the first to the last day; (b) the health profile scores improved from the first to the last day; and (c) lifestyle diary scores improved. Specifically, the number of visits to the doctor and number of cups of coffee decreased, and the number of social phone calls increased; and (d) The stress hormones norepinephrine and epinephrine levels decreased.

The data analyses suggested the following for receiving massages: For the pre-post massage comparisons: (a) Affect improved after the massage but only on the last day; (b) mood was less depressed after the massage but only on the last day; and (c) cortisol levels were lower after the massage but only on the last day. For the first day-last day comparisons, depression decreased from the first to last day (see Table 2).

Discussion

Although other studies have documented the positive effects of massage therapy on depression and stress hormones (Field et al., 1992; Ironson et al., 1996), this study was the first to measure the benefits for elder volunteers serving as massage therapists. As expected, the study showed that elder volunteers benefited from giving massage therapy. Massaging the infants

Table 1. Means for Giving Massage Therapy (standard deviations in parentheses)

Variables	First Day		Last Day	
Pre-Post Therapy	Pre	Post	Pre	Post
Affect	7.7 (2.1)	8.7 (.7)*	8.3 (1.6)	9.4 (.9)*
Anxiety	.6 (.5)	.1 (.3)*	.3 (.3)	.1 (.3)*
Depressed mood	1.4 (.6)	.7 (.7)*	1.7 (.6)	1.1 (.7)*
Saliva cortisol	1.9 (.1)	1.3 (.2)****	1.7 (.4)	1.3 (.2)****

First Day-Last Day	First Day	Last Day
Depression (CES-D)	18.2 (4.3)	14.3 (5.0)*
Health profile	60.9 (14.9)	67.2 (16.4)*
Lifestyle diary	35.9 (2.3)	30.9 (2.1)*
Norepinephrine	52.3 (16.3)	32.9 (6.2)***
Epinephrine	14.1 (.2)	7.7 (1.6)****
Dopamine	330.2 (85.2)	279.6 (24.7)
Cortisol	103.6 (13.6)	104.3 (6.1)

NOTE: Pre-post significance levels are indicated by superscripts after the second and after the fourth column means in the top half of the table. Superscripts in the bottom half of the table indicate first day-last day significance levels (*$p < .05$, *** $p < .005$, **** $p < .001$).

Table 2. Means for Receiving Massage Therapy (standard deviations in parentheses)

Variables	First Day		Last Day	
Pre-Post Therapy	Pre	Post	Pre	Post
Affect	8.9 (.7)	9.0 (1.0)	8.0 (1.0)	8.9 (1.0)*
Anxiety	.4 (.4)	.2 (.3)	.6 (.4)	.7 (.7)
Depressed mood	.9 (1.0)	.8 (.6)	.8 (.6)	.4 (.7)**
Saliva cortisol	1.5 (.8)	1.2 (.2)	1.1 (.2)	.8 (.3)*

First Day-Last Day	First Day	Last Day
Depression (CES-D)	14.4 (1.4)	11.9 (2.1)**
Health Profile	70.9 (9.5)	74.6 (13.5)
Lifestyle Diary	36.1 (2.3)	34.4 (2.1)
Norepinephrine	48.9 (5.9)	40.7 (13.2)
Epinephrine	15.6 (1.7)	13.8 (.4)
Dopamine	310.9 (86.9)	307.2 (85.2)
Cortisol	111.5 (19.3)	109.9 (12.8)

NOTE: Pre-post significance levels are indicated by superscripts after the second and the fourth column means in the top half of the table. Superscripts in the bottom half of the table indicate first day-last day significance levels (*$p < .05$, ** $p < .01$).

immediately affected the elder volunteers, as evidenced by their improved affect, their decreased anxiety and depressed mood, and their decreased stress hormone (salivary cortisol) levels. Their decreased stress levels probably contributed to their decreased depression over the 3-week period, their lifestyle changes (including drinking less coffee, making fewer trips to the doctor's office, and increased social calls) and their improved health. The decreased stress hormones (cortisol and catecholamine levels) would predictably lead to enhanced immune function (Ironson et al, 1996).

These positive effects may relate to the important function of touch in enhancing well-being, especially in the context of a structured activity involving social responsibility. Presumably, both of these mechanisms were operating, inasmuch as fewer positive effects were noted over the 3-week period when the same volunteers were receiving massage therapy. For that treatment period, the positive effects were only noted on the last day of the study. The fewer effects noted for receiving massage may have related to the elder volunteers feeling awkward about the initial massage sessions, noting that they had "never been touched in that way." Thus, the initial anxiety about being massaged may have attenuated the expected immediate effects of receiving massage therapy.

One limitation of this study was the lack of a control group, as only the order of giving versus receiving massage was counterbalanced. Having a control group would help determine the extent to which giving or receiving massage can benefit elder retired people. In addition, assaying immune function would be an important additional measure insofar as waning immune function is a problem at this age. Further, cost-benefit analyses would demonstrate the cost-effectiveness of massage therapy benefiting both groups of people (the elder retired volunteers and the infants) at the same time. If the value of massage therapy for the giver, and specifically for elder volunteers, is confirmed in future studies with larger samples and with control groups (missing from this exploratory study), then this service might be adopted on a more widespread basis for elders and for infants to enhance their health and well-being.

REFERENCES

Field, T., Morrow, C., Valdeon, C., Larson, S. Kuhn, C. & Schanberg, S. (1992). Massage reduces anxiety in child and adolescent psychiatric patients. *Journal of the American Academy of Child and Adolescent Psychiatry, 31*, 125-131.

Field, T., Schanberg, S., Scafidi, F., Bauer, C., Vega-Lahr, N., Garcia, R., Nystrom, J. & Kuhn, C. (1986). Tactile/kinesthetic stimulation effects on preterm neonates. *Pediatrics, 77*, 654-658.

Hendrie, H., & Crosset, J. (1990). An overview of depression in the elderly. *Psychiatric Annals, 20*, 64-69.

Ironson, G., Field, T., Scafidi, F., Kumar, M., Patarca, R., Price, A., Goncalves, A., Hashimoto, M., Kumar, A., Burman, I., Tetenman, C., & Fletcher, M. (1996). Massage therapy is associated with enhancement of the immune system's cytotoxic capacity. *International Journal of Neuroscience, 84*, 205-218.

Kuhn, C., Schanberg, S., Field, T., Symanski, R., Zimmerman, E., Scafidi, F., & Roberts, J. (1991). Tactile/kinesthetic stimulation effects on sympathetic and adrenocortical function in preterm infants. *Journal of Pediatrics, 119*, 434-440.

McCullough, P. (1991). Geriatric depression: Atypical presentation, hidden meaning. *Geriatrics, 46*, 72-76.

Ottenbacher, K., Muller, L., Brandt, D., Heintzelman, A., Hojem, P., & Sharpe, P. (1987). The effectiveness of tactile stimulation as a form of early intervention: A quantitative evaluation. *Journal of Developmental and Behavioral Pediatrics, 8*, 68-76.

Parkerson, G., Gehlbach, S., & Wagner, E. (1981). The Duke-UNC Health Profile. *Medical Care, 19*, 806-828.

Radloff, L. (1977). The CES-D scale: A self-report depression scale for research in the general population. *Applied Psychological Measures, 1*, 385-401.

Radloff, L. & Locke, B.Z. (1986). The community mental health assessment survey and the CES-D scale. In Weissman, Myers, & Ross (Eds.) *Community Surveys*. New Brunswick, NJ: Rutgers University Press.

Ruegg, R., Zisook, S., & Swerdlow, M. (1988). Depression in the aged: An overview. *Psychiatric Clinics of North America, 11*, 83-108.

Scafidi, F., Field, T., Schanberg, S., Bauer, C., Tucci, K., Roberts, J., Morrow, C., & Kuhn, C. (1990). Massage stimulates growth in preterm infants: A replication. *Infant Behavior and Development, 13*, 167-188.

Scafidi, F., Field, T., Schanberg, S. Bauer, C., Vega-Lahr, N., & Garcia, R. (1986). Effects of tactile/kinesthetic stimulation on the clinical course and sleep/wake behavior of preterm neonates. *Infant Behavior and Development, 9*, 91-105.

Zuckerman, M., & Lubin, B. (1965). *MAACL-Multiple Affect Adjective Check-List*. San Diego, CA: Educational and Industrial Testing Service.

Article accepted November 12, 1997.

Tiffany M. Field, Ph.D., is the director of the Touch Research Institute at the University of Miami School of Medicine, and a professor of pediatrics, psychology and psychiatry. She has been conducting massage therapy research for approximately 20 years, primarily with infants, including preterm infants, cocaine-exposed infants, and HIV-exposed infants. This research program has basically demonstrated the pain-relieving (less distress behavior) and stress-alleviating (reduced heart rate respiration and cortisol levels, and increased oxygen tension levels) effects of massage therapy during invasive procedures in the neonatal intensive care unit and growth-inducing effects for preterm infants. More recent studies have focused on immune and autoimmune disorders in children and adults. In children, preliminary studies have been conducted on asthma, diabetes, dermatitis, juvenile rheumatoid arthritis, and pediatric oncology. In adults, immune-autoimmune studies have been conducted on fibromyalgia, chronic fatigue syndrome, HIV, and breast cancer.

Maria Hernandez-Reif, Ph.D. is a senior research associate and the director of the Massage Therapy Research Program at the Touch Research Institute. In collaboration with Dr. Field, she has designed and conducted more than 30 massage therapy studies and has more than 20 articles on massage therapy published, in press, or in review. In the past 3 years she has been responsible for organizing research programs to study massage therapy effects on cancer patients' immune functioning, improving pulmonary functioning, alleviating painful conditions, and reducing stress as a mechanism for improving glycemic control in diabetes and lowering hypertension. In addition to her research experience in designing, conducting, and directing massage therapy programs, Dr. Hernandez-Reif has supervised the activities of more than 30 staff members, including first-year postdoctorate associates, Ph.D. candidates, clinical psychology interns, post-bachelor's-research associates, undergraduate research assistants and interns, and high school candidates for Westinghouse Scholarships.

Olga Quintino, B.S., is a research associate at the Touch Research Institute. In collaboration with Dr. Field, she has designed and conducted massage therapy studies for the past 2 years.

Saul Schanberg is a professor of pharmacology and biological psychiatry at Duke University Medical Center. His research interest over the past 20 years has focused on the influence of mother-infant interactions on the expression of genetic potential either adaptive or maladaptive in establishing the physiological processes involved in the growth and development of the neonate.

Cynthia Kuhn is a professor of pharmacology at Duke University Medical Center. Her research over the past 20 years has focused on the ontogeny of specific neurotransmitter systems that mediate stress responses and responses to psychoactive drugs.

ISSN: 2167-7182
Gerontology &
Geriatric Research

Review Article

Centenarians: A Narrative Review

Tiffany Field*

Departments of Pediatrics, Psychology, University of Miami/Miller School of Medicine and Fielding Graduate University, Florida, USA

ABSTRACT

Centenarians (100-109- years-old) were as many as 573,000 as of 2020. Most of the recent literature has been focused on identifying the unique characteristics of centenarians or predictor variables for their longevity. These have included genes, female gender, personality traits including extroversion and optimism, stress avoidance, resilience, social engagement, nutrition (especially Mediterranean or other Blue Zone diets), no smoking or chronic diseases, and physical biomarkers including low BMI, LDL and diastolic blood pressure. Although many negative effects have been expected for being centenarians, loneliness and frailty were the only prevalent problems in this recent literature. Although the lifestyle factors already mentioned have contributed to longevity, the most frequently discussed underlying mechanism has been chronic inflammatory status called "inflammaging" which has apparently been adaptive and less detrimental for centenarians than for younger aging samples. Unfortunately, studies on centenarians have been limited to cross-sectional or retrospective data, as the research on predicting extreme longevity has been relatively new.

Keywords: Social engagement; Cognition; Longevity

INTRODUCTION

This narrative review involved entering the term centenarians to find literature from the last five years on PubMed and PsycIN-FO. The search yielded 265 papers. However, following exclusion criteria including case reports and non-English papers, this review is a summary of the research reported in 34 papers. The recent literature on centenarians is predominantly focused on predictors of longevity or positive characteristics of being a centenarian. This narrative review is divided into sections on prevalence of centenarians, predictors/positive features, and expected negative effects. These are followed by sections on potential underlying mechanisms for longevity and methodological limitations of this recent literature. Among the contributory factors to the onset of cachexia we can list anorexia and metabolic alterations, i.e. increased inflammatory status, increased muscle proteolysis, impaired carbohydrate, protein and lipid metabolism. Inflammation does play a crucial role in its pathogenesis and its presence allows for cachexia identification.

Prevalence of centenarians

The first article on longevity as a human desire was published in 1838 when the average life expectancy was 40 years [1]. And, in 1842, although the average lifespan in Belgium was only 32 years, 16 centenarians were living there (the oldest being 111) [2].

The prevalence of centenarians (age 100-109) has increased from 417,000 in 2015 to 573,000 in 2020 (a 38% increase in just 5 years). And the prevalence is predicted to reach 19 million by the year 2100 [1]. As these authors have suggested, most children born in developed countries since the year 2000 will become centenarians. Reputedly, most centenarians will reach that age because they can postpone age-related pathologies (e. g. heart disease, stroke, COPD, cancer, respiratory infection, type 2 diabetes, osteoporosis and dementia). And they have several positive lifestyle activities like a nutritious diet and physical activity as well as positive attitudes including stress avoidance and resilience.

These large numbers of centenarians are surprising given that the average global life expectancy is 71 years, although significant variation has been noted across countries, e.g. Sierra Leone at 48 years, U.S. at 79 and Monaco at 87 [2]. Some places like the Blue Zones are home to many centenarians including Okinawa in Japan, the Nicoya peninsula in Costa Rica, Ikaria in Greece, Sardinia in Italy and Loma Linda in California [1]. The longevity of these centenarians has been attributed to a genetic predisposition, stress avoidance, resilience (an increased ability to respond to minor stressors of daily life) and a positive lifestyle in general with good nutrition in particular. The Blue Zones are said to have nine principles including strong family connections, close social engagements, meaningful life purpose, low intensity physical activity throughout

Correspondence to: Tiffany Field, Departments of Pediatrics, Psychology, University of Miami/Miller School of Medicine and Fielding Graduate University, Florida, USA; E-mail: tfield@med.miami.edu

Received: 04-May-2023, Manuscript No. jggr-23-21212; **Editor assigned:** 6-May-2023, Pre QC No. P-21212; **Reviewed:** 18-May-2023, QC No. Q-21212; **Revised:** 23-May-2023, Manuscript No. R-21212; **Published:** 30-May-2023, DOI: 10.35248/2167-7182.23.12.667

Citation: Field T. (2023) Centenarians: A Narrative Review. J Gerontol Geriatr Res.12:667.

Copyright: © 2023 Field T. This is an open-access article distributed under the terms of the Creative Commons Attribution License, which permits unrestricted use, distribution, and reproduction in any medium, provided the original author and source are credited.

the day, staying stress-free, moderate alcohol consumption, belief in a higher power and especially good nutrition (high amounts of legumes, nuts and vegetables, avoiding over-eating and applying caloric restriction) [1].

Predictors or positive characteristics

Many predictors or positive characteristics have been noted for centenarians. These include genes, female gender, demographics, personality characteristics including extroversion and optimism, stress avoidance, resilience, social engagement, nutrition, no smoking, no chronic disease and biomarkers including lower Inflammation (Table 1).

Genes

Hundreds of genes have been implicated as influencing longevity (300-750 genes) [2]. These authors have given examples including oxidative stress genes (SOD3, HSPA) and a glucose metabolism gene (IGF-1) and they claim that heritability approximates 30 per cent, although other estimates have suggested 38 per cent. Phenotypic variation, as expected, has been partitioned into genetic and environmental variance components. Given that the research on genetic components of longevity is larger and more complex than the 750 genes reported, this literature review does not include a discussion of genetics, except to acknowledge their importance.

Demographics

Some demographic variables were addressed in a study from China. In what the authors labeled "the largest sample of centenarians in the world ", centenarians (100-109 years-old) were compared with nonagenarians (90-99 years), octogenarians (80-89) and younger elders (65-79) from the Chinese Longitudinal Health Study which involved face-to-face interviews (N=12,047 centenarians) [3]. Eighty-eight per cent of the males were widowed and 98% of the females. The majority of the centenarians lived with family members. Fewer of the rural centenarians were satisfied with life compared to urban centenarians (62% vs. 69%). But, a greater per cent of the rural centenarians were performing better on activities of daily living (54 vs 37%). The authors suggested that this finding was related to the centenarians living in a more natural environment that was healthier and that they continued gardening. The gardening and the natural environment variables were, of course, confounded in this study.

Gender differences

Gender differences in centenarians have frequently been reported, typically suggesting that female centenarians live longer. In the longevity study from China already mentioned, women lived longer but experienced worse health [3]. A greater number of males had better health (56 vs. 51%), had more active activities of daily living (51 vs. 46%), better cognitive function (43 vs. to 25%) and less disease (39 vs. 46%). However, significant gender disparity was noted for several confounding variables including males having greater socioeconomic status, education and outdoor activity and less disease.

Other gender differences that might affect longevity were noted in a study from Belgium (N=3000) [4]. In that sample, male centenarian lived two times longer with spouses than female centenarians. Females lived alone for more than half their lives. Males also had younger spouses and females had older spouses. Most of the centenarians from the sample ended their lives in a nursing home, but very late in life.

In a study entitled "Centenarians born before 1919 are resistant to COVID-19", the oldest females in the Sicilian sample were the most resistant (Caruso, et al.). The authors related that finding to the women's exposure to the 1918 Spanish flu epidemic, giving them antibodies.

Most of the super centenarians (110-122 years-old) are also females [5]. These authors noted that this sex gap in longevity is also common in non-human animals, especially mammals. They related this to the "cost of sexual selection and sexual dimorphism". They further elaborated this mechanism as mitochondria being transmitted through females in most species, a phenomenon that has been labeled "the mother's curse". They noted that in Calabria (southern Italy) there have been twice as many female centenarians. The sex gap has also been noted there in super centenarians with the oldest female being 122 years-old (a longevity record). Another theory they advanced is that estrogen with its antioxidant and antinflammatory properties, in contrast to testosterone, is protective against many diseases.

Personality characteristics

Personality characteristics have also been the focus of research on centenarians. In one study, 65% of centenarians were noted to be extroverted, 50% open-minded and 35% emotionally stable [6]. The authors suggested that these personality characteristics contributed to more than 50% of the sample being free of depression ananxiety. In the Chinese longevity sample, centenarians were noted to be more resilient than other age groups [3]. Resilience was defined as the ability to adapt positively to adversity including having personal tenacity, optimism, secure relationships and self-control and coping with negative mood. Nonagenarians (90-99 years-old) who had psychological resilience had a 43% greater likelihood of becoming centenarians.

In a study entitled "Storytelling reveals the active, positive lives of centenarians", 16 healthy centenarians from the UK were living as independently as possible and continuing their growth and development and their ongoing close relationships [7]. Their stories revealed a positive picture of aging, thus counteracting negative stereotypes. When asked about difficulties and loss, their expressions were "accept whatever life brings", "just plod on", and "do what you can to make things better and then move on".

Social engagement

Although social engagement or social connection is one of the nine principles of the Blue Zones, only one study on social connection could be found in this recent literature on centenarians. In

Table 1: Predictors/positive characteristics of centenarians.

Predictor	First author
Genes	Eovirdaraju
Demographics	Zheng
Gender differences	Zeng, Poulain, Caruso, Marais
Personality characteristics	Tafaro, Zeng, Koch
Social engagement	Hso
Nutrition	Dakic, Dominguez, Crous-Bou, Gu
Chronic diseases	Barak, Ioakeim-Skoufa
Biomarkers	Hai, Zeng, Dakic

this study from Taipei, typologies of loneliness, social connection and living alone were formed to determine their relationships with psychological well-being [8]. The largest group was the not lonely, socially connected and living with others (53%). The not lonely, not socially connected and living with others comprised a smaller percent of the sample (27%). And very small numbers were noted for the lonely and socially connected (5%) and the lonely, not socially connected but living with others (7%). As might be expected, the lonely groups were more depressed and had less life satisfaction, but the lonely only comprised 12% of the sample and only 5% lived alone, so the living arrangement was not the determinant of loneliness or the lack of social connection. Although loneliness has been a negative effect of being centenarian in several studies, it was infrequent, at least in this sample.

Nutrition

The Blue Zone diets have been described in a couple recent reviews of the literature. In one of the reviews, the Okinawa diet was described as being calorie restricted starting at an early age in young children and continuing years later among septuagenarians [1]. The diet of Sardinia in this review was described as a plant-based diet with high cereal intake and some poultry. The centenarians of Ikaria were noted to follow the Mediterranean diet. However, other variables like family solidarity, social interaction and physical activity have, not surprisingly, confounded the nutritional effects in these Blue Zones.

In the second review, the Okinawa diet was described as being 80% calories from veggies, small amounts of fish and limited lean meat, and sweet potatoes was the main source of carbohydrates [9]. The Japanese diet was described as being rice, veggies, fish, soy, green tea and seaweed and 80% less fat than the Mediterranean diet. These authors described Japan as having "the longest life expectancy and having the greatest number of centenarians". The Nordic diet includes fish, cabbage, root veggies, berries, potatoes, rapeseed oil and fish (salmon, sardines, mackerel and herring). The Mediterranean diet was said to have the largest number of publications and was plant-based including colorful veggies, fruit, nuts, grains, olive oil, fish, dairy products, eggs and wine and only occasional animal-derived food. The Loma Linda, California diet was suggested to be the only fish-vegetarian (pescatarian) diet with the centenarians residing there reputedly having the "lowest incidence of mortality". However, as many as 9000 of those living in Loma Linda belong to the Seventh Day Adventists, which has potentially confounded the effects of their diet.

The authors of this review suggested that fruits and veggies have been inversely associated with non-communicable diseases because of their antioxidant and their anti-inflammatory properties [9]. In addition, they increase energy, fiber, satiety, glycemic control, blood lipids and gastrointestinal function. They are also sources of phytochemicals such as polyphenols, carotenoids and phytosterols.

In a paper entitled "Plant-rich dietary patterns, plant foods and nutrients and telomere length", telomere length was shortened by inflammation and oxidative stress [10]. But plants as antioxidants as well as anti-inflammatories slowed this process. The authors suggested that centenarians were following a Mediterranean diet for that purpose, i.e. consuming seeds (nuts, grains and coffee) and colorful veggies (providing carotenoids).

In a study from Canada that highlighted the importance of diet, centenarians (N=122) were compared to aging adults 65-86-years-

old (N= 12,626) [11]. The frequency of food consumption was measured over the last 12 months. The aging adult group had a western diet (french fries, red meat, processed meat) more frequently than nutrient rich vegetables, fruit, nuts and whole grains. The aging adults also used alcohol more frequently. The authors attributed these findings to the aging not only having a poor diet but also being less educated and more frequently living alone. They suggested that the aging adults may have been more fatalistic as they "approached the end of their lives". Further, they mentioned that the national dietary guidelines were not modified until the 1980s in Canada. Physical activity was not measured in this study and methodological problems included the two groups being from different generations and having unequal sample sizes, thus limiting the reliability of the findings.

Chronic diseases

Centenarians have also reputedly been free of chronic diseases as compared to older adults. This has been demonstrated in a few studies. In a paper entitled "The great escape: Centenarians exceptional health", centenarians (N=292) were compared with elderly adults (N= 103,377) from New Zealand [12]. As would be expected, there were more women in the sample (75%). The centenarians were not only free of chronic diseases compared to the older adults but they were not smoking and there was a greater rate of social engagement in their group. In still another study, centenarians were compared to octogenarians and nonagenarians [13]. Centenarians had less prevalent chronic disease, drugs and polypharmacy. Once again the unequal sample sizes limited the power of these analyses resulting in lower reliability of these findings.

The Seven Countries Study that included prospective observations and trials on diverse samples attributed the absence of chronic non-communicable diseases to the Mediterranean diet that was being followed [14]. The Mediterranean diet was thought to be responsible for the prevention and management of age-associated, non-communicable diseases including cardiovascular, metabolic, neurodegenerative and respiratory diseases as well as cancer, depression, and fragility fractures. Other variables were not reported for this seven countries study.

Biomarkers

Biomarkers of centenarians have been highlighted in a few studies in this recent literature. In a paper entitled "BMI, blood pressure and plasma lipids among centenarians and their offspring", centenarians (N=253) were compared with their offspring (N=217, mean age=70) [15]. The centenarians had a lower BMI (body mass index), lower LDL (low density lipoprotein) and lower diastolic blood pressure but higher systolic blood pressure. They also had less previous obesity but more previous hypertension. In a much larger sample (N=12,047), lower diastolic blood pressure was also reported [3]. In this sample, lower triglycerides were also noted as well as greater HDL (high density lipoprotein). In a review on the Blue Zone diets, the biomarkers that were noted included lower LDL, diastolic and systolic blood pressure [1]. These lower biomarkers likely relate to calorie restriction and nutritious diets reported for centenarians in these studies/reviews, although they may also be heritability factors.

Expected risk factors

Some risk factors have been noted for centenarians, but several of the expected risk factors based on the aging adult literature have not been problematic for centenarians. For example, loneliness and frailty have been reported for centenarians by several investigators. But some of the problems that have occurred for those in their 70s, 80s and 90s such as feeling useless, having depressive symptoms, cognitive impairment and multi-morbidity have not been prevalent in centenarians. Most of these problems have been studied as individual predictors, although they could also be confounding factors.

Loneliness

As has already been mentioned, loneliness has been studied along with isolation in the context of living alone or with others [8]. In that study from Taipei on different combinations of loneliness, being connected and living with others, only the lonely groups were experiencing less life satisfaction and more depression. And, surprisingly, only 15% of that centenarian sample were experiencing loneliness.

In contrast, as many as 50% were experiencing loneliness in another study [16]. In this sample (N= 94), 30% were classified as isolated and lonely, 21% were lonely but not isolated and 29% were neither isolated nor lonely. In a sample from the Canadian Longitudinal Study of Aging (N=30,079), the socially isolated and lonely were more psychologically distressed, but the "only lonely" individuals were more distressed than the "only socially isolated" [17]. In a comparison of psychosocial variables associated with loneliness in centenarians vs. elderly individuals in New Zealand (N=191 centenarians with mean age of 101 and 73,095 elderly with mean age of 81), centenarians were more often female and widowed (89 vs. 43%). However, the prevalence of loneliness in centenarians was 32% less frequent and the prevalence of depression was 22% less frequent than was noted in the significantly larger sample of the elderly averaging 81 years [18]. Loneliness was more often associated with living alone and being depressed. The significant difference in the sample sizes, again, limits the reliability of these data.

In a review entitled "Social isolation and loneliness: the new geriatric giants", social isolation and loneliness were surprisingly more associated with morbidity and mortality than smoking, alcohol, obesity and frailty in centenarians [19]. Several effective interventions were suggested including social facilitation (including technology), exercise, psychological therapies, health and social services, animal therapy, befriending, leisure and skill development.

Perceived uselessness

Perceived uselessness is another psychological variable that has positively differentiated centenarians from non-centenarians. For example, in a paper entitled "A comparison of perceived uselessness in centenarians and non-centenarians in China" (N=5778 centenarians and 20,846 non-centenarians), centenarians had a 31% lower risk of experiencing perceived uselessness [20]. Perceived uselessness was 36-39% less prevalent in the centenarians than those who died at 91-94 years of age. Having purpose in life, as one of the nine Blue Zone principles, was apparently a protective factor for longevity in this sample.

Depression and anxiety

The prevalence of depression and anxiety has been low in the centenarian samples. And, typically, it has been studied in the context of activities that diminish depression and anxiety. For example, in a sample from China (N=288), 13% were expressing depressive

symptoms and 9% anxiety [21]. Diet diversity was negatively correlated with depression but not with anxiety. Directionality, of course, cannot be determined in this cross-sectional study. In another sample from China (N=1547), a greater prevalence of depression was noted at 20% [22]. However, this sample ranged in age from 80 to 116, so it included octogenarians and nonagenarians who were notably more depressed. And lower levels of red blood cells and hemoglobin were also noted in this multi-age sample, potentially confounding the findings.

In a paper entitled "Is the Sardinian blue zone the new Shangri-la for mental health? Significant associations were noted between depression symptoms, physical health and time spent gardening (N=318) [23]. Seventeen percent of the variance in the CES-D depression scores was predicted by perceived physical health and gardening, suggesting that those who engaged in gardening and had better physical health were less depressed or vice versa.

In another study, high religiosity and spirituality were negatively associated with anxiety and depression and positively associated with life satisfaction, meaning in life, social relations and psychological well-being [24]. This review on 102 studies (N=79,918) also showed that centenarians had less fear of death which may have related to their greater religiosity and spirituality.

Frailty

Frailty has been one of the negative effects of being a centenarian. It is typically based on the Fried Frailty Phenotype including at least three clinical signs of exhaustion, weight loss, weakness, slowness and low physical activity level [25]. In this study the Fried Frailty Phenotype was used and the most prevalent sign in this sample (N=1991, mean age =101) was weakness. Six percent of the sample was robust, 43% were pre-frail and 52% were frail. The Geriatric Depression Scale was also administered. And, based on the scores from that measure, 35% of the sample was depressed and of this group, 51% were frail, 21% were pre-frail and 0% was robust.

In a study on frailty and associated factors among Chinese centenarians (N = 1043), a logistic regression was conducted to determine risk factors for frailty [26]. In the logistic regression, the factors that predicted frailty were having less than 23 teeth with dentures, living alone or in an institution, lacking exercise, having insufficient financial resources and being female (Table 2).

Multi-morbidity

In a 13-year longitudinal study, Swedish centenarians (N=222) were compared with folks less than 100 (N=3573) [27]. When the centenarians were less than 85 they had slower health changes. After age 85 there was an acceleration of those problems. Four to nine years later, the sample of centenarians had multi-morbidity, disability and cognitive impairment. However, at 100 years, 39% of the sample was cognitively intact and 55% had escaped disability,

Table 2: Risk factors/negative effects of longevity for centenarians.

Negative effects	First author
Loneliness	Hsu, Zaccaria, Menec, Leitch, Freedman
Perceived uselessness	Zhao
Depression and anxiety	Li, Sun, Ruiu, Cielho-junior
Frailty	Ribiero, Zhang
Multimorbidity	Vettano, Croize-Pourvelot, Liu

but only 5% were free of multi-morbidity. At that time, the centenarians vs. the less than 85-year-old adults had more years of multi morbidity (nine vs. seven years), disability (four vs. three years) and cognitive impairment (six vs. four years).

Geriatric syndrome has been the label applied for multiple problems that have led to dependency for activities of daily living in centarians [28]. In this sample of centenarians (N=23, 77% women), 59% were living in nursing homes and 79% were using walkers. Living in a nursing home was associated with greater cognitive impairment, more comorbidity and fewer hospitalizations. Given that the sample was self-selected as needing a nursing home, the medical staff at the nursing home would make it less likely for the residents to need hospitalization.

Metabolic syndrome is another physical problem that has affected centenarians [29]. In this sample (N= 2493), low levels of vitamin D were noted to lead to metabolic syndrome. Of this sample, 36% had insufficient levels of vitamin D and 41% were considered vitamin D deficient.

Potential underlying mechanisms for longevity

The most frequently proposed potential underlying mechanisms for the longevity of centenarians include inflammation, immune function and exposure to previous epidemics. In a paper entitled "A comprehensive analysis of cytokines network in centenarians", 62 cytokines were studied [30]. An increase was noted in TNF-alpha and IL-6 as well as other pro-inflammatory cytokines like IL-23. No increase was reported for anti-inflammatories with the exception of Th-2 shifting (from more negative immune function) and an increase in the cytokine IL- 19. Several growth factors noted to regulate immunity such as G-CSF were also up-regulated.

Some inconsistent data were reported in a recent review suggesting a decrease in TNF-alpha levels as well as C-reactive protein (both pro-inflammatory cytokines) [1]. These authors suggested that decreased circulating insulin and fasting glucose along with decreased energy expenditure and body temperature were also contributing to longevity.

The chronic inflammatory state called "inflammaging" has been reputedly adaptive and less detrimental for centenarians than for younger people, according to a review of several recent studies [31]. The same authors suggested that centenarians had longevity by being creatures of habit and eating meals at the same time of day which has facilitated circadian rhythms including stable sleep cycles.

In a study entitled "Immunosenescence in aging between immune cells depletion and cytokines up-regulation", the markers of inflammation and adaptive immunity in centenarians are characterized by a decrease in CD*+ cells and an increase in CD4+ cells [32].

This has also been reported by another research group suggesting that healthy aging was associated with a high CD4/CD8 ratio and a low production of pro-inflammatory cytokines [33]. In still another study on immunity and longevity, some drugs (ripamycin, metformin, selegiline) and antioxidants (vitamin C and E) have been noted to improve immunity and prolong the life span, as in a "remodeling of the immune system" [34].

Exposure to epidemics has also been noted in the history of centenarians. As has already been noted, the greater longevity of

females in Sicily has been ascribed to their exposure to the 1918 Spanish flu epidemic [35]. But it's not clear why the men were not also "immunized" by that epidemic. And the extreme longevity seen in the Sardinian blue zone has been attributed to exposure to malaria and shepherds' disease [36]. Even the survival of COVID-19 by women and older centenarians who were born before 1919 has been attributed to the 1918 Spanish flu [37].

Methodological limitations

Several methodological limitations can be noted about these recent studies on centenarians. Significant variability has been reported on the sampling methods, on the sample sizes, and the prevalence and results of the studies. The sample sizes for the centenarians were not surprisingly very small as compared to the less old groups, making the power of the analyses low and the results less reliable. Most of the methods have been self-report surveys. And, most of the data are from records or reports by relatives rather than the centenarians themselves.

The key variables, as often happens, have been "pet variables" or those favored by the authors And, the data have been frequently analyzed via logistic regression analysis which controls for confounding variables that might have instead been risk factors or mediating/moderating variables if they had been analyzed by mediation/moderation or structural equations analysis. An example is that several researchers controlled for gender even though the prevalence data suggest that females have greater longevity perhaps because of estrogen levels. The findings that women were the more prevalent centenarians were not surprising, although their lesser health during their longevity was disconcerting. And does that suggest that estrogen may be less protective of health while its more predictive of longevity?

More studies have reported positive effects vs. data on negative effects. Several of the effects that have been noted could also be bidirectional, reciprocal variables, as in frailty and depression. Several of the scales are short or simply dichotomous which limits the reliability of those measures. Directionality cannot be determined as most of the studies were based on correlational data that have been collected retrospectively, as might be expected for centenarians as they are unknown until they reach 100.

Although many positive effects have been reported for centenarians as in very low prevalence of disease and depression, several studies highlighted the loneliness associated with longevity. The measures of loneliness and its effects are sufficiently variable that reviews have been inconclusive and meta-analyses have not been conducted. Loneliness would be expected to contribute to depression, so the low prevalence of depression was surprising. Despite these methodological limitations, the recent literature highlights the relationships between loneliness and longevity, although it doesn't conclude that aging is associated with more loneliness necessarily than at other stages of life.

The potential underlying mechanism studies have focused primarily on inflammation and immune function as being less problematic for centenarians than the very old (younger than centenarians). It is not clear why inflammation would be a significant problem for folks in their 80s and 90s but not in their 100s unless the younger adults had pre-existing conditions or less heritability of longevity. And the data suggesting that exposure to previous diseases like Spanish flu and malaria was protective highlights the importance of following those who have been exposed to recent diseases like COVID-19. Nutritious diet and physical activity were the most prevalent positive lifestyle characteristics of the centenarians. The most compelling data may come from the five blue zones, although they are largely anecdotal and focused primarily on diet. And only small variations exist in those diets but enough variation that the variance in longevity that is explained by those variations is not known.

Despite these methodological limitations, the recent research on centenarians and the origins of their longevity is informative. At this time the importance of future research on centenarians is highlighted by their expected increasing prevalence. Super-centenarians are also being recognized in various parts of the world. And, the spread of the lifestyles of blue zone centenarians will contribute to growing numbers of centenarians and super-centenarians.

REFERENCES

1. Dakic T, Jevdjovic T, Vujovic P, Mladenovic A. The less we eat, the longer we live: Can caloric restriction help us become centenarians? Int J Mol Sci. 2022;23:6546.

2. Govindaraju D, Atzmon G, Barzilai N. Genetics, lifestyle and longevity: Lessons from centenarians. Appl Transl Genom.2015; 4:23-32.

3. Zeng Y, Feng Q, Gu D, Vaupel JW. Demographics, phenotypic health characteristics and genetic analysis of centenarians in China. Mech Ageing Dev. 2017;165:86-97.

4. Poulain M, Herm A. Centenarians' marital history and living arrangements: Pathways to extreme longevity. J Gerontol B Psychol Sci Soc Sci. 2016; 71(4):724-733.

5. Marais GA, Gaillard JM, Vieira C, Plotton I, Sanlaville D, Gueyffier F, et al. Sex gap in aging and longevity: Can sex chromosomes play a role? Biol Sex Differ. 2018; 9:1-4.

6. Tafaro L, Tombolillo MT, Brükner N, Troisi G, Cicconetti P, Motta M, et al. Stress in centenarians. Arch Gerontol Geriatr 2019; 48(3):353-355.

7. Koch T, Turner R, Smith P, Hutnik N. Storytelling reveals the active, positive lives of centenarians. Nurs Older People. 2010;2.

8. Hsu HC. Typologies of loneliness, isolation and living alone are associated with psychological well-being among older adults in Taipei: A cross-sectional study. Int J Environ Res Public Health. 2020;17:9181.

9. Dominguez LJ, Veronese N, Baiamonte E, Guarrera M, Parisi A, Ruffolo C, et al. Healthy aging and dietary patterns. Nutr. 2022;14:889.

10. Crous-Bou M, Molinuevo JL, Sala-Vila A. Plant-rich dietary patterns, plant foods and nutrients, and telomere length. Adv Nutr. 2019; 10:296-303.

11. Gu Q, Sable CM, Brooks-Wilson A, Murphy RA. Dietary patterns in the healthy oldest old in the healthy aging study and the Canadian longitudinal study of aging: A cohort study. BMC Geriatr. 2020; 20:1-7.

12. Barak Y, Leitch S, Glue P. The great escape. Centenarians' exceptional health. Aging Clin Exp Res. 2021;33:513-520.

13. Ioakeim-Skoufa I, Clerencia-Sierra M, Moreno-Juste A, Elías de Molins Peña C, Poblador-Plou B, Aza-Pascual-Salcedo M, et al. Multimorbidity clusters in the oldest old: Results from the epichron cohort. Int J Environ Res Public Health. 2022;19:10180.

14. Dominguez LJ, Di Bella G, Veronese N, Barbagallo M. Impact of Mediterranean diet on chronic non-communicable diseases and longevity. Nutrients. 2021;13:2028.

15. Hai PC, Yao DX, Zhao R, Dong C, Saymuah S, Pan YS, et al. BMI, blood pressure, and plasma lipids among centenarians and their offspring. Evid.-based Complement Altern Med. 2022; 2022.

16. Zaccaria D, Cavalli S, Masotti B, Gomes Da Rocha C, Von Gunten A, Jopp DS. Social isolation and loneliness among near-centenarians and centenarians: Results from the fordham centenarian study. Int J Environ Res Public Health. 2022;19:5940.

17. Menec VH, Newall NE, Mackenzie CS, Shooshtari S, Nowicki S. Examining social isolation and loneliness in combination in relation to social support and psychological distress using Canadian Longitudinal Study of Aging (CLSA) data. PloS one 2020;15:0230673.

18. Leitch S, Glue P, Gray AR, Greco P, Barak Y. Comparison of psychosocial variables associated with loneliness in centenarian vs elderly populations in New Zealand. JAMA Netw Open. 2018;1:183880.

19. Freedman A, Nicolle J. Social isolation and loneliness: The new geriatric giants: Approach for primary care. Canadian Family Physician. 2020;66:176-182.

20. Zhao Y, Fu H, Guo A, Qiu L, Cheung KS, Wu B, et al. A comparison of perceived uselessness between centenarians and non-centenarians in China. BMC Geriatr. 2018;18:1.

21. Li R, Zong ZY, Gu XX, Wang DN, Dong C, Sun C, et al. Higher dietary diversity as a protective factor against depression among older adults in China: A cross-sectional study. Ann Palliat Med. 2021; 11:1278-89.

22. Sun Z, Lin J, Zhang Y, Yao Y, Huang Z, Zhao Y, et al. Association between immunoglobulin A and depression in Chinese older adults: Findings from a cross-sectional study. Immun Ageing. 2022 23; 19:21.

23. Ruiu M, Carta V, Deiana C, Fastame MC. Is the Sardinian Blue Zone the New Shangri-La for mental health? Evidence on depressive symptoms and its correlates in late adult life span. Aging Clin Exp Res. 2022; 34:1315-1322.

24. Coelho-Júnior HJ, Calvani R, Panza F, Allegri RF, Picca A, Marzetti E, et al. Religiosity/Spirituality and mental health in older adults: A systematic review and meta-analysis of observational studies. Front Med.2022:1330.

25. Ribeiro O, Duarte N, Teixeira L, Paúl C. Frailty and depression in centenarians. Int Psychogeriatr. 2018;30:115-124.

26. Zhang J, Xu L. Frailty and Associated Factors among Chinese Centenarians. J Nutr Health Aging. 2022; 26:806-813.

27. Vetrano DL, Grande G, Marengoni A, Calderón-Larrañaga A, Rizzuto D. Health trajectories in Swedish centenarians. J Gerontol A Biol Sci Med Sci. 2021;76:157-163.

28. Croize-Pourcelet C, Nouguerede E, Rey D, Daumas A, Gentile G, Villani P, et al. Geriatric syndromes in a centenarians population. Aging Clin Exp Res. 2022;9:1-6.

29. Liu L, Cao Z, Lu F, Liu Y, Lv Y, Qu Y, et al. Vitamin D deficiency and metabolic syndrome in elderly Chinese individuals: evidence from CLHLS. Nutr Metab. 2020; 17:1-1.

30. Pinti M, Gibellini L, Lo Tartaro D, De Biasi S, Nasi M, Borella R, et al. A comprehensive analysis of cytokine network in centenarians. Int J Mol Sci. 2023;24:2719.

31. Franceschi C, Ostan R, Santoro A. Nutrition and inflammation: Are centenarians similar to individuals on calorie-restricted diets? Annu Rev Nutr. 2018; 38:329-356.

32. Ventura MT, Casciaro M, Gangemi S, Buquicchio R. Immunosenescence in aging: Between immune cells depletion and cytokines upregulation. Clin Mol Allergy. 2017 Dec;15:1-8.

33. Alves, Amanda Soares, Mayari Eika Ishimura, Yeda Aparecida de Oliveira Duarte, Valquiria Bueno. "Parameters of the immune system and vitamin D levels in old individuals." Front Immunol 9 (2018): 1122.

34. Csaba G. Immunity and longevity. Acta Microbiologica et Immunologica Hungarica. 2019;66:1-7.

35. Caruso C, Accardi G, Aiello A, Calabrò A, Ligotti ME, Candore G. Centenarians born before 1919 are resistant to COVID-19. Aging Clin Exp Res. 2023; 35:217-220.

36. Caruso C, Marcon G, Accardi G, Aiello A, Calabrò A, Ligotti ME, et al. Role of sex and age in fatal outcomes of COVID-19: Women and older centenarians are more resilient. Int J Mol Sci. 2023;24:2638.

37. Soloski MJ, Poulain M, Pes GM. Does the trained immune system play an important role in the extreme longevity that is seen in the Sardinian blue zone? Front Aging. 2022;3.

Printed in the United States
by Baker & Taylor Publisher Services